"*They Were Just People* is an important contribution to the literature of rescue during the Holocaust. Tammeus and Cukierkorn have brought to the fore many gripping stories never before told, forming an inspirational narrative of courage and survival. These are the experiences of people who had the courage to care and the courage to act in a time when caring for others meant endangering oneself and one's family. A readers' guide supplements the poignant stories and compels the reader to reflect and discuss the implications of choice and action. The stories are individual, the lessons universal."

— **Stanlee J. Stahl, Executive Vice President,**
The Jewish Foundation for the Righteous

"A wonderfully written, engaging book providing a perspective that sadly is often missing when reading about the Holocaust. It shows that at least a few people saved the honor of humankind and witnessed God, even in the midst of such terrible times."

—**Dr. Carol Rittner, RSM, Distinguished Professor of Holocaust**
and Genocide Studies, The Richard Stockton College of New Jersey

"By sharing these personal accounts, authors Bill Tammeus and Rabbi Jacques Cukierkorn provide for their readers a glimpse into the dilemmas and decisions faced by Jewish victims of Nazi persecution in Poland and by non-Jews who played a role in their survival. This book offers a useful perspective for those wanting to learn more about the Holocaust and the context in which rare acts of rescue occurred."

—**Midwest Center for Holocaust Education**

"*They Were Just People* is a clear-eyed documentation of compassion during the Holocaust. The harrowing hunt to capture and exterminate a Jewish population in Poland is recalled by a score of survivors aided by rescuers—family, friends, and strangers—whose moral code and humanity transcended their own fear of Nazi retribution. But the stories do not sentimentalize nor analyze. Each account, carefully researched and corroborated, bears witness both to the survivors' will to live and their rescuers' determination to do the right thing. Authors Bill Tammeus and Rabbi Jacques Cukierkorn triumph in a journalistic achievement about the innate spiritual resilience of humanity."

— **Suzette Martinez Standring, Past President,**
National Society of Newspaper Columnists

They Were Just People

They Were Just People

Stories of Rescue in Poland
During the Holocaust

**Bill Tammeus and
Rabbi Jacques Cukierkorn**

UNIVERSITY OF MISSOURI PRESS
COLUMBIA AND LONDON

Copyright © 2009 by
The Curators of the University of Missouri
University of Missouri Press, Columbia, Missouri 65201
Printed and bound in the United States of America

5 4 3 2 1   13 12 11 10 09

Library of Congress Cataloging-in-Publication Data

Tammeus, Bill.
  They were just people : stories of rescue in Poland during the Holocaust /
Bill Tammeus and Rabbi Jacques Cukierkorn.
       p. cm.
  Includes bibliographical references and index.
  Summary: "Tammeus and Cukierkorn interview Jewish survivors and their
non-Jewish rescuers, capturing for future generations stories of how, through
courage and ingenuity, a few Jews in Poland escaped the Holocaust, and re-
vealing how individuals can preserve civility and compassion even in the face
of overwhelming evil"—Provided by publisher.
  ISBN 978-0-8262-1876-6 (cloth: alk. paper)
  ISBN 978-0-8262-1860-5 (pbk.: alk. paper)
  1. Jews—Poland—Biography. 2. Holocaust, Jewish (1939–1945)—
Poland—Personal narratives. 3. Righteous Gentiles in the Holocaust—
Poland. 4. Holocaust survivors—Poland—Biography. 5. Holocaust
survivors—United States—Biography. 6. Poland—Biography. I. Cukierkorn,
Jacques. II. Title.
  DS134.7.T36 2009
  940.53'180922438—dc22
                                              2009013438

∞™ This paper meets the requirements of the
American National Standard for Permanence of Paper
for Printed Library Materials, Z39.48, 1984.

Designer and Typesetter: Kristie Lee
Printer and Binder: Integrated Book Technology
Typefaces: Minion and Constantia

To all those individuals who have chosen—and
continue to choose—to put integrity, decency, and humanity
above convenience, expedience, and self-interest.

May the stories in this book inspire others
to make similar choices.

Contents

Acknowledgments

No book of this sort can be the work of just its two authors. We had considerable help in many ways, but first we want to express our gratitude to the people who opened up their homes, gave us their time, and shared not only their personal stories but also their very hearts with us. Without their willingness to contribute to our effort to add additional details to the story of the Holocaust, there would have been no book at all.

We also want to thank those who helped us find people to interview, who guided us as we imagined the shape of this work, who helped us as we traveled and did interviews both in the United States and in Poland, and who covered our research costs with their generous donations. For an important part of that funding we are particularly indebted to Ed Porter, Michael Rosenblum, David Vittor, and David and Shirley Wurth for their especially generous support. We're also much indebted to Claudia and Jack Mandelbaum for helping us with some of our interviews in Poland. Jack served as translator for several of them. Others who donated money or helped us in other ways are included in the alphabetical listings below:

Kristin and Bill Amend, Amanda and Jason Anderson, P. Ashcraft, and Severyn Ashkenazi.

Carol Barnett, Michael and Nancy Barr, Irvin Belzer and Sue McCord-Belzer, Andrew Stuart Bergerson, James Bernard Jr., Magda Bielska, Howard and Elizabeth Birky, Allen and Gloria Block, Eliot S. Berkley, Bernard Brown, and Bernard and Jean Brown.

Robin Carroll, Dorothy Clarke, Barton and Mary Cohen, Robert and Lynne Cohen, Congregation Ohev Sholom of Prairie Village, Kansas. Georgine Cooper, Yvonne Cordeiro, Kate Craddy and the staff of the Galicia Jewish Museum in Kraków, and Denisse Cukierkorn.

Elaine Dalgleish, Jean Daugherty, Heywood Davis, and Bob Dillon.

Monika Elliott, Brad and Virginia Epsten, and Gloria Eurotas.

Tasha Fabela-Jonas, Chris Fawley, Sally Firestone, Don and Laurie Fisher, Barbara and Jim Fyfe, Laurence M. Frazen, and Joyce Fulps.

Ed and Susanne Garay, Barbara and J. Peter Gattermeir, John and Mary Ann Glenski, Lance and Terry Goldberg, Fran Goldschmidt, Ann and Ralph Goodrich, and Robert and Melanie Griffey.

Margaret Hage, Andy and Margaret Hansen, Nicoya Helm, Barnett and Shirley Helzberg, John and Reesa Helzberg, Walter and Jean Hiersteiner, Betty and George Hoare.

Susan Llanes-Myers, Ira D. Perry, Linda Toyota, and others on the staff of the Holocaust Museum, Houston.

Victoria J. Barnett, Ellen Blalock, Aleksandra B. Borecka, Andrew Hollinger, and others on the staff of the United States Holocaust Memorial Museum, Washington, D.C.

James and Barbara Holzmark, Leonard and June Horwitz, David Hughes, Doug Hundley, and Jean Hunter.

Esther Ingber, Beverly Jarrett, David and Lydia Jeter, Dr. Robert Johnson, Carolyn and Buddy Jones, and Sherman Jubelirer.

The Joy Group of Northminster Presbyterian Church of Kansas City, Barbara Kaufman, Haven and Dan Kiernan, Marilyn Klaus, Mark and Judith Konikoff, Magdalena Koralewska, William B. Kort, Stephen and Marilyn Koshland, Gayle and Bruce Krigel, Krouse & Co., Bill and Susan Krusemark, Charles Kuluva, and Andrew Kureth.

Karen and Peter LaFauci, Lake Quivira Community Ministry, Robert B. Langworthy, Rolland and Carolyn Larson, Hal and Annie LeMert, David and Linda Levine, Renee Lichtman and the International Conference of Holocaust Child Survivors, Robert Litan, Louis Memorial Chapel of Kansas City, and Shirley Lytle.

Mark Mandelbaum, Sylvia Manko, Lisen Tammeus Mann and Richard P. Mann, Thomas Manson, Henry and Betty Jo Marder, Denny Matthews, Tom and Judy McClanahan, Chris and Larry McDonald, Karin McPhail, Mary Kay McPhee, Harold and Marilyn Melcher, Jim Melching, Howard Mick, Frank Milewski, Craig and Patty Miller, Jerry and Lauren Miller, John and Mary Ann Miller, Donald and Diane Mnookin, Clarabeth Moore, Jim Mueller, and Julia Mykovet.

Dr. Mark Nanos, Mark and Mary Neustrom, and Notre Dame de Sion School.

Marian Oldak, Jane and Bill Ostoff, and Steve Owens.

Karen Pack, Allen and Debra Parmet, Teresa Piechota, Miriam Pepper, Laurence and Rita Poisner, Magda and Jacek Pokrzycka, David and Carol Porter, Aron Primack, Keith Purcell, and Marek Purowski.

The Reed Family Foundation, William and Victoria Reisler, Joel and Diana Resnick, the Rockhill Tennis Club, Sigmund A. Rolat, Abe and Marilyn Rosenberg, James Rosenblum, Janet Rowlands, Michael and Gloria Rudd, Christopher Rutkowski, Elaine Ryder, and Barbara Rzeznik.

St. Andrew Christian Church of Olathe, Kansas; St. Charles Borromeo Catholic Church of Kansas City; St. Michael and All Angels Episcopal Church of Merriam, Kansas; St. Paul School of Theology of Kansas City; Daniel and Vivien Schlozman; Rabbi Michael Schudrich; Howard and Barbara Schwartz;

Second Baptist Church, Liberty, Missouri; Barbara Shelly and Jonathan Rand, Cantor Paul Silbersher, Kamala Singh, Robert and Betty Slegman, Beth Smith, Bill and Joyce Smith, and the Sosland Foundation of Kansas City.

Stanlee Joyce Stahl and the staff of the Jewish Foundation for the Righteous.

Ann Stapleton, Suzette Martinez Standring and David Standring, Helen Stefanov, Ira and Pat Stein, Arthur and Barbara Stern, the Strauss Philanthropic Fund, Frank and Adelaide Szabo, Marcia Tammeus, Temple Avodah, Susan L. Throckmorton, Karl Timmerman, Robert Uhlmann, James and Agniezka Van Bergh, Dorrie Virden, and Leslie and John Von Bargen.

The Wally Foundation, Kay Walkup, R. J. and M. L. Walter, James and Mary Jo Ward, Ward Parkway Presbyterian Church women of Kansas City, Mo., Julie and David Warm, Mary and Gary Watanabe, Rachel Watkins, Irene Weiner, Tom, Anita and Steven Wertz, Norman and Marcia Whitcomb, Priscilla and Rodney Wilson, Steve Winn, Yankee Cowboy Publishing, and Dewey Ziegler.

Special thanks go to the Midwest Center for Holocaust Education, at 5801 West 115th Street, Suite 106, Overland Park, Kansas 66211–1800, 913-327-8190, info@mchekc.org, www.mchekc.org.

All photos in this book, unless otherwise noted, were taken by Bill Tammeus. All maps in this book were created by Tasha Fabela-Jonas.

POLAND

1939

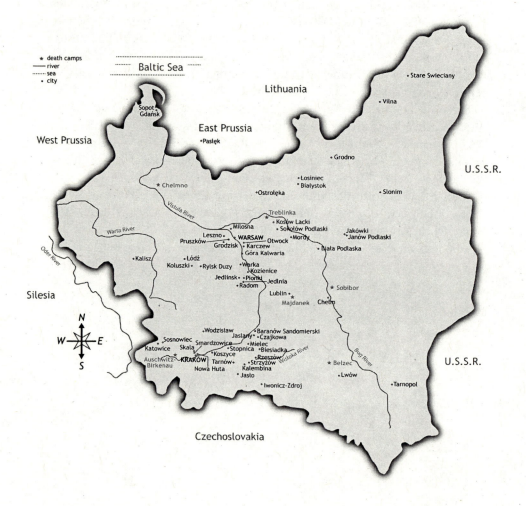

Baltic Sea

* death camps
— river
— sea
• city

Lithuania

• Stare Swieciany

West Prussia

Sopot
Gdańsk

East Prussia

• Vilna

•Pasłęk

U.S.S.R.

• Grodno

★ Chełmno

•Łosiniec
• Białystok

• Słonim

Vistula River

•Ostrołęka

Treblinka

Warta River

• Miłosna

• Kosów Łacki
• Sokołów Podlaski

Leszno
Pruszków

• WARSAW

Grodzisk

Otwock
• Karczew

•Mordy

Jakówki
•Janów Podlaski

•Łódź
Koluszki

• Góra Kalwaria

•Rylsk Duzy

• Biała Podlaska

Oder River

•Kalisz

• Łądlińsk

• Werka
• Kozienice
•Pionki

Jedlnia

•Radom

Lublin

★ Sobibor

Majdanek

Chełm

Silesia

• Wodzisław
Jaslany

Sosnowiec

Smardzowice

Katowice

Skala
•Koszyce

•Stopnica

• Baranów Sandomierski
• Czajkowa
•Mielec
•Biesiadka

Auschwitz-
Birkenau

★ KRAKÓW

Tarnów
Nowa Huta

•Rzeszów
•Strzyżów
Kalembina

•Jaslo

Wisłoka River

Bug River

★ Belzec

•Lwów

U.S.S.R.

N
W   E
S

•Iwonicz-Zdroj

•Tarnopol

Czechoslovakia

This map shows Poland as its borders existed at the start of World War II in 1939. The cities and towns on this map are mentioned in one or more stories in this book. It also shows the location of the six death camps operated by German authorities in Poland. After the war Poland became smaller, especially as it lost territory in the east to the Soviet Union.

POLAND
Today's Borders

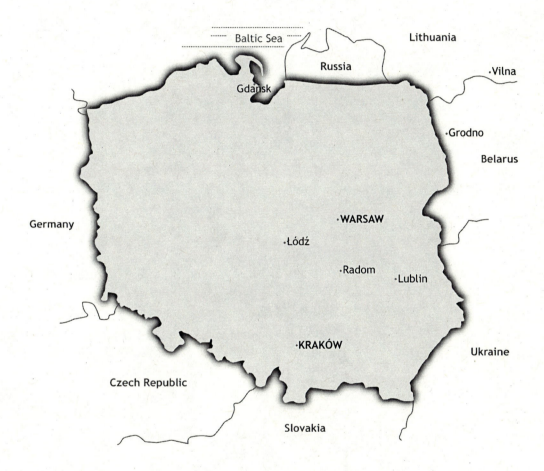

This map shows Poland's borders as they are at the beginning of the twenty-first century.

They Were Just People

Introduction

When Felix Zandman knocked on Anna Puchalska's door near Grodno in eastern Poland that cold afternoon in early 1943, he was looking for someone who would help to save a life—his. But Felix knew that the Germans would kill any non-Jew in Poland who helped Jews, so if Anna agreed to his request to hide him even for one night, she would be putting her entire family—her five children, her husband, and herself—in jeopardy. Still, Anna said more than yes.

Instead of agreeing to hide Felix for a single night, Anna said he could stay until the war ended. In that welcoming act, Anna Puchalska became one of the rare individuals who helped to save Jews during the Holocaust. In the end she allowed not just Felix but also his uncle and several other people to hide for nearly a year and a half in a hole dug in the soil under a bedroom of her small home. In recognition of her actions Yad Vashem, the Holocaust memorial authority in Israel, has honored her as one of the "righteous among the nations."[1]

How did it happen that a few Polish Jews like Felix managed to survive by finding a few Polish non-Jews like Anna to help save them from genocide?[2] In trying to find an answer to this question, we traveled across the United States and Poland, interviewing such survivors and members of the families who helped to save them. And in this book we record some of their stories. Here you will find Zandman's story, as well as stories of more than a dozen other Polish Jews who survived despite the staggering odds against them.

Adolf Hitler came to power in Germany in 1933 and almost immediately began to implement anti-Jewish policies, although it was not clear then that eventually the aim would become the annihilation of European Jewry.[3] As time went on, the denial of rights became ever more severe for Jews as well as for other groups, including the mentally and physically disabled. The violation and abrogation of the rights of Jews happened incrementally in Germany, but in Poland, which Germany invaded on September 1, 1939, all of these anti-Jewish policies were implemented quickly. Hitler's policy of genocide was not fully implemented until three years after World War II began. Holocaust scholar Nechama Tec describes how Jews needed the most immediate help when "the orders came to abandon their homes and move to these specially designed ghetto areas. . . . In a sense, then, Jewish rescue was a human response to the Nazi measures of destruction. The appearance of righteous [individuals] signaled an opposition to, an interference with, the German policies of Jewish annihilation."[4]

Jews had been living in Poland for hundreds of years. The first immigrations started in the twelfth and thirteenth centuries.[5] By 1939, more Jews lived there than in any other country. Although Jews were killed soon after Germany invaded, most were murdered in death camps between 1942 and 1944, and the majority of those died in 1942 and 1943. In all, more than 90 percent of Poland's Jews were murdered.[6]

We chose to focus on Poland for several reasons. The first was the huge numbers of Jews who were killed there. We selected Poland (using its boundaries as they existed in 1939) because the Germans established six death camps there: Auschwitz-Birkenau, Belzec, Chelmno, Majdanek, Sobibor, and Treblinka.[7]

Poland attracted us also because some of the people whom Yad Vashem has honored as "righteous" lived there (though certainly in small numbers),[8] despite the fact that punishment for helping Jews there and in eastern territories occupied by the Germans (which almost always entailed death) tended to be more uniformly and quickly executed. Poles now account for a little over six thousand of the nearly twenty-two thousand persons recognized by Yad Vashem as "righteous." Those figures may not seem significant, statistically, but our hope is that the individual stories of rescue that they represent—and the stories we tell here—can be positive influences today as efforts to reestablish a Jewish presence in Poland move forward, and as Jews and non-Jews there acknowledge the bleak reality of history and seek to live together in peace. There were rescuers in many other countries too, where, instead of immediate death, the penalty for helping Jews usually was imprisonment and confinement in concentration camps, from which most never returned.

Two-thirds of Europe's approximately nine million Jews perished in the Holocaust, most of them in Poland. Survival turned out to be much more a matter of chance than anything else. Any choices Jews might make to try to survive were, in the end, not choices at all but, rather, hopeful guesses that their decisions would make a difference. In hindsight we know that the scope of the Holocaust simply overwhelmed such individual decisions and actions, meaning that the survival of Jews was essentially out of their own hands. Most of the Jews who found non-Jews to help them—and even some of those rescuers—were killed anyway.

The stories we have collected do not and are not meant to constitute an academic study of this aspect of the Holocaust. Rather, our purpose is to tell these compelling stories because we find them fascinating and illuminating and believe you will too.[9] Because one of us is Jewish and one Christian, we approached these stories with different perspectives and, frankly, different interests. It turned out that the Jewish author, a Reform rabbi, often was more interested in the actions of the non-Jewish rescuers, while the Christian author, a Presbyterian elder, was more engaged by the stories of the Jews themselves. The Christian author was born in the United States in January 1945, the day after Soviet troops liberated Warsaw. The Jewish author was born in Brazil in

1967, a full generation after the Holocaust. So neither of us brings to this task any personal experience of the Holocaust—only personal roots. The Christian's paternal great-grandparents were Germans who came to the United States in the 1860s. Many of the Jew's ancestors were rabbis who called Poland home for more than four centuries. When Germany invaded Poland, the histories of the authors' families began to clash.

If the widespread current public discussions about finding harmony among and between different religious traditions are to be useful, they must come to terms with precisely these kinds of divergent and intersecting personal histories. So there are lessons to be learned not just from the authors' experience of writing this book together, given their own backgrounds, but also from the various ways in which Jews and non-Jews interacted for centuries in Poland before World War II as well as during the Holocaust. The stories we recount can provide some insight into those relationships.

What we found so compelling about those relationships was their variety, ranging from deep-rooted antisemitism to profound friendship, and how the particular circumstances in each case led to a non-Jew helping a Jew. For both of us, these stories also raised questions, at least by implication, about whether and under what circumstances each of us might aid others being threatened with death—and about how we might react if we were members of a targeted group. We concluded that these are questions that cannot be answered with any certainty unless and until we face such circumstances.

These accounts also reminded us that even Jews who had non-Jewish help had to work hard and give up a great deal to try to save themselves, which is why we think the word "rescuers," the term commonly applied to non-Jews who helped, is at least somewhat problematic. The word itself seems to imply that the Jews were passive victims. They were not. Holocaust historian Yehuda Bauer put it this way: "Victims are not passive, except in their last moments."[10] Assistance from non-Jews was crucial for the survivors whose stories we tell here, but this alone was not enough. Survival also took ingenuity, creativity, sometimes money, and what some survivors labeled simple good luck. Yet most Jews even with those advantages died anyway. In various ways, each story in this book clarifies some aspect of that harsh reality.

Some of the people who helped to save Jews seemed to do so out of a sense of compassion and obligation that they had learned in their churches. Others had motives for acting that had no apparent religious antecedents at all but were, rather, drawn from humanitarian motives and ideologies or from a simple impulse given the immediate circumstances. In many cases it was difficult for us to determine their motivations for helping, though scholars studying rescue have been spending more time analyzing this area in recent years. One reason for our difficulty was that such a concise determination would require a psychological analysis of the rescuers, delving into personal histories and values at various times in their lives, and this was beyond the scope of our work. Besides, the rescuers themselves often could not articulate their motivation in any exhaustive way, partly because their memories had faded and partly because some of the non-Jews we interviewed were young at the time of the Holocaust and thus had not yet developed a sharp sense of self-awareness or self-knowledge. It is also true that a few people who saved Jews were antisemitic but acted because they knew and liked individual Jews or were somehow convinced to help despite their fear and reluctance.

A prominent, though not universal, theme we found among the rescuers we interviewed was that, no matter the source of the motivation, their families—whatever their backgrounds or situations—taught them that all people were worthy of dignity and respect. It is difficult, more than sixty years later, to know how clearly this value was articulated within rescuing families at the time, and how much of this conclusion was formed by family members later based on their families' actions to save Jews. As one author put it, rescuers "came from every walk of life. They were teachers, students, shopkeepers, factory workers, housewives and farmers. They ranged in age from their late teens to their eighties."[11] What does seem clear and of great importance, however, is that in a majority of cases the decision to help save Jews was based on the fact that the rescuing families already knew the Jews they helped. In many cases, thus, it was simply friends helping friends. It also was evident that in many ways the members of the rescuing families we interviewed had at least attempted to live out the principle of respect and dignity for everyone in their postwar years, even if that principle was not the primary motivation for helping Jews during the war.

The explanations about such values that we heard all these years after the Holocaust and the testimony of the survivors themselves raise an old question with which Holocaust scholars often wrestle. How useful is witness testimony, especially when it is given decades after the events being recalled? This is a legitimate concern. After all, as Holocaust scholar Christopher Browning has noted, "memory is a problematic thing," and some historians have been "very leery about survivor testimony."[12] Again, this is a reasonable position to take. Personal memory—particularly of events during periods that were stressful and even traumatic—can be distorted. So even though we believe that the oral and written recollections of the people whose stories we tell in this book are their authentic memories, recalled with as much accuracy as possible given the trauma they survived, it is possible that some of the personal recollections we report are inaccurate, embellished, or misinterpreted. When they spoke to us of events taking place in a larger historical context that could be verified (such as dates of an invasion or liberation), then we have compared their memories with the record of history. And at times, the memories of the survivors we interviewed differed on some points from the memories of the family members who saved them. See the Felicia Graber story for an example of this. In such cases, we simply have noted the different recollections in the text.

We did not write this book so we could identify some kind of redemptive meaning in the sufferings the Nazi regime forced on Jews, some kind of silver lining to the Holocaust. No such silver lining exists. Seeking to create one would cheapen history with naïve words about happy endings or about heroism in the midst of evil. Rather, our goal was to tell compelling stories that describe some of the ways in which a few non-Jews acted to aid Jews—some for noble, some for mercenary, some for intensely private reasons. In the end, it may not much matter why they tried to save Jews. What mattered was that they tried at all, and that because of their actions the total number of murdered Jews was not higher. Their actions encouraged a few Jews to keep trying to outlast the Germans even though there appeared to be little or no hope of succeeding. As Yehuda Bauer wrote, "The Holocaust has . . . become the symbol for genocide, for racism, for hatred of foreigners, and, of course, for antisemitism; yet the existence of rescuers on the margins provides a hope that these evils are not inevitable, that they can be fought."[13]

Finding people willing to tell us these stories was fascinating work. Sometimes we found survivors eager to describe what had happened to them and happy to give us contact information so that when we went to Poland we could interview members of the families who helped to save them. Sometimes we found survivors who were reluctant to talk but who finally saw the value of sharing their histories. We also interviewed a few survivors—and wrote chapters about their stories—only to have them decide for various reasons that they were unwilling to be included in the book.

Some of the stories we heard were impossible for us to verify, despite the fact that people continue to pass them along as fact. For instance, in New York we spoke with a Polish immigrant who insisted that his whole village in Poland knew his family was hiding a young Jewish girl but did not reveal that secret to authorities. We went to that village, which turned out to be just a few houses, and spoke with the man's brother as well as with others there. But the story disintegrated, the more we learned, until finally it focused not on this family at all but on a long-dead Catholic priest who helped to hide and save several Jewish children. There were not enough verifiable details of the story left to include it here, however, though clearly some version of the story has become important to family lore.

In another case we interviewed a survivor who preferred that we not get in touch with a man who was a member of the family that rescued her because she feared he would come after her for money. This woman insisted that, if we ever did talk to him, we could not tell him she was alive. Because we were curious to hear his side of the story, we found the man in Poland and interviewed him, but we honored the survivor's privacy request. The man turned out to be difficult and, in the end, unwilling for us even to take his photograph. So you will not find that story in this book, either. And yet we mention it here because talking with him was a lesson to us that to be a rescuer did not require one to be a saint. Rather, these were just ordinary people who elected to take actions in opposition to the German policy of genocide. And if the rescuers were just ordinary people, what of the people they saved? One of the rescuers we spoke to drew a parallel between rescuers and those they saved by describing the survivors exactly as we have described the rescuers: "They were just people."

The Stories

Zygie Allweiss

When the German soldiers came that day, the teenage brothers Zygie and Sol Allweiss were in their usual hiding place—in the Dudzik family barn behind bales of hay. But this time the Germans had come to find hay, not necessarily to search for hidden Jews. Hearing the demand for hay, Zygie and Sol steadied their racing hearts and felt for the triggers on the guns they had acquired while on the run—Zygie had a German Mauser, and Sol a French weapon.

The soldiers hauled out bale after bale, getting closer and closer to the boys, who had found refuge with non-Jewish family friends in Czajkowa, not far from their native village of Jaslany. Zofia Dudzik, wife of Maciej and mother of the eight Dudzik children, recognized what was about to happen and quickly came into the barn to divert the soldiers: "She was like a fireball" is how Zygie later described her.

"What are you taking that stuff for?" Zygie heard her say to the soldiers. "It's wet. Why don't you come and I'll give you some good, dry stuff."

So the soldier who was about to remove the last of the hay bales hiding Zygie and Sol, ready to shoot, simply turned around and followed her.

"We most likely would have finished off the German because we had the drop on him," Zygie said. But by the narrowest of margins they avoided not only killing that soldier but also what almost certainly would have been their own deaths—and the death of the whole Dudzik family.

Even if the Germans had simply found Sol and Zygie hiding, unarmed, everyone, including the Dudziks, would have been killed. And the Dudziks knew this of course. In fact, given the close call that day, Zygie and Sol expected the Dudziks to ask them to leave and move to some other location. But Zofia and Maciej would not hear of the boys taking their chances elsewhere. They told the boys, "Leave our safety up to the Lord in heaven. Stay with us." And so Zygie and Sol did.

Why did the Dudziks do it? The simple answer, Zygie and two Dudzik sisters said decades later, is because they saw Jews as fellow human beings, and that they had been friends before the war. So Zygie survived to tell this story in an interview at a hotel near his Detroit home more than sixty years later. After World War II, Zygie and Sol both moved to Detroit, where Sol also lived until his death in 2004 and where Zygie, who turned eighty in 2007, still lives.

The boys' experience behind the hay bales in the barn that day was far from the only time they almost died in the Holocaust. Zygie can recount many times

Zygie Allweiss

Wladyslawa "Lottie"
Dudzik Rzeznik
(photo courtesy of Barbara Rzeznik)

Helena Dudzik Hajnas

·WARSAW

·Lublin

Jaslany·Baranów Sandomierski
·Czajkowa
·KRAKÓW ·Biesiadka
·Tarnów
·Lwów

when it looked as if the end had come for him. There was, for instance, March 7, 1943.

He was riding in the back of a truck crowded with about eighty people, including three of his sisters, from the Biesiadka labor camp in south-central Poland. The Germans had forced him and other camp inmates into the truck because they were not useful workers at the camp any more. This was one of six transports to a nearby killing pit on that day.

Zygie was riding in the truck's flat bed, which was covered with canvas. Thinking about his dire circumstances he turned to a passenger beside him, an older boy from Berlin named Irving, and whispered, "I'm going to try to get out of this."

But Irving had given up. Resigned to die, he declined to take part in any escape plan: "I don't want to go with you. I know I'm going to die today," Irving said.

Zygie did not say another word to him. Instead, he felt for the small knife stashed in his pocket, found it, and made his plan. He would cut an opening in the canvas near a grommet and make the slit large enough to stick his legs through. Then he could slip outside the moving truck and hang on as it dragged him along until the time was right to let go. The three Germans in the truck's cab could not see him even with their side-view mirrors as long as he stayed in the center at the back of the truck. Zygie was familiar with the road they were traveling on, so just before they came to a sharp right turn that he knew was coming, he released his hold on the back of the truck and fell off, praying not to be noticed.

When he let go and rolled into a nearby ditch, he looked at his knees. What he saw was mostly bones and blood. The skin and tissue above them had been worn off by the dragging. But he had made it. He had calibrated his chances, devised a plan, carried it out, and survived, at least for the moment. He was, however, a long, long way from ultimate safety.

Zygie and Sol, the only Holocaust survivors from their large family, received help from several non-Jews, primarily the Dudziks. They also employed their own ingenuity and a willingness to take extraordinary risks, though even those elements combined with help from non-Jews did not guarantee survival for any Jew in Poland then. Zygie was born May 8, 1927, in the small village of Jaslany, about ten miles northwest of Mielec, which is east and a little north of Kraków near the Vistula River. His given name was Zygmunt. Later he became Zyga and then Zygie. His Jewish name, Zalman, came from his maternal grandfather, Zalman Jochnowitz. He was one of nine children, five boys and four girls: Sarah, Loeser, Gittel, Mendel, Rachel, Fishel, Salek (Sol), Zyga, and Frimcha.

Zygie's father owned some land and also bought and sold horses. And the Allweiss children had a good childhood. They would play with the grasshoppers and butterflies and seek out rabbits sleeping in the cabbage patch in the daytime. Sol was one year and three months older than Zygie, and they were very close. One day Sol found a crow's egg and somehow got a chicken to hatch it. Sol trained the crow so he could call it and the bird would come to him from anywhere. It would land right on Sol's arm.

Zygie said, "So you can imagine how jealous I was that the bird didn't come to me." Sibling rivalry and jealousy, all mixed with fun. It was like that for the Allweiss boys in Jaslany before the war.

Zygie was twelve years old when Germany invaded Poland. His father, Jacob Allweiss, and older brothers Mendel and Fishel went east to the section of Poland that soon would be taken over by the Soviet Union. There they planned to join the fight on behalf of Poland. Another older brother, Loeser (also known as Leo), was a dentist in Tarnów, southwest of Mielec. He had opened a clinic there with a friend from the Polish army. But the war meant Leo had to return to military life.

The war had just begun when Leo, wearing a Polish military uniform, came back to Jaslany to say goodbye to his family. He stood on the front steps of the house and hugged his mother. Overcome, she cried. And Zygie never forgot the scene, especially because it was the last time the family ever saw Leo.

Zygie, his mother, and the rest of the family stayed in Jaslany, which was home to seven Jewish families. His oldest sister, Sarah, married in 1940 and moved away. A well-to-do evacuee from the east named Max Federgrün met Sarah, a dressmaker, and they fell in love. But Sarah and Max did not survive the Holocaust. Nor, as far as Zygie knows, did their daughter.

The Friday the war started, Zygie came home from school, and bombs started flying. The Germans were trying to hit the Jaslany railroad station, but they were not even close, sometimes missing by miles. Zygie and Sol ran around gathering up pieces of the bombs—coppery, shiny parts that they found exciting. But soon German troops advanced toward the town, so Polish soldiers pulled out their artillery to oppose them. Some of the villagers, drinking coffee in the Allweiss house before heading out for combat, were upbeat and falsely confident. One of the soldiers, a man with a mustache, bragged about what they would do to the Germans. Hearing him boast made Zygie and his family feel good, at least briefly. When the soldier finished his coffee, he stood up and said, "That's it. We gotta stop them [Germans]."

But the fight was a breathtaking mismatch. The Polish troops were not even mechanized, pulling their artillery with horses. By contrast, when Zygie looked toward the nearby village of Czajkowa, he saw dust rising from the road and thought it must be something he had never seen in his life—cars or military equipment powered by internal combustion engines. What he was seeing was, in fact, the well-equipped German army, which soon streamed by and surrounded the residents of Jaslany. When the shooting started, the villagers ran into fields to lie on the ground. They stayed there all that warm day, bullets flying overhead. Finally, late in the afternoon, the shooting stopped and the residents of Jaslany got up slowly to assess the damage.

The Polish army was gone—captured or destroyed by the Germans. So Zygie and his family started walking home. But when they looked toward their village, their hearts broke. Jaslany was aflame. About half of the three hundred houses burned to the foundations, including Zygie's family home and that of his uncle Yossel Muhlbauer. It was a sickening sight. And cows that had been tied to buildings to keep them from running off were burned alive. So Zygie's first experience of German soldiers opened his eyes to the brutal realities that Poles—and especially Polish Jews—were to face in the war.

Zygie had known a Jewish woman in Jaslany named Miriam Schlissel, who was considered smart and knowledgeable about the world. Just before the men and boys ran east, Zygie said, "the people in our village asked her what she thought would happen to us if the Germans came here." She tried to put everyone at ease, saying the German people were "infused with great culture and would never kill women and children." But she was wrong. Zygie said he and other villagers immediately knew things would not happen the way "that smart woman said." The German troops would kill men, yes, but also women and children. The Germans would target Jews, especially, though they also had little use for most Poles. That much was now clear to Zygie. He would not be fooled into thinking otherwise.

Zygie, his mother, Esther, and his remaining siblings now were without a home. But Jews in Jaslany tried to help each other. So a single Jewish man in his sixties named Chaiml came to Esther and asked if she wanted to move into his house with her children.

There really were no alternatives. Chaiml took in the remaining Allweiss family members and charged them nothing. At the same time, a well-to-do farmer with lots of land gave bundles of wheat or rye for food to everybody who lost a house. The man was a Christian, Zygie said, and gave the same to everybody who needed help, Christian or Jewish. This would be the first help from a non-Jew for Zygie in the war, but not the last.

The Germans were taking control of the area of Poland where Zygie and his family lived, but they had not yet started rounding up local Jews. Labor and death camps were yet to come. But the Allweiss family was hearing disheartening rumors about what the Germans might do to the Jews in the area. Zygie's older sisters talked about going east to the region controlled by the Soviets, thirty or forty miles away, as a way to survive. They even made rucksacks to carry things in as they traveled, but they never had a chance to leave.

The year 1940 was a traumatic year for Zygie and Sol, in effect moving from boyhood to manhood because there was no choice. Sometimes at night they would jump onto moving trains carrying coal toward Germany. The boys would toss pieces of coal off the train into the ditches. Then, when the train neared the local station at Jaslany, they would leap off. The next day the boys would get a small toboggan and load it up with the coal from the ditches. The coal helped provide warmth that winter because there was no wood for the stove in Chaiml's house.

In June 1942 the Germans forced all the Jews of Jaslany to gather in front of a Catholic church there so they could be moved to a new ghetto in the town of Baranów Sandomierksi. That morning Zygie saw two German soldiers on horses using their guns to try to direct about three dozen women, older people, and children to gather for the forced march to Baranów. In the group were Zygie's uncle and two aunts, his father's sisters—Yossel Muhlbauer, Hencha Muhlbauer, and Rachel Allweiss. The older people had a hard time keeping up with the pace of the march. In fact, the group had traveled barely a mile when the Germans' patience ran out. A soldier moved in behind Zygie's two aunts and his uncle, who were walking right next to Zygie. The German shot the three of them in the head, one after the other. Startled, Zygie jumped, and thinking he would be next he began to cry. But the German soldier shoved the boy forward, and Zygie knew if he made one wrong move he might lose his own life. So he shut up. As they continued the trek to Baranów, the soldiers killed most of the older people walking behind Zygie.

Zygie now understood in a profound way the fragility of Jewish life in Poland, the precariousness of his own life, and his diminishing chances of surviving. The survivors continued walking, and by the time they got to Baranów, perhaps thirty miles away, Zygie was thinking hard. He told Sol, "We're not going to stay here with those animals. I can't take it. I'm going to leave." So Zygie went to his mother and told her that he and Sol were going to run away when it got dark. They would not wait until morning when, he was sure, the Germans would start taking down names.

"I don't want to worry that they're going to kill you because I left," he told her. "I can't do that." So the boys planned to take off before the Germans figured out who their relatives were in the group.

Zygie was becoming more aware of the threat German policies posed to his survival. He was doing his best to stay a step or two ahead of them. When it got dark in Baranów, Zygie and Sol sneaked off. They believed they had the skills needed to survive. They spoke Polish well and knew farming—knew how to plow, how to thresh, how to cut the chaff, and how to take care of horses. So Zygie dreamed up a new name for himself (a name he no longer could remember when we interviewed him), and he told farmers that he was old enough to work.

He and Sol managed to get jobs as farmhands in the same village, Krzem- ienica Gawłuszowice, north of Mielec. Zygie told people he was from a village many miles away, and he was sure no one would check. There were, after all, no telephones or other modern methods of communication at that time. If someone was from a village fifty miles away, Zygie said, "it might as well be Tibet."

But Zygie and his brother were in grave jeopardy, nonetheless. They had no papers they could show to pretend to be Polish non-Jews. And they were circumcised. Anyone who saw that would know immediately they were Jews. Although Zygie was confident of his ability to avoid getting caught, he had decided that if anyone figured out his identity and tried to kill him, Zygie would get shot in the back, because he would not stand around and wait for death. He would run.

Zygie and Sol worked for different farmers in Krzemienica. The farmer who employed Zygie was doing quite well, considering—at least well enough to be able to bake bread every week. One night on the Krzemienica farm, Zygie, who often slept in the stable, woke up to the sound of voices screaming in German. He leaped up and pushed the stable door open just far enough to see flashlights all over the farm. Zygie figured soldiers had come to get him. He knew he could not escape through the stable doors. There were just too many Germans around. In fact, they were all over the place. So Zygie climbed up a ladder to the roof and jumped to the ground. Jumped—and landed right on top of a German soldier, knocking him down. Zygie did not have a gun then, but he had fast legs—in fact, he had been the fastest runner in school. So Zygie ran. And ran and ran, darting right and left to avoid bullets the soldier began firing at him. But by the time the German got up, found his gun, and started shooting, Zygie was almost out of range.

That soldier and others chased Zygie, but they could not keep up. Zygie kept running until he came to a swamp near the confluence of the Vistula River and its tributary, the Wisłoka River. The swamp, which had big branches growing out of it, was relatively deep, so Zygie knew he had to stop. He did not know how far behind him the Germans were, so he lay down and kept quiet in the dark. The Germans, it turned out, were already close. When they arrived at the swamp's edge, they waded into the water. Zygie, lying in the muck, was close enough to see their boots. But they did not see the frightened, exhausted boy desperately trying to be invisible. Eventually the Germans gave up. They turned and left, though Zygie did not know how far away they had gone. He figured they might be trying to trick him by pretending to leave while in fact they were waiting around the swamp until he emerged. So the boy lay still in the darkness for a couple of more hours, listening and hoping.

As daylight broke, Zygie got up and carefully checked his surroundings. No Germans. But also no food, no water to drink, and no obvious plan for how to proceed. He decided not to go back to the farm. He figured that because he had run away, the farmer would suspect he was Jewish. Zygie began to search for his brother so the two of them could decide what to do next. As Zygie walked along, he saw a farmhouse and, feeling hungry, got some milk directly from the cow.

Then he kept going. As night began to fall, he noticed someone walking toward him. It was, in fact, Sol, who was looking for Zygie. Sol had heard that something had happened on the farm where Zygie worked, but he did not know exactly what until he saw Zygie and heard the story of his escape.

Zygie and Sol were happy to find each other, but they knew they were running out of options. They felt it would be nearly impossible to get another farm job in this area, given the Germans' persistence in searching for Jews. So they decided to look for their mother and sisters. This task would require help from another non-Jew, a man with a bad reputation but one who turned out to be friendly to the boys. His name was Jantek Kloda, and he lived by himself. Before the war Kloda once had stolen chickens from the Allweisses. Zygie's father quickly figured out who the thief was and went straight to Kloda's house—an easy task because it was snowing and Kloda, clearly not a clever thief, had left tracks. Kloda returned the chickens and apologized. Case closed.

But when the war had started, Kloda told the Allweiss children that if they ever needed news of what was happening they should come to his house. Later Zygie said this about the man: "Jantek may be a thief, but the heart of this guy and what he did for us—believe me, God can forgive him a few chickens." So the boys walked at night the five or six miles it took to reach Kloda. There they learned that their mother and sisters probably were in a work camp named Biesiadka. Laborers in that camp were cutting down trees and breaking up stones to make new highways through the forest.

With directions from Kloda, the boys began walking toward Biesiadka, moving quietly at night and sleeping and hiding during the daylight hours. To sleep they would tunnel under the hay of a barn or find a secluded spot in a small forest. To avoid getting caught together, they did not sleep in the same spot, but they were close, nonetheless. When evening came, nearby dogs inevitably started making noise and woke them up. Then Sol and Zygie would move toward the edge of the woods and slowly sneak out, trying not to provoke the dogs. The Biesiadka camp was eight or twelve miles from Jaslany, and it took several days for the boys to reach it. When they finally got there, they walked up to the fence surrounding the camp. Almost immediately, a man ran toward them with a rifle.

"What do you want?" he demanded.

"Our mother and sisters are working here and we'd like to join them," Zygie told him. The man went inside the camp gate to ask someone what to do and then returned to let the boys come in.

Zygie and Sol, thus, became voluntary inmates at a labor camp because they felt it was the best option available to them at that moment. They joined about four hundred camp inmates, including their mother. She did much of the cooking for the camp with help from her youngest daughter. Cooking mostly meant making a thin soup out of potato peels. Sometimes the Jewish inmates would bring bark from the pine trees to Zygie's mother because the bark was quite juicy. People also brought her grass and other things from the field to use. Otherwise there was nothing in the soup but a few potato peels.

The reality of life in such places is reflected in the fact that, when interviewed, Zygie did not remember going to talk with his mother and sister as soon as he and his brother arrived at the camp. He was "so heartbroken [because] I know what's going to happen to them. I felt pretty bad about it. I don't recall me sitting down and having a conversation with them."

"Yes," he said, his mother observed that her two sons were there, but here, in Zygie's words, was the emotional reality of the camp: "Nobody laughed and nobody cried. We were just frozen. So when I saw my mother, what am I going to talk to her about?"

Zygie said the inmates were starved, and many died within a year of arrival. Then they were simply replaced by new workers. Biesiadka was not run directly by Germans. Rather, a man named Rabiega was in charge. Zygie believed he was a Ukrainian, and he kept careful track of the prisoners for the Germans, who would make regular visits. Rabiega lived in a large motor home without wheels but with its own kitchen.

German authorities would come on their motorcycles and say to Rabiega, "Give me the list of your Jews."

Rabiega would do as ordered, though on his own the man did not beat or otherwise harm the inmates as far as Zygie remembers. The Germans would point to this or that name on the list, and Rabiega then would announce a name. The person named would step forward. Then the Germans would shoot him. They did this every Saturday, the Jewish Sabbath.

Life in the Biesiadka camp was miserable and fragile. In the barracks the three levels of bunks were so close together that prisoners had to go in sideways to get to their beds. When Zygie and Sol arrived at the camp, they got the middle bunk, and Zygie immediately noticed a big nest of spiders there. Well, he thought they were spiders, but when they kept falling on him, he realized they were lice—a constant problem for everyone.

Each morning at the camp, the brothers would walk to a road construction site. They and other prisoners were each given three or four wheelbarrows full of large stones to break up. They spent the day smashing them with hammers and sledgehammers. Later, bulldozers would roll over the crushed rocks, now the size of eggs. Guards at the site shot anyone failing to make his quota of crushed rock. Zygie and Sol easily made the daily quota because they were young and strong. And when they first got to the camp, unlike people who had been there for months, they were not severely malnourished.

Each morning Zygie and the other inmates were given a piece of hard white bread. It was about as thick as a deck of cards. More experienced prisoners told

Zygie and Sol what to do. "Don't eat it all. Just take a bite now and put it in your pocket and when you get hungry later take another bite. It will last you until late in the afternoon."

Usually they got no more food until the next day. There was supposed to be soup, but often his mother was ordered to use the soup pot to boil and wash clothes. On those days she was unable to make soup.

Toward the spring of 1943, the middle-aged and older adults started dying at night in the camp. They would scream out loudly in the night and then die, Zygie said. Younger people got typhus, also called *Fleckfieber*. Sol got typhus first. For four days he was in a coma, running a high temperature. Then he pulled out of it. But then their mother got sick, and so did Zygie, who did not know anything for several days as he fought off the fever and accompanying delirium. When he finally came to, Sol was there.

"Where is Mother?" he asked him.

Sol's answer was direct and hard. "Our mother died."

But Zygie was not sad. In fact, he felt relieved, believing her to be much better off dead instead of seeing her children killed. Zygie by now had concluded that sooner or later everybody in the camp would die.

In early March 1943, a couple of weeks after his mother's death, Zygie saw some people walking by the outside of the camp. They passed along information that shot fear through Biesiadka. The Germans had dug a hole with a big power shovel at the edge of a nearby forest. Zygie knew what the hole would be used for—mass burial. That was exactly what the Germans had in mind. Which is why, early on Sunday morning, March 7, a big truck came in and transported a load of people from the camp, most of whom were sick or frail. When the truck returned, Zygie noticed lots of shoes in it, including the new wooden shoes of his cousin Blima Allweiss. Immediately Zygie concluded that she was dead. On this day, Zygie was just recently off the sick list. He felt certain that he was going to be taken on the truck, and this is what he was thinking: "How is it going to feel when they shoot me?"

Deciding he would not get on the truck, Zygie went up on the barracks roof and hid in an attic that contained pine needles put there to keep people warm in the winter. Sol had been in the barracks, working on some project, and knew that because Zygie had been on the sick list he would be put on the next truck-load. So Sol came up to where Zygie was hiding.

"Run away with me," Sol said.

"I can't run. I can hardly walk," Zygie replied. "You run away and save your-self."

"You go with me," Sol demanded, pulling on Zygie's shirt.

"I'm not going," Zygie said. And he did not go.

So Sol covered Zygie with pine needles on the roof and said again to Zygie, "You run away." Then Sol left and he ran.

Zygie then could hear the Germans shooting at his brother, but he had no immediate way of knowing whether he escaped. Only later did he learn that Sol made it, but the Germans murdered a young friend of Sol's who had run with him. So, again, Zygie and Sol were separated. Up on the roof, Zygie knew the Germans were aware of his location and of his still-sickly condition. Things could hardly have been more perilous for him.

While Zygie was on the roof, Germans came into the building and sent an inmate named Phil Winter up the ladder to tell Zygie to come down.

"Yeah," Zygie told him. "I'll go down if the guy won't shoot me on the ladder."

Zygie had wanted to go down the ladder earlier, but a trigger-happy German, a camp security chief with a bad reputation, was standing there with a gun. Winter backed down the ladder and talked to the man. Somehow he said something that persuaded him to leave. So Zygie came down and began walking toward the truck. He passed the first barracks for women, and as he did, he heard them calling the name of one of his sisters. Then he heard another sister saying, "Me, too," so they could go together. Everyone whose name was called went into the truck, but Zygie's little sister did not want to go. She came to him, thinking that because he was her big brother he could help her.

"Why do I have to die today?" she asked him. Zygie could find no words to tell her. So he said nothing at all.

That was a bright and sunny day, and Zygie knew that March 7 is the day when certain swallow-like birds called *skovroneks* traditionally return north from warmer lands. Indeed, Zygie saw a *skovronek* come in to sing his song. To Zygie, the bird was saying goodbye to him.

But if the bird's message was farewell, it was not meant for Zygie. Standing in the back of the truck, right in the center, Zygie cut his way through the canvas of the truck's cover and escaped into a nearby ditch. Once off the truck, the still sick and now injured boy started crawling. He got away from the highway and into a small forest and kept crawling until he collapsed. At midnight he woke up to see the stars above him and realized he was still alive.

Zygie decided to try to go back toward his native village. He knew his route would take him by the Biesiadka camp, and this would give him the chance to see if anyone still was there. As he got to the camp, he slowly and carefully crawled and listened. But the place was empty. No Jews, no guards—no anything. Everyone was either dead or taken elsewhere.

Moving toward Jaslany, Zygie returned to his old pattern of traveling at night and hiding by day. He helped himself to milk and eggs from farms he passed. In the dark he would feel around for an egg and, when he found one, open it up and drink it down. Along the way, Zygie began to heal. Able to walk better, he sometimes slept with dogs—or figured out how to neutralize them. Zygie once saw a watchdog that a farmer had hooked up by a wire chain that ran from the house to the stables and barn. This German shepherd, trained as a killer, was running back and forth on the chain inside a tall gate and fence, protecting the property. Zygie wanted to get inside the fence to go to the stable to sleep, but he had to avoid arousing the dog so people would not come and investigate the commotion. Zygie jumped the fence, and the dog started running toward him even as Zygie ran toward the dog. But when they got about five or ten feet apart, the dog suddenly stopped. And he never barked. Instead, he looked at Zygie and came over by him and lay down. Relieved, Zygie scratched the dog's back, went to the barn, and lay down next to the dog to sleep. Zygie decided that the dog felt sorry for him.

After a journey of twenty or thirty miles, Zygie finally neared Jaslany. But now what? He was fourteen years old. He had been on the road now for nearly three weeks. Already he had lost much of his family. And he had no idea where Sol was or how to locate him. So Zygie passed by Jaslany and went toward the village of Krzemienica, where he had worked on a farm and escaped a raid by Germans. And he thought this: "How can I find my brother? How long will it take before I find out if he's alive or not?"

As Zygie was moving along the road, thinking about all of this, he saw a house out in the field and decided to see if he could find some eggs or something else to eat. So he pushed the stable door open and started to hunt for food. He stuck his hand in the pigs' trough—and discovered another human being in there. It was, of all people, Sol. Zygie calculated the odds that both of them should go to the same place and find each other in that dire situation as one in a million.

Sol had good news for Zygie. Their father was still alive. Sol had been able to meet up with their father at night in farm fields. So that night the brothers met their father.

In June 1944, Jantek Kloda told the boys that Americans had landed on the French beaches of Normandy. For the first time Zygie and Sol had hope that Germany might lose the war. So they went to get their father, Jacob, from where a farmer was hiding him. The three of them were in a field celebrating the war news when they got ambushed. Suddenly flares came out and lit up the night like daylight. They were surrounded, but at least they had their guns. Feeling trapped, they split up so that they might not all get killed. Zygie and Sol made it out of the tight spot, but not their father. After being caught Jacob was tortured and then murdered.

Now orphaned, the boys went back to the shelter their father had helped them find in 1943, staying with Maciej and Zofia Dudzik in nearby Czajkowa. Maciej let them stay in the Dudziks' wheat field, and when it rained they were allowed to come in and warm up in the stable, which was attached to the house. That stable door was always open and looked out on a field. There also was another stable and a barn in which the boys sometimes slept on the hay.

Before daylight came each day, they would go into the Dudziks' field, lie down, and stay there until it got dark again. Then they would go in search of food to add to the provisions that it took to feed them and the Dudzik family. There were only a handful of other homes near the Dudzik farm, so the relative isolation of a twenty-acre field made it a more effective hiding place.

The Dudzik girls would bring out water from the well to Zygie and Sol. Helka (now called Helena) was the oldest. Then came Wladyslawa (now called Lottie), Franka (now called Ania), Marysha, Stanislawa, and two younger brothers, Janek and Jusef, both of whom live today in Mielec. Another sister, Bronia, died when she was quite young.

Quite often the boys were invited to eat breakfast indoors with the family. A huge pot that took more than one person to carry would be brought from the stove to the dirt floor of the living room. They would all sit down and use wooden spoons to eat from the communal pot. It was often a soured potato soup called *zolivanka*. Zygie and Sol hid with the Dudziks for about a year and three months, until the Soviet Union liberated the area around August 1944.

That was the last time the Dudziks saw the boys. They lost touch with each other until Lottie Rzeznik's daughter, Barbara Rzeznik of Chicago, initiated an Internet search for Zygie and Sol in 1999. She found them living in suburban Detroit, émigrés to the United States, as were many members of the Dudzik family.

"Why did the Dudziks risk their lives for two Jewish boys?" Even with the passage of time, this question for Zygie was still relevant.

This is how Zygie answered: "Me, my brother and Ania Olszewska, who is one of the Dudzik girls, were interviewed in 1999, after the Dudziks found us again. The interviewer asked Ania, 'Why did you risk your life?' And she said, 'My father said, "These boys are good boys, and they should not have to die."' That's what their father said."

And it was one reason that the Allweiss brothers later petitioned the Holocaust Memorial Center in suburban Detroit to honor the Dudziks.[1]

Maciej Dudzik's statement about the boys being good and not deserving death is simple and yet profound. And Maciej's daughter Lottie's response to the "why" question reflected that same approach. Jacob Allweiss and her father were friends, she told us when we interviewed her at her home in Pell Lake, Wisconsin. So there would be no question that, if their children were in trouble, each would help out the other. "Yes," she said, some people thought it was crazy that her parents would risk their lives and the lives of their children to hide Zygie and Sol, "but not all people are bad. Besides," she added, "the boys were like our brothers."

When pressed about whether she ever got angry at her parents for risking her own life to save the boys, Lottie did not criticize their choice.

"I'm always thinking God saved us. Nothing happened to us. I never thought that they did wrong because they [the Allweisses] were our friends. My father, he was a good man." Beyond that, she said, neighbors who lived around the Dudzik farm were aware that Jewish boys were hiding there but chose not to betray the family. "In the village, if one knows something, everyone knows. They were our neighbors and they were good people."

In fact, Lottie said she still does not understand "why there's hatred always and why they killed people. I don't understand to this day." And she pointed out the truth that the Germans killed not only Polish Jews but also many Polish non-Jews, as well as prisoners from the Soviet Union.

We interviewed Lottie's sister Helena Hajnas in her home in Chicago, and she recalled that before the war Jacob Allweiss often came to talk with her father in the evening. The old friends had met through business. Helena and her family went to Jaslany, home of the Allweisses, to attend church every Sunday. When the war started, Jacob came to the Dudzik farm seeking help with food and other necessities. He and his nephew Zygmunt Muhlbauer frequently were allowed to hide with the Dudziks. Eventually, Helen said, Jacob brought the boys to the farm to hide.

But why did her parents hide them?

Helena's answer was in Polish and was translated by her daughter, Teresa Piechota. It was as simple as her father's and her sister's. "They knew each other. So they did not refuse any help." What other reason could one need?

The only time Helena was angry at her parents, she said, was when the Dudziks did not have enough food. The parents insisted that the children not eat all the soup and bread for dinner so the Allweiss boys could have something later.

After the War

When the Soviet Union liberated Czajkowa and the surrounding area, Zygie and Sol were afraid they might be killed by the local villagers if they went back to Jaslany. The brothers had to decide what to do next. Zygie wanted to join the Soviet army but was told he was too young to join up.

The brothers caught a freight train east to Lwów (now L'viv in Ukraine) where an agency recorded them as Jewish survivors. Zygie got a job as a janitor maintaining the furnaces in a Lwów hospital, but Sol could not find work. Before long the Soviet army decided to accept Zygie, and he gave Sol his hospital job. Zygie enlisted, using the false name of Zygmunt Dudzik, in honor of the family that sheltered him.

In September 1944, after he had trained for a month in Rzeszów, Poland, the Communists asked Zygie and other soldiers with Polish-sounding names to transfer to a newly established Polish Communist military force in Lublin. He accepted and later traveled close to Berlin with the Polish unit attached to the Soviet force. The unit fought the Germans alongside the Soviet soldiers near Berlin. Zygie believes a bomb struck when they were near the Oder River on the German-Polish border. The attack left him in a coma. When he woke up in a Soviet hospital in Włochy, a suburb of Warsaw, it was August 1945. Zygie had missed the end of the war in Europe.

After recovering, Zygie's next assignment in the Polish army was with the military police. He was assigned to guard the home of Marian Spychalski (1906–1980), the marshal of Poland, who headed the government's political affairs from September 18, 1944, to March 1945. Spychalski and his family lived in Włochy.

Sol found Zygie in the army—Zygie doesn't know how—and persuaded him to go with him to the displaced persons camp at Foehrenwald in Germany. They intended to go to Israel, but Zygie got into a fight and ended up in jail. Eventually, the brothers sailed to America as part of a quota of orphans. They took the SS *Marine Flasher,* along with their cousin Zygmunt Muhlbauer and his wife, Sallah (or Sarah). The ship arrived in New York in November 1947. An immigrant from Jaslany, Charlie Schneur, met them at the harbor, and they drove with him—their first car ride—to the Manhattan apartment of their aunt Beila (Allweiss) Greenberg. She had come to America before the war.

Soon afterward, the promise of work in the auto industry enticed Zygie and Sol to leave New York for Detroit. World ORT, an international agency assisting Jewish refugees, helped the brothers to get vocational training. They learned auto mechanics at the Washington Trade School and picked up English along the way.[2]

Zygie studied at both Wilbur Wright High School and Wayne State University. Both he and Sol worked at assembly line jobs for Chevrolet Gear & Axle before going into business for themselves. The brothers operated Mobil and Standard gasoline stations under the name Sol & Zygie's for many years. Each eventually owned an auto and truck repair service.

Sol graduated from Cass Tech High School in Detroit. He married Frieda Schiller, a native of Poland who survived the war with her parents in Russia. They had four children—three sons and a daughter.

Zygie married Irma Burg, who was born in the Bronx, New York, and they had five children, four daughters and a son. One daughter, Esther Ingber, traveled to Jaslany in 1985 and wrote an account of her trip for the *Detroit Free Press.* Esther returned to Poland in September 2006. She accompanied her father on his first trip back to Jaslany since the war. They were treated like relatives, staying in the home of Janek Dudzik and his family. Esther also reported on this trip for the Jewish *Forward* and the *Detroit Jewish News*.

In recent years, the Holocaust Memorial Center in Detroit has asked Zygie to speak to groups of young people about his experiences in the Holocaust.

"When I talk to kids, I say, 'I want you to know that the horrible thing that happened was caused by a nation regarded as the most cultural and fair and technologically advanced. And all this equipment they killed with was produced by people with degrees in engineering and other fields. I want you to know that, just in case you think you're safe somewhere.'"

Then he warns them, "You're not safe nowhere. You have to watch the world. You have to watch others, otherwise you've got no control and you cannot stop another Holocaust."

Irene Bau

At night, hiding in a Polish woman's barn, Irene Landesdorfer and her mother could hear the chilling screams and moans of Jews who were locked in collection points at nearby railroad tracks, waiting to be sent by train to death camps the next morning. But after Irene and her mother, Regina, had been in the barn just two or three days, the woman who owned it ordered them to leave. When this happened Regina could see no alternative but to give up, turn themselves in, and face certain death, too. So, taking no precautions, simply walking along a rural road in the daylight of that cold November day in 1942, Regina and her thirteen-year-old daughter headed toward the police station in the nearby village of Koszyce, northeast of Kraków.

They had lived in Koszyce since 1940. Then the Germans ordered them to move at least thirty kilometers from their native Kraków.[3] The German order to rid Koszyce of Jews in early November 1942 caused Regina and her daughter to go into hiding.

As they walked toward the police station, to their surprise, they saw walking toward them Irene's friend, seventeen-year-old Zbigniew Bolt, who had a romantic interest in her. Zbigniew, who went by the nickname Zbyszek, was accompanied that day by one of his friends, the son of the local chief of police. And they were looking for Irene and her mother. Zbigniew was shocked to see them walking in the open, knowing full well they were putting themselves in danger.

"Where are you going?" he demanded to know of Irene and her mother, as Irene recalled the story. "Are you crazy?"

Regina explained that the woman who owned the barn they had been staying in (space the woman offered only because she had been given furniture and other goods from Irene's mother) had told them to leave because it was too dangerous to hide Jews. Without any alternative, they were heading back to turn themselves in.

"No, no, no," Zbigniew said. "You go back. I will go talk to that woman." So Zbigniew and his friend went with Irene and Regina to see the woman, who knew Zbigniew because his father was the only doctor in the area and was known by almost everyone. Zbigniew promised the woman that if she would keep Irene and Regina for just another day or two, he would arrange for them to be transported to a safe location elsewhere. Reluctantly, the woman agreed.

To find an alternative hiding place, Zbigniew spoke to his uncle Stanislaw Kwiecinski, an unmarried teacher who lived with his two single sisters in the

Irene Bau

Zbigniew Bolt

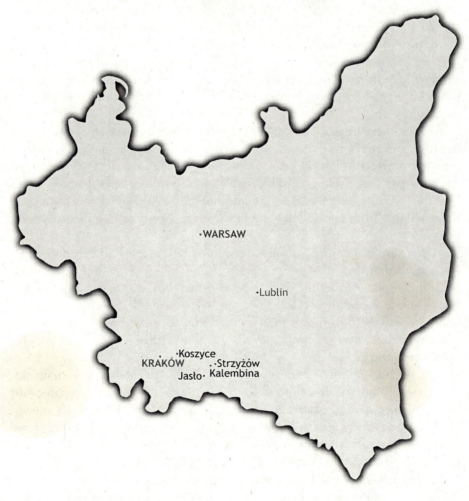

·WARSAW

·Lublin

·Koszyce
KRAKÓW ·Strzyżów
Jasło· Kalembina

26

village of Kalembina near the town of Jaslo, almost one hundred miles east-southeast of Kraków. Zbigniew also spoke with a cousin who lived in Płaszów, the location of a concentration camp near Kraków. Arrangements were made for Irene and her mother to go to the home of a cousin and aunt of Zbigniew, while his uncle Stanislaw, the brother of Zbigniew's mother, prepared more permanent arrangements.

Zbigniew arranged for a driver with a sled to pick up Irene and Regina at the woman's barn and take them across the snow to the train station, where they caught a train to Płaszów to stay with Zbigniew's cousin. They were not yet able to move to the uncle's house because the space there was taken. The fiancé of Zbigniew's cousin was Jewish, and he was already hiding there.

So, without yet having a permanent hiding place, Regina and Irene were told to head to a mountain village for a week or two and to tell people that Irene had bronchitis and needed mountain air. That was how they wound up temporarily in Osielce, where they rented a room. But Irene needed some kind of documentation of her alleged bronchitis from a doctor, so they made an appointment to see a physician, though they feared how he might treat them, even with their false identity papers. When they got to the doctor's office they were tired and hungry—so hungry, in fact, that while the doctor was examining Irene, her stomach was growling loudly.

"Would you excuse me?" the doctor asked her.

Within a few minutes he returned with two bowls of very welcome warm soup for Irene and Regina. He had figured out that he was dealing with two Jews, but he kept quiet about it, provided the necessary health papers, and even suggested a place for them to rent a room.

Regina and Irene had some money, but they were so scared of being found out that they did their best to stay out of sight. Regina also had another resource—jewelry, which she had buried in the ground while living in the village of Koszyce. In fact, later, she told Zbigniew where she had hidden the jewelry, and he and his uncle went at night, dug it up, and brought it to her. Uncle Stanislaw, at Regina's request, periodically sold pieces of the jewelry so she could have money to support herself and Irene. She wanted to pay him for his help out of the proceeds, but he refused.

Irene and Regina were supposed to stay in the rented room in Osielce until they got word that it was safe to move to Zbigniew's uncle's house. But they were forced to leave earlier than they planned because Irene ran into a priest who had taught in her former school and who knew she was Jewish. Irene told her mother that the priest had seen her and recognized her.

"That's it," Regina said. "We're getting out of here." Which is exactly what they did, quickly traveling by train and then by sled to the home of Zbigniew's uncle Stanislaw in the village of Kalembina and showing up there unexpectedly.

It could have been an awkward situation had Stanislaw, who had never seen them before, answered the door and reacted to their unexpected presence in a shocked or hostile way in front of the sled driver. But he came out of the house, immediately realized who they were and what their situation was, and said loudly, "Oh, my God, am I happy to see you. How wonderful you made it," just as if he were expecting them.

Decades later, as we interviewed Irene in her condominium in West Orange, New Jersey, she still marveled at Stanislaw Kwiecinski's goodness. "He was a saint," she said.

Irene and her mother crowded in with Uncle Stanislaw, his sisters, and the fiancé of Zbigniew's cousin for about a week while Stanislaw located another house for them to rent in a village just west of Kalembina, Wiśniowa. The people from whom they eventually rented had no idea they were Jewish. That was a secret that Stanislaw kept as he helped them in various ways.

In their new rental situation, their disguise was aided by the fact that they spoke fluent Polish. In addition, they had false identity papers. Regina's, which a priest in Koszyce helped her get, said she was Zofia Glowacz. Irene's, which Stanislaw obtained for her, said she was Irene Glowacz.

In reality Irene was, originally, Irena Landesdorfer, born November 9, 1929, in Kraków, the only child of Regina and Samuel Landesdorfer. Indeed, Irene said she was considered a "miracle child," because physicians had told her mother she would never be able to have children. Her father ran a wholesale and retail hardware and farm equipment store. They were not Orthodox Jews, but they were observant and kept a kosher home because otherwise Irene's grandparents would not have visited their home. Until the war started, Irene went to public school and her only religious education came in a one-hour weekly class taught by a rabbi.

When the Germans invaded Poland in 1939, Irene was no longer allowed to attend school because she was a Jew. She even felt that some of her best friends did not even want to look at her any more. A *Volksdeutsch* man was made manager of her father's store soon after the outbreak of war, but by then her father, reacting to rumors of what the Germans would do to Jewish men, had escaped to Lwów, in Soviet-controlled territory.[4] From there the Soviets sent him to Siberia for the remainder of the war, but eventually, in his early forties, he died of typhus in Kazakhstan. When Regina's husband left, her sister and husband (both of whom died in the Holocaust) moved in with them.

Irene and Regina Landesdorfer not only pretended to be Irene and Zofia Glowacz, they also regularly went to church, pretending not to be Jews. And they were helped with this by the fiancé of Zbigniew's cousin, with whom they hid for a time at Stanislaw's house. Although Jewish he knew a lot about Catholicism—indeed, he later married Zbigniew's cousin and became a Catholic. In the week or so that he and Regina and Irene all lived in Stanislaw's house, he taught them the basics of Catholicism.

In fact later, when Irene was attending high school, still as a Catholic, the priest who taught a class on religion regularly called on her because she seemed to know more about Catholicism than children who were born into the faith.

"If I didn't know the answer," she said, "he'd say, 'OK, I don't have to ask anybody else.'" And when she attended church, she regularly took Communion and went to confession. In fact, she said, she came to be a believer, at least for a time—even though she was exposed to church teachings about Jews as Christ killers. "And Easter was the worst holiday" for this, she said. "I hated that holiday." Even some of the choral music, she remembered, "said the Jews crucified Jesus." One reason she remembered this so clearly is that "I was in the choir singing the songs."

This was quite a change from Irene's girlhood in Kraków, where she was surrounded mostly by Jews and rarely heard antisemitic talk, even among her many non-Jewish friends. But one day when they came home from church, the people at whose house they lived told Regina that "people are saying that you don't know how to pray and you don't know how to use the rosary." But Regina credibly dismissed the complaints, saying that in the big city of Kraków, where she came from, they did things a little differently. Regina had other explaining to do, too, such as why they had left Kraków. She told people who asked that her family was active in the Polish underground and that several family members had been arrested, so they left to find a safer place to live. However, whenever she and Irene saw any Germans coming near, they would slip away and hide in a potato cellar.

After a time in their new place, Regina was deported to Germany and employed as a Polish forced laborer. Left alone, Irene would make more regular visits to Stanislaw's house. Sometimes Zbigniew, who was still very fond of Irene, would be there visiting his uncle.

Once in the middle of the night, while Irene was sleeping at Stanislaw's, two Polish policemen came and took her away to the police station on suspicion of being Jewish. Stanislaw came running after them, yelling, "What do you want? She's just a little girl. She's not Jewish."

But the police hit him in the head with a rifle and said, "Go back home if you don't want your house to be burned and you end up in a concentration camp."

One of the arresting officers then left to look for Polish people the Germans wanted for forced laborers. The other officer stayed with Irene and prepared to take her to the police station. But he offered her a way out.

"Look, little girl," he said. "I will look this way and if you want to go I won't see you."

Irene, however, refused. This girl, now fourteen, already understood clearly what she would be required to do if she hoped to survive.

"I'm not going," she told him. "I have nothing to hide."

She knew that if she ran away, he would know for sure she was Jewish and not only would her life be in even more danger but authorities would come after Stanislaw, too. So Irene and the officer went to the police station, which was little more than a chicken coop, with live chickens and with bars on the windows. There he began to interrogate her at length.

"What was your mother's name?" he wanted to know. "What was your father's name?" Irene knew all the right answers, and despite her habit of blushing when she failed to tell the truth, her face never once got red. Next, however, a German soldier was brought in to question her. Because he was *Volksdeutsch*, he spoke to her in Polish, but he finally concluded that Irene was not Jewish.

The chief of police had a reputation for being harsh on Jews and was known to have helped kill many of them. But somehow he liked Irene, who was not afraid to confront him. In fact, after being in jail for two days, she said to him, "I cannot just sit here. Either you do something or let me go."

"You can go," he replied. "I have all your papers. You can go, but come every morning at 10 o'clock and report to me and I'll see if those papers are real."

They were not real, of course, and all the man had to do to discover that was to pick up a phone and trace them, but he never did. Something kept him from deciding to end Irene's life, and she attributed it to her own spunkiness and her lack of fear in his presence. In fact, one day she came to the police station as ordered and found it full of Germans.

When the police chief saw her, he quickly and quietly said to her, "What are you doing here? Get out."

Irene is convinced that if her mother, who was afraid of such people and could not but show it, had been with her at the police station, they both would have died. But, on her own, Irene was able to get through the experience.

However, without her mother and without her papers, she was stuck. She had no way to buy food or to compensate the people from whom they rented the room for feeding her—to say nothing of not being able to pay the rent. Those people, however, had grown fond of Irene and even called her their baby. But she did not want to live there without money, completely beholden to them. Unsure what else to do, Irene went to confession at church and told the priest that she was a Jew in hiding.

And then an amazing thing happened. Instead of turning Irene over to authorities, the priest went to the police station. There he said this to the police chief, "Give the girl back her papers. I knew her parents. The girl is not Jewish."

After that, Irene returned to see the police chief, who said to her, "I don't know what it is with you and that priest. But he came here and he told me that he knew your parents and that you are not Jewish. So here are your papers. Go."

This turn of events revealed that here and there some Poles who never risked their lives by hiding Jews nonetheless performed one or two smaller acts that helped to save Jewish lives. Why did the priest do this? Irene does not know. He soon moved elsewhere and she lost touch with him.

With her papers back, Irene found a job in a grocery store stocking shelves. She continued working there until the area was liberated by the Soviet Union in the fall of 1944. And although she lost her rented room because others needed it more, the family from whom she rented simply took her in and let her continue living in the same house.

As the Soviets were driving out the Germans, bombs and bullets were flying in and over the village where Irene was living. It fascinated her, so sometimes she would stand outside and watch until the woman who owned the house would spot her and, yelling, drag her to safety in a cellar.

After the War

Once her area had been liberated, Irene began to attend a high school that had been reopened by the Soviets in the nearby town of Strzyżów, and during the week she lived with a fellow female student there. The girl was not very bright, so in compensation for Irene tutoring their daughter, the girl's parents paid for both their lodging there. School officials, in fact, let that girl pass tests and courses so she could keep up with Irene, because they knew that without this girl and support from the girl's parents Irene could not afford to go to school.

A month after the war formally ended in May 1945, a friend told Irene that she had just seen her mother get off a train at Strzyżów, the town where the high school was. Irene grabbed a bicycle and rode back to the other village where she had lived before, thinking her mother, finally released from forced labor in Germany, would go there to look for her. Along the way she ran into her mother riding in a wagon.

At the mother-daughter reunion, everybody cried—Irene, Regina, the wagon driver, everybody.

Irene and Regina soon returned to Kraków, their original home, where Zbigniew had become a medical student.

"He wanted to marry me," she said. Irene recalled that Zbigniew's parents may not have been too happy about their son marrying a Jewish girl, but when we interviewed him in Kraków, Zbigniew insisted to us that "my parents never disapproved of it." Irene thought about the possibility of marriage, but her mother wanted to come to the United States. She had two sisters in America, and she did not want to stay in Poland.

Zbigniew understood. He later became a physician and married another woman after the war. But he and Irene have stayed in touch throughout the years. Today Zbigniew lives in Płaszów, the town where his aunt used to live.

After the war Irene and her mother first moved to Germany, where they lived for two years. Then they received permission to come to the United States in 1948. Irene married a Holocaust survivor from Kraków, Marcel Bau, whom she had met in Poland, and they had one daughter, Celia, who now lives in Chappaqua, New York. Irene worked as an administrator in a property management office and continued to work on a part-time basis well past normal retirement age.

Our Visit with Zbigniew Bolt

We met Zbigniew Bolt and his wife, Zofia, on the main market square in Kraków and sat down to talk in a nearby coffee shop. Bolt was a retired medical doctor, an internist. He was an elegant soft-spoken man whose eyes twinkled as he spoke of his wartime experiences and his pride at having helped to save Irene and her mother.

When Bolt was a boy (he told us through an interpreter), his family lived in Koszyce, the town to which Irene and her mother moved when they were forced out of Kraków. Irene became part of a group of young friends that spent lots of time together there.

"We were really good friends. We'd spend all day together," he said.

What Bolt described as the crucial event in saving Irene happened when he ran into Irene and her mother as they were walking on the way to turn themselves in. He said he had previously arranged for them to be taken from the barn in which they were staying to another hiding place, but somehow Irene and her mother had failed to get the message about this plan. Thus, when the woman who owned the barn demanded that they leave, they felt they had no choice but to surrender.

"So she started walking toward Koszyce, where the Nazis were waiting. But we met on the road as I was walking to get her. She was walking from one direction and I'm walking from the other direction, and we see each other from across the street. This was the most important moment. I gave her a sign to go back to where they were staying because I have a plan to help them. Everything went fine then."

We asked Bolt if he was, in fact, in love with Irene then.

"It wasn't a big love," he said, "but I liked her." So much, in fact, that he later thought about marrying her. In fact, his father expressed the hope that he would do exactly that.

"Maybe if she hadn't gone to the United States and I wasn't studying medicine in Kraków we might have gotten together," Bolt told us. But Bolt stayed in Poland, finished medical school, became a physician, and was married in 1951. He and his wife, Zofia, have two sons and five grandchildren.

We wanted to know whether he was fearful as a young man for his own life or the life of his uncle. Both of them were at risk for helping Jews.

"I wasn't afraid of helping, although I knew it was putting my life and my uncle's life in danger. But I belonged to an underground organization, the *Armia Krajowa,* which was well organized.[5] There was much help within the organization. And one of my friends had a Jewish girlfriend. This man advised me how to hide Irene where it would be safe."

Within the A.K, he said, there were many subgroups, "but the group I was with was really focused on helping Jews.[6] And it wasn't just me, it was my entire family." Indeed, his uncle's sister and others in the family also helped to save Jews.

"We were just very human," Bolt said. "And there were a lot of people like that. There were probably even more people helping Jews but we don't know it. In our family's upbringing, we were taught that everyone is the same. There was no antisemitism. This is how we were brought up and it's how we've tried to bring up our children and grandchildren. There is no place for antisemitism." The murder of millions of Jews in the Holocaust, he said, means that only a tiny number of Jews now live in Poland, which has resulted in the problem that "the younger generation in Poland today doesn't know Jewish people."

We asked him whether he would do the same thing today to save desperate people.

"For sure," he said. "In fact, I would do it even better. My uncle and I would help even more people."

We asked whether he considered himself a hero.

"No," he said, "it was just a normal human act."

Bolt brought to our meeting the Yad Vashem medal designating him as "Righteous among the Nations," as well as the one awarded to his uncle, now deceased.

"When Yad Vashem started giving these medals," he said, "Irene asked me if I wanted to get one. I said yes, but the only reason I said yes was that I wanted others to have a good opinion of Polish people. I'm no hero. I just wanted Polish people to be seen in a good light."

Sheila Bernard

The man was dying of cancer, and he knew it. He also knew that as a Polish policeman he had done things that did not make him proud. So he decided he wanted to do something good and courageous for the world before he left it. Against his wife's bitter protests this man did exactly that, and having accomplished it, he died two weeks after the war. He saved the life of Sala Perec (sometimes spelled Peretz), who was later known as Sheila Bernard, and her mother, Bela Perec, by hiding them from the Germans.

Had the man listened to his wife, he never would have done that, Sheila told us, and her chances of making it would have been, by her own estimate, zero.

"He said he did a lot of bad things as a policeman," Sheila told us when we interviewed her near the U.S. Holocaust Memorial Museum in Washington, D.C., where she did volunteer work.[7]

"And before he died he wanted to save us."

Sheila was an only child, born in early 1936 in Chełm, east of Lublin, not far from today's Poland-Belarus border. Her parents, Bela and Isaac Perec, named her Sala, or Sara. Her mother always called her Sala. She adopted the name Sheila after she moved to the United States from Israel in 1963.

Isaac Perec was the manager of a Singer Sewing Machine business, and the family owned a big U-shaped apartment building at 25 Lubelska Street in Chełm. The building faced three different streets and had a courtyard in the center that included a small stable for horses. One wing of that structure eventually would form a border of—and be within—the Chełm Ghetto.

When the war started in 1939, Chełm was home to about eighteen thousand Jews, most of whom died in the Holocaust.[8] The city contained many Jewish institutions such as schools and synagogues.

"There were Jews in Chełm for a very long time," Sheila said. "And actually the Germans destroyed one synagogue that was seven hundred years old."

Sheila's mother was one of ten children and her father was one of three brothers. So Sheila grew up with many nearby family members in this active Jewish community. Her parents would take her on occasional summer vacations.

"I remember our last vacation. We went to a country house, and there were chickens and horses there. It was beautiful. Then the war started. I was about four years old." The fighting prevented the family from returning home immediately because, among other disruptions, passenger trains were no longer running. Eventually Sheila and her parents started walking back to Chełm.

34

Sheila Bernard

"I remember my father carried me on his back for a long time. Finally, I think, he must have hired a horse and buggy and we finally made it back to Chełm." That was a region that Soviet troops controlled temporarily after they invaded Poland from the east a few weeks after Germany invaded. But soon German troops turned on the Soviets and drove them out.

"As soon as the Germans came, our life completely changed," Sheila said.

Her family was forced to move to Chełm's open ghetto. That meant moving to a smaller apartment in a different section of the same building they owned and already lived in. (Just that section of this large building became part of the ghetto.) They moved in with Sheila's aunt, uncle, and cousins—her mother's sister, her husband, and their three children. "It was very small, but at first it was OK," she said.

In addition to a different, smaller living space, another aspect of life that changed for Sheila under German rule was language. Her mother forced the little girl to quit speaking Yiddish. Now she had to speak only Polish instead.

When Sheila's father, Isaac, learned that the Germans first were killing Jewish men, he and several other men, including Sheila's uncle, organized a group to try to escape the killing by going to the Soviet Union. But by the time he made it as far as Lwów, south-southeast of Chełm, he learned that women and children also were targets of the Germans. So he turned around to rejoin and protect his wife and daughter. "He was trying to come back, but the Germans conducted a raid in which they killed a lot of Jews. My father was shot and my uncle at the same time. My father died running away. They shot him in the back. That's what my mother told me."[9]

This meant that Sheila and her mother were now on their own, so Bela began selling things she owned to get money to buy food. "She was trying to buy things and sell to others. I remember one time she bought two big sacks of flour for baking bread and she was selling them by the kilo. And somehow the Germans came and raided and found the flour. Jews were not supposed to sell or have any business. And they took her to jail."

Jewish policemen were in charge in the jail, but Bela knew someone whose authority trumped theirs. Her family was longtime friends with a Polish policeman named Chizuk (Sheila did not remember his full name). One of Sheila's younger cousins went to Chizuk "and told him that they arrested my mother. So he came to the police and went to the jail and took my mother out. So that's how she survived that." Later, Chizuk would prove to be even more helpful.

When the ghetto first was created, most able adults there were required to be forced laborers for the Germans, including Bela and her uncle. "But my aunt stayed home with the children."

Life in the ghetto grew increasingly difficult and ever more fragile. There was never enough food, and the Germans forced Jews in Chełm, like Jews throughout Poland, to wear items on their clothing identifying them as Jews. Sheila also told us she remembered seeing German authorities murder Jews by shooting them "in the street. Sometimes you see them lying in the street. Then, later on, a wagon would come and collect them. I saw a few bodies in our courtyard."

One day German authorities came to the apartment in which Sheila lived. "And they found my aunt. She was babysitting a few other children. She had papers showing she was sick and couldn't work at that time. But they didn't care. They took her and shot her. My aunt was shot in front of me. I was standing at the top of the stairs. We lived on the second floor, and they shot her as she was walking down the stairs. She rolled down the flight of stairs and died."

Right after that they shot some other children. "And then it was my turn. They were going to shoot me. They told me and another boy to walk down the stairs. That boy became very hysterical and started laughing. And I was crying very hard. It was very funny to those Germans that I was crying and he was laughing. The [man] in charge said, 'Well, we already killed enough Jews today. We can let them go.'" Sheila said she knew Yiddish and this helped her decipher the German words that the man spoke. Sheila was not quite six years old when she was spared from death that day on the whim of one soldier.

Several other times German soldiers came to find Jews, and Sheila hid with her cousins in a closet under the stairway. Sometimes she also hid in a small shed in the courtyard that once housed horses. But as time went on, Sheila's mother, while she was gone during the day to do forced labor for the Germans, got increasingly worried about her daughter's safety back in the ghetto. So she paid a Jewish policeman to sneak Sheila out of the ghetto one morning before dawn and bring her to the place where Bela was assigned to dig ditches.

Bela found places in nearby bushes and trees for Sheila to hide while she worked. After some time Bela and other workers were transferred to a factory in Chełm. In this location Sheila hid in an attic on the roof with other children.

"Some of the Germans even knew we were hiding there, but they didn't tell. My mother said those were the good Germans."

Chizuk eventually found Bela and told her that the Germans planned to close the ghetto and to send everyone to a death camp. Chizuk said Bela should escape the ghetto and come to his house to hide, "but my mother wouldn't go without me, so he agreed to take me, too."

So, late that same night, they sneaked out of the ghetto with "clothes and blankets and whatever we could carry with us," and they came to Chizuk's home at the edge of Chełm in a semi-isolated area.

"At first we stayed in his house, but his wife was afraid that the Germans would catch us there and kill them also or send them to a concentration camp," Sheila said. "She didn't want us there, but he insisted. He knew he had cancer and he knew he was going to die soon. He was a Catholic and he said he had done many bad things as a policeman and now said he wanted to do something good before he died. Also, he knew my mother and grandfather and was a friend of the family."

Chizuk and his wife had two grown children. But the wife had sent the children to live with her brother on a farm for the rest of the war. Chizuk's wife was "not nice to us. She didn't want us there. She stayed away from us. She never gave us food or anything, and she never talked to us."

One day Sheila's two younger cousins, who somehow had survived when the Germans closed the ghetto, came to Chizuk's house, but the wife would not let them come in. "She chased them away from the house. We saw them from the window. I cried and my mother cried because we knew we'd never see them again, and we never did because they were killed."

After they had stayed two weeks in the house, Chizuk decided to move Sheila and her mother to a nearby bunker where he kept potatoes for the winter. With the onset of winter, however, the potato bunker got too cold after some weeks. So next he moved them to a chicken coop with fifteen or twenty chickens not far from the house and they fixed up a corner with the clothes and blankets they had brought with them. "We slept there in the corner."

Each day, Chizuk would bring them a bottle of water and a loaf of black bread that Sheila and her mother would cut in half. But sometimes he had to leave his property for a day or two, and "his wife would never bring us food. I remember I was more thirsty than hungry. But that's all we ate and we were grateful we had that."

Sheila and Bela hid in the chicken coop for almost two years. "It was very boring there. There were a few cracks in the wall, and I was able to see the people walking in the street. I even saw Germans walking, marching in their boots. When I hear the boots still today, it bothers me, because in the ghetto they used to come walking in their boots over the cobblestone making a lot of noise."

Looking through the cracks in the wall—"that was my entertainment. I was so scared in the chicken coop that they would find us. My mother said we should keep quiet. So during the day we talked very little. We had no pencils, no paper, no toys, nothing," including nothing to read. Mother and daughter would talk quietly so as not to give themselves away. In the chicken coop, Sheila said, she "used to ask my mother, 'Why do they want to kill us? Why do we have to hide? What did we do?' And my mother didn't really have a good answer."

Sometimes the ailing Chizuk would come and talk briefly to her mother at night. And periodically Bela "used to sneak out and clean out the pot that we used [for bathroom purposes]. But I never went out."

Not far from the chicken coop, on property owned by someone other than Chizuk, there was a potato field. Farmers would work the field in the day. "At the end of the day, they would roast the potatoes and make a fire, and they were sitting and eating the potatoes and the smell of those potatoes was so good. I love roasted potatoes. But they couldn't know that we were there. The smell was driving us crazy because half a loaf of bread a day was not enough."

Chizuk suffered from stomach cancer, and toward the end of the war his condition worsened steadily. By the time the Soviets began driving the Germans out of the area, "he could barely walk," Sheila said. Bombs were exploding overhead, and Sheila and Bela were hoping Chizuk would last until the Germans were gone.

The Soviets finally arrived, and the Germans retreated from the area on July 22, 1944. Chizuk was still alive, but several weeks earlier when the bombing started his wife abandoned him.

"His wife, near the end of the war, when the bombing started—she ran away and left him alone." So Bela would sneak out at night and slip into the house to help this dying man.

When the Soviets liberated the area, Sheila and Bela moved from the chicken coop into Chizuk's house. "The first time I went outside, my mother let me walk in the street near the house. It was so strange to me. And right away I heard Polish people saying, 'Oh, here are Jews walking.'"

Just two weeks after liberation, Chizuk died. "If he would have died before the war ended, his wife probably would have thrown us out," Sheila told us. Bela and Sheila could not attend Chizuk's funeral because his wife, who returned after he died, did not want them there. She did not want anyone to know that he had saved Jews.

After the War

After leaving Chizuk's home Bela and Sheila moved back into a small second-floor apartment in the building they owned in Chełm before the war. They met a few other Jews who emerged from hiding in the forest around Chełm. Bela began working again, mostly as a cook. She put Sheila back in school where, she said, other children treated her as an unwelcome eight-year-old in first grade. But Bela was weakened from living in the chicken coop and from eating only bread and water. Before long she injured herself when she was hauling a large piece of furniture up the stairs.

The result was that Bela got a blood clot in her leg and was in great pain. Although she got some medical treatment, "the clot traveled through her body to her brain and two days later she died. So I was left alone." This was just before Sheila's ninth birthday.

To bury her mother, Sheila had to rely on the few Jews who had come back to Chełm after the war. Bela was buried in a cemetery that the Germans had not destroyed in the war. But to pay for this, whatever her mother had, including her wedding ring, had to be sold. Even so, there was not enough money to put Bela's name on a gravestone. Her name was added sometime later, something Sheila learned about only later.

After Bela's death, a Jewish couple who had returned to Chełm after the war (the husband was a shoemaker) took in the orphaned girl and made sure she continued to go to school for the next year.

Once the war finally ended in May 1945, representatives of a Jewish organization called *Koordynacja*, a Zionist group funded by the American Jewish Joint Distribution Committee, came to Poland looking for Jewish children who had survived the Holocaust. Sheila was found and taken to an orphanage west of Munich, in Dornstadt, Germany, where she lived for two years with about forty other children. By then Sheila was the only survivor from among members of her family who had lived in Poland in the war, although she had some relatives in the United States and in what was then Palestine, and a cousin who escaped to Russia who survived.

"I'm the only survivor and we had a very big family. I didn't have anything when I left Poland. Everything was gone, even though technically I still own the building on Lubelska Street."

While at the orphanage Sheila wrote to an uncle in Israel and an uncle in the United States, both brothers of her late mother who had left Sheila their addresses. They tried to get papers for her to be able to leave Germany. But the process took most of two years because the British set a limited annual quota on Jews who could come to Palestine. Eventually, however, at age ten and a half she was able to go to Palestine in 1947 and enter the fifth grade.

The state of Israel was established the next year, and Sheila lived in Israel for sixteen years. She attended nursing school there. She also served in the Israeli military. While there she married a native of Lithuania, Eli (later Eric) Etons, also a Holocaust survivor. She gave birth to a daughter, who today is the mother of Sheila's two grandchildren in the United States. She and Eric were married for more than twenty years. Later she married an American named Bernard.

Sheila came to the United States in 1963 and worked as a nurse for thirty years in a large hospital. She was an active member of her synagogue. In recent years she was a regular speaker for the U.S. Holocaust Memorial Museum.

Sheila never spoke about any of her experiences until the early 1990s. Then, "every time I was talking about it I used to cry and especially I would cry when I was telling about my younger two cousins—whom Chizuk's wife would not let into the house—because it was so traumatic for me." She continued to talk about it because "the world should never forget that six million Jews were killed in the Holocaust, including my family. There are some people who want to re-write history as if the Holocaust never happened. I lived it. It did happen. Also, I am, after all, the only member of my family who stayed in Poland during the war who survived and I am able to tell the story. I want people to know what happened, though it's not easy for me to speak about it."

Sheila said she would be forever grateful to Chizuk for his kindness, but she also credited her mother's wits for her survival. "She was a remarkable woman."

Maria Devinki

For more than two years—from September 28, 1942, to January 16, 1945—Maria Devinki lived under barns.

For more than a year and a half, it was in a hole dug in the soil under the wooden floor of a barn at the edge of the village of Droblin, outside Wodzisław, northeast of Kraków. Then fear of being discovered drove her and her family to another nearby farm, where she hid for eight more months until Soviet troops liberated the area. She, her husband, and her mother, and sometimes others were paying a lot of money for the privilege of hiding from the Germans in a hole in the ground, as much as two thousand dollars (in today's dollars) a month.

The young woman who emerged from those unspeakable places of darkness saw the realities of the world with remarkable clarity. We had barely sat down with her in her suburban home in Kansas City when Maria, more than sixty years after the end of the war, said this: "Just to make it short and sweet before we go any farther, that generation, my generation, will never forgive. Pardon me for making this statement, because I wouldn't be here if it weren't for a Polish army officer."

That officer, Jozef (or Jusick) Gondorowicz, was a non-Jew in the *Armia Krajowa*. He had been a business partner of Maria's parents, Solomon and Regina (or Rivka) Braun. Maria was known then as Mala Braun. Jusick acted as a trusted go-between, paying money the Brauns gave him to compensate a Polish farmer and his wife for hiding Maria, her husband, her mother, and sometimes her brothers and their wives as well. Maria's father was murdered at the Treblinka death camp.

The Devinki story contains a range of characters—from the good-hearted Jusick Gondorowicz to farmers who risked their lives by hiding Jews—but did it for money. Maria Devinki said she believes the first farmer to hide them, Wladyslaw Chelowski, probably did not realize how much danger he was putting himself in. The second was just desperately poor.

When Maria, born June 1, 1920, was a small child, her family moved to Wodzisław from Hanover, Germany, where her parents had run a successful export business. Maria said she believed that at the start of World War II Jews made up more than half the population of Wodzisław.[10]

Maria had two brothers. She went to a public school as well as to a Bais Yaakov, a religious school for girls. Her goal was to become a teacher. But when the war came, she and some members of her family relied on a trusted business

Maria Devinki

friend to survive. "Jusick [Gondorowicz]," she explained, "he was a very close friend to us. Matter of fact, we had a partnership."

The Braun family business was shipping merchandise, eventually getting it "to the Baltic and from there shipping to the United States, Canada, and other countries," Maria explained. "So we had trucks and buses. There was a whole group of us. Because of Jusick we got the license to do that."

When the German threat to local Jews became clear, Jusick "came to me and he said, 'I have a place for you. If you feel comfortable, I will take you to a farm and they probably will hide you. But we have to make an agreement with him [the farmer]. To make it very short, I'm not going to go into every little detail.'"

One detail Jusick told Maria about only later was that when Jusick (an army man long before the war) first talked to the farmer about hiding Maria as well as her mother and husband, he pulled out a gun and pointed it at the farmer as he said, "If anything happens to those Jews, it will be bad." The farmer understood Jusick's clear meaning.

"So," Maria said, "that was our guarantee that he's not going to do anything to us."[11]

In a written statement that Jusick made much later to the Jewish Historical Institute in Poland, he said that he believed "my visits at the bunker played a very important role in the life of the Jewish families. On one hand, I had to make sure that the farmer was still willing to provide a shelter for them, and on the other hand I was reassuring the Jewish families that they were in a safe place, providing them with news, trying to keep their spirits high, and giving them hope to continue. Several times, we were pressured to stop helping the Jewish families and deliver them to the Nazis, but having the support of our relatives and friends who worked in conspiracy, we managed to resist the blackmailing and survive the occupation with dignity."

Maria and her mother decided that, if things got really bad, they would accept Jusick's offer. They would leave money with Jusick, who in turn would pay the farmer on a monthly basis.

"It was never for free," Maria said. "It was ten thousand zloty a month." This was, in fact, an enormous sum for a farmer, and the farmer's carelessness with so much money could have cost Maria and others their lives.

"Here's my choice," Maria said of what the farmer offered to Jusick. "There was no bargaining. It was not like merchandise. I don't know if he wouldn't go for less or whatever. I have to be very frank with everybody: The farmer took a chance. His life was as much at risk as our lives." If German authorities came to that farm and found Jews, she said, "then he has the same execution that we would have. But the farmer was not smart enough to think of this. He was thinking of the big chunk of money he would get."

In Wodzisław, Maria's family lived across the street from the burgomaster or mayor, and the families were friends. One day, Maria said, she learned through that family that the Gestapo was in the area, "and they said next week going to be bad," meaning Jews would be rounded up and sent to death or labor camps.

The man who soon would become Maria's husband, Fred Devinki (born Froim Dziewiecki), was staying not far from her at the time. They had known each other before the war. "He came in the middle of the night," she said. "He walked to the city. It was seven kilometers to the city and he came into our place. We were in the ghetto then." Fred told Maria he had heard the upcoming *Aktion* in Wodzisław would happen on the eve of Yom Kippur (1942). Maria and Fred were young and believed their age and their ability to work would help them survive.

"For example," she said, "in my case, I was like a sanitizing commission. The city broke out with typhoid [fever]. Of course, the Germans were afraid of that. It was spread around between soldiers and whatever. So they separated parts of the city. And who should go there and who should do something in case of a death or in case to help them? Girls like me. So that's why they let us live longer."

Fred told Maria, "It would be a good idea for us to get married as long as there are still a few Jews in town and can get us Chuppah Kiddushin, like marriage blessing."

Maria pressed Fred on why they should do that. She said he replied, "If we are a couple, you have a better chance. I'll be with you. By yourself, your mother is going to be separated from you because she's older. Now older persons go right away to Auschwitz or something. So you'll be by yourself."

Maria thought that made sense. "I said, 'fine.'"

So that same Thursday evening they were married. The mayor's sister-in-law, who had gone to school with Maria, came to be the witness. The marriage lasted almost fifty-one years and produced three children, Sam, Karen, and Ida, seven grandchildren, and two great-grandchildren. Three days after Fred and Maria were married, the feared *Aktion* to round up the Jews took place.

That evening Jusick found Maria, Fred, and Maria's mother and "made us hide in the hay" on a wagon, Maria said. "He put us under the hay, me, my husband, and my mother, and we went and lived in a barn," which was about ten kilometers from the city.

Fred Devinki and the farmer dug a hole under the floor of the barn, and that became the hiding place. They placed floor boards on top of the hole and covered it all with hay. When it was done, it was about ten feet by fifteen feet, but not deep enough even for Maria, barely five feet tall, to stand up. It was, she said, "like a grave."

Because it was September and hay-harvesting time, "the whole place was full of hay," Maria said. "If the Germans come in they couldn't possibly look in that spot unless the Polish tell them that there were Jews hiding on the farm and how they're hiding and what they're doing. Then they would start coming with their bayonets. If the ground is soft, somebody's hiding under there. If the ground is hard, they walked away. That's what happened. It was hard because there were boards. So they walked away."

As many as ten times authorities came to check out the first farm to see if Jews were hiding there. And each time they failed to discover Maria and others living under the barn floor.

Maria said the farmer who first hid them eventually told them the village had been cleared of Jews, and that some farmers who had agreed to hide Jews "got tired of it." So these farmers called the Polish police and told them there were Jews on their property who had come to rob them. In response to this allegation, Germans went out to those farms, "and they killed those Jews right on those places," Maria said.

This kind of betrayal was not uncommon, even claiming members of Maria's family as victims. Her husband's brother, for instance, gave his family's flour mill business to local non-Jews and told them they could keep it if his family did not survive the war. So, Maria said, those people told authorities where to find that Jewish family, guaranteeing they would not survive.

"After several months," she said, the man hiding her brother-in-law and his family "called the Polish police saying, 'The robbers have come to rob us.' The police came out. He opened the door and the police saw Jews.

"'They came to rob you?' [the police asked.]

"'Yes.'

"They killed one after another."

There were lots of cases like that, Maria said. "Matter of fact, I had a girlfriend where the two sisters were hiding also on a farm and they had a store of leather goods. And they also signed over their store to a farmer, and he did the same thing."

In this hostile and volatile atmosphere, Maria said, "the Polish police were going around looking for Jews and making themselves important for the Germans." Indeed, when Polish authorities, collaborating with the Germans, found Jews in hiding, she said, they usually killed them, but not before calling in "the Gestapo to be witnesses to what they're doing. They didn't do it on their own."

As Maria discovered, sometimes the life of a Jew was not deemed to be worth two suits of clothes.

One of her brothers, David, escaped from a camp to which authorities had sent him, she said. Jusick managed to pick him up and bring him "to our hiding place. And, of course, we didn't have enough money to pay for one more man.

We couldn't get much money." Whatever money they had they already had given to Jusick so he could use it to pay the farmer for hiding them. Others could not be added to the original deal without more money changing hands.

To raise more money to cover the cost of hiding him, "my brother had to go find the places where we had left some goods from our business." So one night, between midnight and four o'clock in the morning, he slipped out of the hiding place and went to pick up some men's clothes he had stored away. His thought was to give them to Jusick to sell to raise funds.

"But," Maria said, the man who was keeping his brother's merchandise told him, "I'll buy from you a couple suits." His brother agreed and sold him two suits for thirty zloty, she later learned (zloty are still the Polish currency).

"My brother was happy because he felt that would help to buy some fruit. He started to walk back to our place. He had to go through a cemetery in order for nobody to see him. He could hide behind the stones. He came into the middle of the cemetery, and somebody walked out from the stones."

It was, Maria said, the man who had bought the two suits. He killed Maria's brother and took back the thirty zloty he had paid for the suits.

"I have to be honest with you. My life was like that. Maybe somebody else's was different."[12]

A second brother, Shmuel, and his wife also spent some time in the hole under the first barn floor with Maria, her husband, and her mother, as did Maria's sister, Pola Rubinek, and her teenage children, Shmuel and Alek. Pola survived and lived until age sixty-four in the Kansas City area. One of Pola's sons was murdered when Polish police caught him outside his hiding place. The fate of the other boy is unknown.

In the hole the hours dragged. The place was cold and dirty. There was almost nothing to do but talk or sleep. And the food was barely edible.

"At the farm," Maria said, "the only time in the night when we got out of that hole was like between 12 and 4 [a.m.]. And my husband went out and got some water from the well and that's the way we bathed and that's the way we drink. Otherwise the farmer's wife was cooking one time a day for the pigs—potatoes. That's what she brought down to us." It was gritty, and "we had to clean it up and eat that and the water that we brought in the middle of the night. That was our food for twenty-seven months. Never, ever any meat or any eggs or anything. You know what else she [the farmer's wife] did? She baked bread. Once a week, on Saturday, she bakes bread. But she doesn't give us a loaf of bread for all of us for the week. She waits. When the week is over and she bakes fresh bread, she gives us an old loaf. That's why we don't eat a lot because we break our teeth." At telling this so many years later, Maria was able to laugh.

During the day they took heavy blankets from the horses in the barn and put them on the ground in the hole "because the ground was wet." Maria said that because she knew how to crochet and sew, the farmer's wife "brought me down material to make a little dress by hand for the [couple's] child. She had a six-month-old girl and a six-year-old boy. She brought with her a light, a lamp, kerosene. And by this I would sit and cut and sew and make a little dress."

That filled up one day. The next day the farmer's wife had no work for them to do, so "I tell her bring me the Bible, bring me anything." The farmer, she explained, "didn't want to go to the city to buy a newspaper because he didn't know how to read. He said if you buy a newspaper they would accuse him of something. But they had a Bible and they had little children's books. I was twenty-two then. Anyway, we didn't take anything from home because we didn't have enough time. Whatever we wear, the clothes, that's what we had all the time." By the time Soviet troops liberated that part of Poland, she had no shoes to wear because "my feet was still growing and I couldn't get into the shoes what I had." So she wrapped her feet in horse blankets.

In late spring of 1944, the farmer returned from church one day and told Maria and her family that someone in church had said to him, "Vladick, you holding some Jews?"

And he said, "Why?"

The man replied, "How do you have money to build a house?"

Maria explained that the farmer, using the money he received for hiding the family, was building a house using bricks as a replacement for what she called his "little shack." The farmer denied hiding Jews.

"No," he said, "I just accumulate the brick, picked up from the cemeteries" and elsewhere. Maria said that her husband, who was six years older than she was, thought the farmer's story was a warning for them to get away.

"That was Sunday," Maria said. "Monday night we all—five of us were left because my brother was killed already—we all left his place and go into another place." This second farm was not one Jusick arranged. Rather, one of Maria's brothers had met the farmer while in the wheat business, and he knew him to be terribly poor.

"He was a poor, poor farmer," Maria said. So Maria and the others just showed up and asked to be hidden. They agreed to pay him what little money they had left—and they promised him more if they survived—and "he was pleased with it."

To get to the second farm, in the nearby village of Olszowska, they got dressed in farm clothes and carried baskets as if they were going to or returning from market. They "walked in the middle of the night," picking a path that avoided the German army. That meant walking through an area controlled by *Volksdeutsch*.

As they passed by a school, a man said in German, "Where are you going?"

Maria said they told him in German, simply, "Home."

"And he said, 'What do you have?' thinking we had vodka or something because usually the farmers used to buy on Monday. And I answered him, 'Eggs.' Eggs they're not interested in."

In response, the man said, "Go to hell!" in Polish.

So, she said, they "walked through. We didn't walk through because he let us go through but because Somebody above us make that possible. We call it a *nes,* a miracle."

At the new hiding place, Maria said, the farm family "hardly had food for themselves." The farmer there was a poor sharecropper who nonetheless shared whatever he had. "We didn't have too much but we survived."

In January 1945, Maria said, she and her family learned that Soviet troops were getting closer, and thus, liberation would not be long coming. One day the farmer came to tell them what they suspected based on the noises they had heard in the middle of the night. The Soviets had arrived. But Maria and her family were skeptical.

"Go and get a newspaper," they told him.

But he said, "I don't know how to read."

So Maria and her family said, "We're not taking chances." And they remained hidden for another day.

The next day they heard Soviet troops on the farm coming in for baths and for food. So they came out of hiding and found a Soviet soldier in a military vehicle. They asked if it was possible now for them to go to their city without fear of dying at the hands of the Germans, and they were told it was safe.

"There were too many people for them to take us [to the city] and we didn't have the nerve to ask for this," she said. "Nobody really could speak good Russian, but we could speak German, we could speak Polish. He understood us even in the Polish language and he said, 'No, you don't have to worry about it. We all are occupying this part of Poland, the cities.'"

Because Maria had no shoes, the farmer gave her rags from the blankets used by the horses. She and the others walked eleven miles to Wodzisław. "There were two Jews in the city already. They had come out from the place where they were hiding."

Finally, a few more Jews came into the city, but Maria said the non-Jews there were not happy to see any of them. "They didn't treat us like we were welcome."

In fact, the cold-shoulder reception got personal for Maria. She went to see the woman whom she had called her best friend, a member of the mayor's family. Maria had left all her clothes with her when she went into hiding. And, as Maria explained, these were not just ordinary clothes. "We had nothing but the best and I left her everything. And she was not even my size. She was taller than I was."

But when Maria knocked on the door, she didn't get the happy welcome she expected. Instead the woman simply said to her, "You still alive?"

"I thought she was going to grab me and hug me and be so happy that I survived," Maria said. Indeed, it is one reason Maria Devinki never returned to Poland.

After the War

Maria and her husband soon moved to a bigger city, Sosnowiec, just northeast of Katowice. There, they opened a grocery store. Her mother stayed in Wodzisław to be with Maria's brother, Shmuel, but she joined them in Sosnowiec after people Maria identified as antisemites killed Shmuel in May 1945.

"I start operating a store and started making good money," Maria said. "We were doing wonderful." Before long, however, Jusick came to Sosnowiec. "And he said to me in Polish, 'I want you to leave the city, leave the business, leave everything.' I said, 'What I did wrong now?' He said, 'They killed your brother. And they were looking for your husband.' I said, 'Who?' He said, 'The A.K. [*Armia Krajowa*],'" the very militia in which Jusick served as part of the Polish resistance.

"I said, 'You were at the meeting [of the A.K.] and you heard this?' He said, 'Yes.'"

So she had to pack up and leave. She could not "even go back to the funeral of my brother. So they buried my brother. I don't know where."

Maria and her husband had some money as well as jewelry and clothing that they had picked up back in Poland after the Soviets liberated their territory. So they went to Kraków to speak to a lawyer there whom they had known before the war.

"I said to him, 'I have money. I got a grocery store and I made a good chunk of money. I give you all the money. Work out something for me to go over the German border.' And he arranged a truck, a Russian truck, to take me to the Czech border. From there we got into Prague, and from Prague we got into Regensburg, Germany. This was 1945, November."

There Maria and Fred created a textile business, and Maria gave birth to their son, Sam. From there, in 1950, the family, including her mother, moved to Kansas City.

Maria kept in touch with Jusick after the war. "In his eyes," she said, "it was not the money. In his eyes it was he's going to save human beings. Now, I tell you frankly, I was sending Jusick money all through the years. The minute I arrived in Germany and we opened a business and we would make money, I would send money to Jusick to help. And we got to the United States and bought a truck, Chevrolet, and send it to Jusick, because I know that the Germans took everything away from him. They still had something but they didn't have enough. And I was sending money until he passed away [in the 1990s]. But I never sent a penny and I never got in touch with the first farmer." Maria learned from Jusick that the second farmer died "a long time ago, before we even got to Germany."

Maria's niece from Canada once went to Poland and took with her some money for Jusick, but he told her he really did not need the money any more. Maria reported that instead, he said, "'I need pictures. I want to know if she's still as pretty as she was.' He didn't care about my money, he cared about just me. And because of me he saved my husband, though he had no interest in my husband. And because of me my mother was saved."

When Maria and Fred Devinki first moved to Kansas City, they ran several grocery stores, and Maria worked for a time in a department store. Then she borrowed a couple of thousand dollars from a cousin and bought a piece of property that the Kansas City Life Insurance Company wanted for a parking lot. Selling this property to Kansas City Life led to the creation of Devinki Real Estate, a Kansas City company that, with her son, Sam, she was still operating at the time this book was researched. Fred Devinki died in June 1993.

Maria has given a lot back to the community through such organizations as the Midwest Center for Holocaust Education, which she served as vice president of the board and for which she has been named a director emeritus.

Aaron Elster and Irene Budkowski

Aaron Elster knew it was almost certainly his only chance to survive. So this sick, frightened, malnourished, lice-ridden ten-year-old boy knocked anxiously on the door of Francesca and Hypolit Gorski's home in his hometown of Sokołów Podlaski, where he believed his sister, Irene, was already in hiding.

But when Mrs. Gorski opened the door and saw him, she was furious. "It is very dangerous for you to be here," she scolded him. "You must leave. Your sister is not here any more."

Aaron, wearing short pants and feeling sickly from wandering fields and forests in the frozen winter air, was out of options.

"No, no," he pleaded. "Please help me. I have nowhere else to go. My mother told me to come here."

Aaron opened his hand and showed Mrs. Gorski the little bit of jewelry that his mother—before sending him out alone into a hostile world—had given him to offer to people who might help him. Hoping that it would make a difference he held it out to the stern woman who was berating him.

But for Francesca Gorski the matter was not about jewelry. It was about the likelihood that the Germans would find out she and her husband were hiding not just one but two Jewish children—and they all would die: Aaron, Irene (who was indeed hiding in the Gorski home), the Gorskis themselves, and possibly even the people occupying the two apartments on the ground floor of the small building.

"No," Mrs. Gorski told him, angrily pointing a finger at him. "You must leave right now."

Hearing what sounded to him like a death sentence, Aaron collapsed. He sobbed. Then he sobbed harder. As bitter tears streaked his gaunt face, somehow the sight of this bedraggled urchin touched something in Mrs. Gorski's hesitant heart. That heart cracked open a little.

"You may stay in our attic," she finally told him, "but only for a few days. Then you must leave and find your mother. It's her job to care for you, not mine."

So the door opened, and Aaron followed her into the house. They went through a hallway, and up to what was called the attic. It was, in fact, a small unfinished space under the sloping roofline behind a low wooden door on the same second floor of the house where the childless Gorskis lived.

Decades later, by the time we interviewed Elster in his office near Chicago, he had come to understand and have more sympathy for the predicament in which the Gorskis found themselves. This couple had been customers of the butcher

Aaron Elster

Irene Budkowski
(photo courtesy of Irene Budkowski)

·Sokołów Podlaski

·WARSAW

·Lublin

·KRAKÓW

shop run by Aaron's parents, Chaim and Cywia Elster, in Sokołów, east of Warsaw. Chaim and Cywia sold non-kosher meat to non-Jews while Cywia's father sold kosher meat to some of the four or five thousand Jews living in Sokołów, a town of roughly ten thousand people.[13] Aaron said that it was only with much reluctance, and thinking it would mean only a few months at most, that Mrs. Gorski had agreed to hide Irene when German authorities were rounding up Jews and sending them off to death camps. Cywia encouraged her with small gifts of food, clothing, and a little money to cover the added cost of an extra mouth to feed. Hypolit Gorski, a retired man, was not happy with his wife's decision but allowed it.

After several months of having Irene in their apartment, the Gorskis took in Aaron, too, even though, as he told us, "they probably didn't know what to do with me. They didn't want me, and quite frankly, they were afraid of the consequences. What if somebody finds out? What if they catch them? You know for a fact that the Germans would have killed them without question and burned their house."

Even though Mrs. Gorski agreed to keep Aaron for just a few days, he said, "unfortunately for her, a few days turned out to be almost two years." In all of that time, Aaron knew that she did not like him. And her husband simply ignored him, almost never even speaking to him except to berate him occasionally.

The problem was, Aaron said, that the Gorskis could not get rid of him or Irene "in a clean way where nobody would be hurt." If the Gorskis had kicked him out and the Germans had caught him, "mostly likely I would tell them who was hiding me. I mean, I'm ten years old. All they have to do is slap me around and beat me up. And I'd say, 'Well, the Gorskis were taking care of me.'"

In fact, when we interviewed Irene in her home in suburban Chicago, she told us that Mrs. Gorski had said exactly that. "Many times she told me, 'If I throw you out, the Germans will catch you and you'll tell where I am and we'll be shot, too.'"

But that did not happen. Instead, Aaron lived by himself in the attic, receiving a slice of bread and some soup once a day. His sister hid in the Gorskis' apartment and visited Aaron when she was allowed to.

"I was afraid," Irene told us. "I was always afraid. She wanted to throw out Aaron so badly."

A few days after Aaron's arrival at the Gorskis, Irene learned of his presence. Although she was happy to know her brother was alive, she knew Mrs. Gorski did not want him to stay. So she told Mrs. Gorski to give her just half the soup and bread she had been eating so Aaron could have the rest and be able to stay.

"She was very unhappy," Irene said of Mrs. Gorski. "She used to swear at my mother all the time. I told her, 'Don't swear at her. I don't know if she's alive or not.'"

The parents of Irene and Aaron had never imagined it would come to this. Before World War II began, they were doing reasonably well as part of a family meat business in Sokołów. Irene was born in 1930. Aaron came along two or three years later (he is uncertain of his birth date), and Sara was born in 1936.

The Elsters owned and lived in an apartment building on Piekna Street. They had a small garden outside, where Aaron's father planted carrots, cucumbers, onions, and sunflowers. Instead of indoor plumbing, there was an outhouse next to the garden, but Aaron had to accompany Irene to this facility at night because she was afraid to go there alone in the dark.[14]

The Jewish section of Sokołów contained a synagogue, a theater, a newspaper, two libraries, a school for religious education, and a number of other schools. On Thursdays, Jewish and non-Jewish Sokołów would meet at the marketplace off Dluga Street, not far from the Elsters' butcher shop on Rogowska Street, part of the *rynek,* or market. It was this area that became the Sokołów Ghetto, which at first was open but by 1941 was closed. In addition to Sokołów's Jews, some two thousand Jews from Łódź, Kalisz, and other places were forced into that ghetto.[15]

Life in the ghetto quickly deteriorated. Several times Chaim Elster was beaten, either by Germans or by Poles, and barely survived. One of their uncles was shot by a German guard as he escaped from a train heading to a slave labor camp, and he died in the Elsters' apartment. Bribes to German authorities managed to keep the butcher shop open for a while. Irene's job then was to deliver non-kosher cuts of meat to customers outside the ghetto.

"My parents used to send me out and take orders from the Polish people," Irene told us. "Then my father would make up the orders. And early in the morning, someone would pull out one board from the [ghetto] gate and push me through [to make deliveries]. The policeman was paid off. But some of the Jewish people in the ghetto were wondering how we were making a living. So they watched and they caught me. They took away my money and started fighting with my Dad, who was such a nice, quiet man. And then I couldn't go any more to do business. So it got very bad in the ghetto."

In 1942 the Elsters were allowed to leave the ghetto to work on a farm just outside Sokołów in the village of Sabnie. While their parents worked, Irene, Aaron, and Sara roamed the farm freely. But in early October, after just a few months on the farm, they were ordered back to the ghetto. Cywia Elster anticipated trouble, however, and arranged for Irene not to return with them but to move in with the Gorskis, who lived just a few blocks from the ghetto.

"What my mother paid Mrs. Gorski, I don't know, but there was some financial arrangement," Aaron told us. Irene said that all her mother ever gave Mrs. Gorski was a little money and some clothing, an amount that barely would have covered the added cost of an extra person in the house and certainly not enough to compensate for the cost of feeding two extra people. The reality was, Aaron said, that Mrs. Gorski "didn't bargain for all this. Had she known in advance what was involved, what was going to be, I doubt very much whether we would have been accepted, especially me."

On October 10, 1942, the Jews of Sokołów were forced into the marketplace for deportation to the Treblinka death camp north of Sokołów. Little Sara, crying, was snuggled up next to her father, who knew that Aaron's only chance was to try to escape and to run to the Gorskis, too. Profoundly frightened by his father's order to do just that, Aaron nonetheless began to crawl behind the line of Jews facing the German guards, looking for a way out. Eventually he reached a sewer opening and dropped into it for a run through muddy waters out of the ghetto.[16]

He made it as far as a small house—still inside the ghetto—that belonged to an aunt and uncle. There he found his aunt and a cousin still hiding. So he got a bit of sleep, and when he could not persuade them into leaving with him, he departed alone. With the help of a friendly elderly Polish woman who was passing by, he slipped through the barbed wire of the ghetto and ran.

While on the run Aaron learned from some other Jews hiding in a field that his mother had survived the ghetto's destruction and was part of a small group chosen to work in the nearly empty ghetto, sorting through and packing up belongings that the families had been forced to leave behind. So he sneaked back to the ghetto and found her. She told him then that she did not know the fate of his father and little sister.

Irene and Aaron later were told that their father and sister were sent with other Jews to Treblinka and that they were murdered there. But Aaron also has a fleeting and uncertain memory of seeing his father as part of a ghetto work crew after the ghetto was destroyed. If so, it would mean that little Sara went to Treblinka alone.

"Certain things become gray," Aaron told us. "Certain things you don't remember. You try to reconstruct them and sometimes you just can't. I have a problem trying to come to some kind of conclusion about how and why I feel I saw my father after liquidation. And maybe there's some guilt involved with that. Maybe there's something I held against him. My little sister went to Treblinka by herself if I saw him after the first liquidation [Yom Kippur, October 10, 1942] as part of a work detail in the marketplace. So I can't quite put this together. Did I imagine this? Did I make it up?"

Within a few days after Aaron rejoined his mother in the ghetto, however, it was clear that the work there was about to end and that the Germans would come back and murder the four dozen people in the work crew. So Aaron's mother and he slipped out of the ghetto just before the Germans arrived. A German Jewish man named Gedala, who had developed a friendship with Cywia, left with them.

For a couple of weeks, the three of them hid in the forest or sought shelter from Polish farmers. A few helped them out, but others chased them away and threatened to notify the Germans. Aaron's mother finally found a former neighbor, a farmer, who allowed her and Gedala to stay in his barn. But Cywia forced her son Aaron to leave. She gave him a ring and a pair of earrings and told him to go to the Gorskis.[17]

Aaron, feeling abandoned, unloved, deserted, stomped off full of rage. Somehow his mother had chosen Gedala over him. For a few days he hid here and there, getting occasional help from Polish farmers. Finally, however, he realized he could not go on like that and must try to get the Gorskis to take him in.

As an adult it took Aaron a long time to resolve his feelings about his mother, who, he learned later, was murdered with Gedala by Germans after being turned in by Poles. He said, "I had a problem with my mother for many years. How could she have done that? I felt that she threw her family over, so to speak, for this man. I finally came to the conclusion that it was done out of love instead of abandonment. Had I stayed with her, I would not have survived. But it was very difficult for me for many years."

Irene said it has taken years for her to understand what Aaron experienced before he arrived at the Gorskis. "I never knew what this kid went through," she told us, her voice quivering with emotion. "And I felt so bad because he felt abandoned by our mother. I felt abandoned, too, but still he went through a lot more. I was in hiding. I had a roof over my head and he didn't."

Once both children were living in the Gorskis' building, something like a routine developed. A teacher and his wife and small daughter lived in one downstairs apartment. Another couple lived in the other downstairs apartment, while the Gorskis occupied the one upstairs unit. The Gorskis also rented some of their upstairs space to a young woman student. Her boyfriend, a member of the *Armia Krajowa*, used to ride his bicycle out to see her. Aaron said that, on an average day, "Mr. Gorski was in church and Mrs. Gorski was downstairs working or whatever."

In fact, Irene said, "Mr. Gorski used to go to church twice a day, at morning and at night." Mr. Gorski got to sleep in the largest bed in the house, while Mrs. Gorski and Irene shared a smaller bed.

In exchange for a little soup and bread, "I just did what she told me," Irene said. Which meant that when the Gorskis were not in the apartment, Irene had to be extraordinarily quiet and never go near a window. "So when I wanted to go into the other room I had to crawl."

Irene missed her family so much that, soon after she arrived at the Gorski home, her mother made arrangements for Mrs. Gorski to bring her to the ghetto just for one night.

"She was a hard-working woman," Irene said of Mrs. Gorski. "And he [Mr.

Gorski] was OK. He didn't bother me as long as I stayed out of his way."

Aaron, however, despite being out of sight of the Gorskis nearly all the time, managed to raise the ire of Mr. Gorski more than once. After Aaron had been in the Gorski attic for about nine months, fall apple harvest time arrived, and Mr. Gorski began to collect the fruit from a tree behind the house. Aaron was able to watch him from the attic, and he longed for a ripe red apple. Some weeks later, when the last ripe apple was picked, Mr. Gorski brought a large basket of the fruit to the attic. Aaron sat motionless in a corner because in all this time Mr. Gorski had never come to the attic.

Mr. Gorski placed the apples on some straw atop the attic's dirt floor, arranging them in well-ordered rows. Then he covered them with more straw to keep them from freezing over the winter. In fact, it was more straw than Aaron had available to him to keep him warm. When Mr. Gorski's work was done, he turned to Aaron and warned him never to touch a single apple, reminding him of the danger he and his wife had put themselves in for hiding Jews.

After days of pining for the apples, Aaron concocted a plan. He would take one small apple from the rows and then replace the straw—but only after he had rearranged the space between the apples to make it look as if nothing had changed. He did this for a number of days in a row until, finally, Mr. Gorski came back up to check on his apples. He immediately knew that apples were missing, so he reprimanded the little boy in the corner. "He calls me every ugly name that he knows and reminds me over and over that he and his wife are good people. He tells me that if it was not for him I would not be alive."[18]

Aaron told us that rearranging the apples "was some of my entertainment. It was a game, but I was also extremely hungry. Hunger played a big part of my life."

He said he tried "to apologize and look down as I keep saying over and over that I am sorry. Mr. Gorski continues to call me names. I retreat into my straw bed and pull my knees into my chest and begin rocking. Mr. Gorski walks to the attic door and slams it, but not before calling me a dirty Jew."[19]

The next day Mr. Gorski returned and removed all the apples.

The seemingly endless and lonely hours caused Aaron to do strange things to pass the time. One day, for instance, he began drawing designs on the dirt floor with his urine. But early one morning Mr. Gorski entered the attic and screamed at him, saying his urine has seeped through the ceiling and dripped below.

In the Gorski apartment, where Irene lived, there was no toilet and no running water. Mrs. Gorski did the laundry in a small outbuilding and carried water into the house. Irene told us that the Gorskis had an outhouse to use, but she was forced to use a pail in the apartment. And, she said, in all the time she was hidden, "I never took a bath."

Periodically Irene would get a toothache, "and they couldn't do anything for me. There were no aspirins. There was nothing. I just had to sit there the whole night. I couldn't cry. I just sat there until it got filled up with pus and then it would pop and go away. And then it happened again, and she comes in and she gives me a little bottle with something red in it. She took it and put it on the tooth and the pain went away.

"She crossed herself and she started crying. So I said, 'What happened?' She said she had a dream about my mother. She dreamt that my mother told her to go down to the backyard, where she grew potatoes. And she told her to find the fifth row and she'd find that bottle." That's just what Mrs. Gorski said she did, and there in the potato field she indeed found a bottle containing a red liquid that healed Irene's toothache. When Irene thought back on this mysterious story, she said simply, "So I believe some things are meant to be."

Before Irene was sent to live with the Gorskis, her mother gave her a small garter belt to hold up her stockings. Her mother had made a pocket in it and put in five hundred zloty. "She said, 'Don't give it to her until you really have to.'" Irene would take it off at night and put it under her pillow. But one morning she found that the money was gone, "but I couldn't confront her."

In the summer of 1944, the war was going badly for the Germans, and Soviet troops were moving relentlessly toward Sokołów. German authorities ordered the Gorski home be evacuated so retreating soldiers could use it for temporary lodging. But the Gorskis somehow managed to convince them to take just the downstairs apartments while they would stay upstairs and Mrs. Gorski would be their maid and helper.

Irene visited Aaron in the attic and told him he must be even quieter than ever because of the soldiers below. So Aaron simply spent his time sitting on his straw bed, praying not to be discovered by Germans. The Germans stayed in the house for four weeks, and there was at least one close call when a drunken soldier was making his way toward the attic and had to be diverted by Mrs. Gorski.

When the Soviets finally arrived, they began bombing the area. Irene joined Aaron in the attic as Francesca and Hypolit Gorski moved into the smokehouse and potato cellar in an outbuilding just behind the house. Bombs hit the roof of the Gorski house.

"When they hit our house," Irene told us, "we had to leave the house. She went into that place, the smokehouse, but she wouldn't let us in. She said she didn't want to die with Jews."

So Irene and Aaron, before abandoning the house altogether, thought about what their uncle, who served in the Polish army, had told them about surviving. "He'd say, 'Always cover your head,'" Irene said. "'You can get hit in the arm, a leg and still live, but once you get hit in the head . . .'"

So as bullets and bombs were flying, Irene and Aaron hid at first partly under the roofline of the house near a big tree. "We lay with our heads in and our tushies out," Irene said.

But explosions next removed most of the roof, so for the first time in almost two years the children left the house and ran to the backyard to hide in some craters made by falling bombs. Aaron and Irene lay on one side of a fence while a man who was a Gorski neighbor lay on the other side.

"And all of a sudden the Russians started shooting at us," Irene said. "We were screaming the *Shema* and he [the neighbor] was praying." The man next to them was killed.[20]

"I didn't care if they heard me saying 'Sh'ma Yisrael,'" Irene said. "The only thing we wanted was some bread."

So when there was a lull in the shooting, the two children ran into the apartment the German troops had abandoned and found bread and jelly to eat. "We ate," Irene said. "We didn't care that they were shooting. We wanted to die with a full stomach."

When things quieted down, the children were lying in the house. Mrs. Gorski emerged from her hiding place and began calling them. "I am mad," Irene said. "I am so mad that she wouldn't let us into that place. I said to Aaron, 'Don't answer her.' But she kept calling me, so finally I answered her."

The attic was destroyed, however, so the only place for Irene and Aaron to stay was a chicken coop in the backyard. That was their home for four or five days until the Ukrainian soldiers who had fought with the Soviet troops began leaving the area and heading back toward their home.

Two Ukrainians entered the Gorskis' backyard looking for food. One of them opened the chicken coop door and discovered Aaron and Irene.

"After two years in hiding," Aaron recounts, "I'm going to die at the hands of a Ukrainian looking for food."[21]

"When the Ukrainian came in," Irene said, "he saw that I was a Jew, so he put his gun in my mouth and he was going to shoot me. But all of a sudden the other guy found butter and eggs and he started yelling, 'Come on, I got this and that.' So, again, I was saved."

Aaron and Irene stayed with the Gorskis another two weeks or so because the couple could not locate other Jews to take responsibility for the children. Eventually Mrs. Gorski found some Jews who had come out of hiding, and she told them she had two children they should take.

So a Jewish woman named Mrs. Rafolowicz took Aaron and Irene and moved them with her to a building in town where the few Sokołów Jews who survived (Aaron recalls the figure was twenty-nine out of about five thousand) were gathering together.[22] This transaction between the Gorskis and the Rafolowiczes occurred at night so neighbors would not see that the Gorskis had hidden Jews.

"She told me, 'Irene, I don't want you to get in touch with me. I don't want you to come over here. I don't want anyone to know that you ever knew me.' So I listened."

Aaron and Irene were in such battered shape by then, however, that they could walk only a few steps at a time. "We walked a little bit, we fell down, we walked, we fell down until we got to their house," Irene said.

The milk and black bread they were fed at the Rafolowicz house almost immediately produced dysentery, so the children had to spend most of the first night outside because there were no toilets in the house.

Still, they had survived for nearly two years because of people who put their own lives in jeopardy, however reluctantly. Now in their later years, both Aaron and Irene realize how much they owe to the Gorskis, even though at the time they felt unwelcome and at times detested.

We asked Irene directly, "Are you grateful to these people?"

"I have to be," she said, even though "it was not a love affair."

For Aaron's part, he has come to believe that Mrs. Gorski "was—she had to be—a very decent person. She was also very religious. And I think that helped. She basically ran the household, so to speak. He was just there in the background. They were very poor people."

Aaron also said that no matter what her motivation was, "she staked their lives every day for two strangers. If they really wanted to, she could have killed us and nobody would have known the difference, nor would anyone have cared. So there had to be extreme goodness in her heart to do this, to share food with us, to keep us."

Still, Aaron said, he continues to think about the paradox that Mrs. Gorski helped to save them even though she sometimes expressed antisemitic views. "At the end, when the Russians were bombing the town, and the roof blew off and Irene and I are sitting in the attic and Irene runs down into that wash house, into that cellar, she wouldn't let us come into that cellar because she didn't want to die with Jews. And this is a woman who staked her life for us. How do you explain it?"

Aaron and Irene, in fact, spent much of their postwar time thinking about that and trying to cope with the long odds of their own survival.

After the War

Right after the war the children had to face the reality that their mother was dead. For their own safety and survival, in fact, they felt forced to sign papers saying that a Polish man named Czeslaw Uzieblo (the man who, in fact, had turned in their mother and her companion Gedala to the Germans) had really helped them by offering food and shelter. Aaron began hearing rumors that if he and Irene did not sign this false statement, they would be killed. Even Uzieblo's wife came to them to plead for them to sign the statement, and other members of Uzieblo's family "say if we do not protect him, there will be retribution upon us and the Jewish community."[23] Despite the false testimony signed by the children, however, a police court eventually found Uzieblo guilty of turning in what the court called a "Polish national" and was sentenced to five years of jail time.

In this process Aaron and Irene learned that their mother was pregnant when she died and that her murderers (although Uzieblo was given jail time, two other men escaped punishment) had cut off a finger to steal a ring from her.[24] Then, when their mother's brother Sam Scherb returned to Sokołów, they discovered that he also had survived the Holocaust. At Sam's urging, the children moved with him to Łódź, where they spent some time in an orphanage. Eventually, the three of them made their way to Czechoslovakia and then to a displaced persons' camp in Germany at Neu Freimann.

In June 1947, after the discovery of relatives in New York and Chicago, Irene and Aaron traveled by ship to the United States. They spent some time in New York, then they moved to Chicago to live with members of the Elster family— and later, it turned out, with foster families. After high school Aaron worked in a shoe store and then served in Korea with the U.S. army.

Aaron and his wife, Jackie, have been married more than fifty years, and they have two sons and two granddaughters. Aaron spent most of his working life in various sales and management positions with the Metropolitan Life Insurance Company. After retirement he continued to do some investing for clients. He also has been active with the Holocaust Memorial Foundation of Illinois, giving many speeches to young people.

Right after the war, Irene moved in with a Polish woman in Sokołów who helped her get back on her feet. Once in the United States, she worked in a factory job. Although barely able to sustain herself on the twenty-nine dollars she made every two weeks, she managed to send the Gorskis some used clothing and a little money. But Mrs. Gorski wrote an angry letter complaining that the clothing was not new.

"So I figured, 'What's the use?'" Irene told us. "I stopped."

Irene and her husband, a Holocaust survivor she met in Chicago named Jack Budkowski, have two daughters, who each have two sons. Jack spent most of his career in the construction business. After their children were grown, Irene spent seventeen years working for the bakery at a Marshall Field's store in suburban Chicago.

Hypolit Gorski died in 1952, and Francesca (Franciszka Gorska in Polish) died in 1969.

In the speeches Aaron has given to students in recent days, he reminds them that Hitler came to power through the vote. "He didn't come in there with tanks and an army. The general population stood by and let it happen. Nobody wanted to get involved. So I warn children that the burden is on their shoulders because they're going to be the decision makers in the future."

Our Visit to Sokołów

We visited Sokołów in late summer 2007 and found the house at 13 Kosciuszki Street where Aaron and Irene hid. As we stopped our car across the street from the dwelling, a man came toward the front fence from the backyard. Almost immediately he asked if we were looking for the house where two Jewish children were hidden during the war.

The man was Bohdan Golos, then seventy-six years old, who said his father-in-law was related to the Gorskis. He had met Aaron when Aaron visited Sokołów in the 1990s. Golos has lived in the house for years, he said, and he helped take care of Mrs. Gorski there until her death.

He invited us to see the potato cellar where, he said, the Gorskis had hidden the children at times.[25] At other times they hid them inside the house. The entrance to that cellar now is inside a room that is structurally attached to the house, though when Aaron and Irene lived there it was in a building separated from the main house. Golos raised a trap door that revealed an old wooden ladder leading down into a dark space filled with spider webs and dust.

"Those Jews," Golos said, looking down into the cellar, "they really wanted to live."

When we went inside the house to talk, Golos gave us an account of the Aaron and Irene story that he had received from Mrs. Gorski in her later years.

"The Gorskis had no children," he said, "so when she saw these two poor children she wanted to help." Later he said that Mrs. Gorski helped people all her life. "She didn't like to see anybody who was hurt."

We asked if he considered her a heroine. "Yes, of course," he said. "She didn't receive any money for this or anything of value."

He did acknowledge that most of the neighbors "were very afraid of Mrs. Gorski because she was very strange. Nobody from the neighbors visited her. But when I lived with her she was a very good woman."

Roman Frayman

When German troops burst into Maria Balagowa's home that day, little Romek Frajman (today Roman Frayman) was wearing only a nightshirt that came down to his ankles. The soldiers demanded to know who this child was.

"This is my nephew, my sister's boy, visiting from the countryside," Maria told them. It was a lie. But somehow the Germans failed to do the one thing that would have proved Maria was lying.

"All they had to say is, 'Raise his nightgown.' Ballgame's over, for her and for me," Roman told us when we interviewed him in his suburban Cleveland home. Just lifting his gown would have revealed he was a circumcised Jew. That's not all the Germans missed that day. Had they conducted a careful search of the apartment house, it would have revealed that Roman's mother, Bajla Gawrylowicz Frajman, was hiding in the basement in a coal bin.

"When I teach the Shoah [Holocaust] to sixth graders," Roman told us, "I tell them that I'm a firm believer in miracles because of all these things that happened. I shouldn't be here. I should have been stabbed with a bayonet. I should have been found when we were leaving Srodula [the ghetto in Sosnowiec where he and his family were confined], I should have been found in Srodula. Kids like me just were not survivors."

But because of Maria Balagowa's willingness to risk her own life and that of her own teenage son, Czcziek, Roman and his mother found shelter and survived. Roman's father survived, too, though he was not hidden with them at Maria's home. Maria was married, but Roman said her husband apparently was arrested by German authorities and removed from the home, so he was not around much when Roman and his mother were hidden by Maria.

Roman was born to Bajla and Aron Frajman on March 16, 1938, in Sosnowiec, northwest of Kraków, not far from Katowice in southwestern Poland. Both his parents were twenty-three years old at the time and had been married for two years. Sosnowiec then was home to some 130,000 people, including about 28,000 Jews.[26] It was Roman's good fortune (though no one knew it was luck at the time) that one of the residents of the apartment building in which this baby dwelled was Maria Balagowa, who took an early shine to him and who helped Roman's mother with her child-rearing duties. Bajla had no immediate family nearby to help her and was delighted to have Maria's assistance and friendship. Although Maria was only in her forties, she already had graying hair, and when Roman learned to speak he called her "Babcia," or "Bobka," which is "grandmother" in Polish.

Roman Frayman

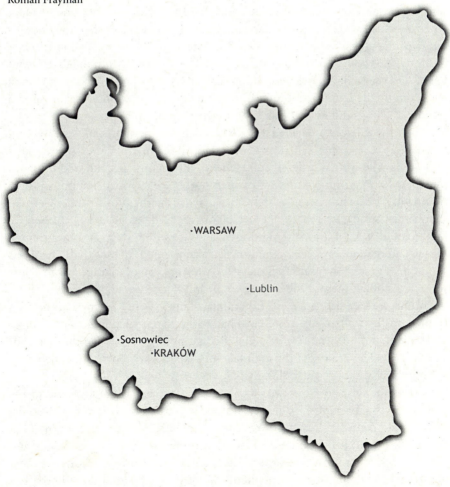

The Frajman family was poor. Aron was a sheet-metal worker who installed gutters on farm buildings. He also worked in a bakery owned by his father-in-law. Bajla was an Orthodox Jew, but Aron was much more secular. He was, in fact, a Bundist.[27] The Frajman family lived on the lower floor of a three- or four-story apartment building. Roman said he remembered looking through the window at street level and seeing German soldiers "goose-stepping by the window."

When the Germans rounded up the Jews of Sosnowiec, Roman said, they sent Roman's family to Srodula.[28] This was an area of the city that became the ghetto. While they were in the ghetto his mother gave birth to another son, Chaim, who later almost certainly perished there, he said. Roman obtained Chaim's birth certificate, which says he was born in 1941.

Although Roman was only three or so years old when he lived in Srodula, he said he had at least one clear memory of that time. "I remember one incident when a woman was sitting on a barrel. A German walked up to her, took out his Luger pistol, and shot her in the head. I still remember this. She had pure white hair, and she was lying on the ground. I went crying to my Mom to tell her what I saw. And she said, 'Romek, you didn't see that.' And I said, 'Ma, I saw it.' I took my Mom by the hand, and I took her over to where the woman was lying in a puddle of blood, and by that point there were flies around."

When the Germans decided to close the ghetto, Roman said, "we were all taken to a work camp." Their fate, thus, was different from most of the Jews in Srodula who were murdered at Auschwitz-Birkenau.[29] Roman told us he remembered seeing the boxcars into which Jews were crowded for transport to Auschwitz. "I remember seeing the Germans loading them on and the German shepherds barking. As a matter of fact, before my Dad passed away [in 1996] we talked about it. My Mom and I and my Dad were sitting there and I was telling him what I remembered seeing, and my Dad said, 'You didn't see that. There was no train.' And my Mom said to him, 'Aron, what are you doing? He saw it. There were trains down there at the bottom of the hill. There were boxcars.'"

In the work camp to which the Frajman family went, German authorities wanted no children, so Aron and Bajla had to figure out what to do with Roman and Chaim, both of whom were being hidden in the ghetto when the Germans destroyed it. The Frajmans chose to take Roman, the firstborn, with them in a secretive way and to come back for Chaim later.

"My Mom somehow was able to obtain some drugs from someone in the ghetto and she thought she'd put Chaim to sleep for about twelve hours so my father could come get him, too. What they did with me—and every time I tell this story I think it's not true because it's a miracle—they took a blanket and covered each other up and had me in the middle. Why the Nazis didn't see me, I don't know. Why the German shepherds didn't smell me out, I don't know. But we started marching from Srodula to a work camp not too far away. And I still can remember the Germans screaming and firing shots in the air. The dogs were barking; they were muzzled. And we made it to the work camp." At this camp workers made boots and backpacks for the German soldiers. That is, the three of them made it to camp. Chaim was still in a drug-induced sleep back where he was hidden in the ghetto.

"After we arrived at the work camp, my Dad went back in the evening to get my brother, but my brother was gone. Disappeared. My Dad told my Mom— and whether this is the truth or not will never be known—that some woman who was crazed found him and decided she was going to take this child with her. And if that happened he would have gone to Auschwitz.

"And yet there's a third hope in my heart, which is that maybe some not- crazed woman, maybe some German or Polish woman, heard the baby crying and just took the baby. And for all I know my brother may be alive in Poland, a man who is [in his late sixties]," though Chaim already was circumcised as an infant and thus was readily identifiable as a Jew.

Roman told us that when his father returned from trying to retrieve Chaim, "I remember my Mom screaming about Chaim, that he's gone. She was quite sick. My father said she turned yellow—from anxiety, stress, all of the above."

This development made Bajla even more worried about protecting Roman. "While I was in the work camp, my Mom would hide me in a suitcase, in a po- tato sack, under the mattresses on the bed. I remember lying in a suitcase under the bed for hours."[30]

But it was clear that hiding Roman inside a busy work camp was no long- term solution. So Bajla made other plans. "My Mom befriended a German sol- dier named Timan. She trusted him. She arranged for me to be taken from the work camp to Maria's in a suitcase. And I don't know how Mom kept in touch with Maria while we were there. My Mom told me they punched holes in the suitcase so I could breathe. He took me out of the work camp to Maria's, and then somehow my Mom escaped," and she made it to Maria's, too.

After the war Roman's father told him that he and Bajla had arranged for another woman to take the boy out of the camp. They had given her jewelry to compensate her for taking such a risk, but "she took the jewelry and then brought me back to the camp. And my Dad told me that a man in the camp came to him and said, 'Aron, there's a little boy out there who looks like your son.' I said, 'Dad, that's not possible. The Germans would have seen me if this man saw me.' But he said, in Yiddish, 'It happened.'"

Roman said that somehow his mother then arranged for the German soldier to carry her boy in a suitcase to the home of Maria Balagowa, and that's where he stayed hidden until the end of the war.

Some things about the time he hid with Maria remained firmly in Roman's memory. One was going to church with Maria one Easter. "The priest came out and blessed our Easter eggs. I remember holding Maria's hand in one hand and the Easter basket in the other hand. I remember when the priest blessed the baskets with holy water a drop of it went in my eye. It's amazing how you remember this trivia."

While Roman lived with Maria, he said, he did not have a sense of his mother's presence in the basement. "She may have come up while I was sleeping. She may have come up other times. In the basement there was a huge coal bin and somehow, my Mom told me, they had a rain barrel that they put inside the coal bin and covered it up. She lived in the barrel. She was down there from 1942 to 1945, a three-year period."

But in all the time Roman stayed with Maria, he could not do any of the things boys his age normally would do, including going to school.[31] Toward the end of living with Maria, Roman said, he has a memory of the time Soviet troops drove out the Germans and liberated their area.

"I remember the bombs falling around Sosnowiec because I fell out of bed, and I remember running to Maria screaming. I also remember before this being told by Maria that the Russians are coming. We walked out in the street and I would gather up cigarette butts and open the paper. I had a little box for saving the tobacco in it for them. And I remember that when they did come into the city in their army trucks, I went into a truck with this little box of tobacco and I gave it to them."

Piecing together the whole story of his survival has been difficult for Roman. For example, what role did Maria's husband play in all of this? Roman said that his mother told him that the man was "antisemitic and he had some shady dealings with the Nazis, so they took him away. So he was not with us much. And he did not survive."

Meanwhile, Roman's father spent much of the war in different work camps and concentration camps, and "after the war he came right back to the building he had lived in," though Roman did not know where his father was when the war ended. His father never wanted to talk about this time in his life.

Why, we asked Roman, did Maria risk her life and her son's life to save him and his mother?

"I think," he said, "it was because she was a religious woman. I think she loved me as her own. And to save me, she saved my Mom. But basically the reason she did that is because I think she felt a commitment to me. She saved me because I think she thought of me as her grandchild. There were many Poles, known now as righteous gentiles, who saved Jews, and if you ask them why they did it, they would say it was the right thing to do."

Would Roman risk his own life now to save others? "It's funny that you should ask that question," he said, "because when I teach the children, sixth graders, and I tell them how Maria saved my life, I say to the children, 'How many of you would be willing to risk your life to save someone else, knowing that if you're caught you'll be put to death?' And, of course, after hearing my story, many of them say, 'Oh, we would, Mr. Frayman, we would.' But I say, 'Put your hands down. Let me tell you honestly, if someone asked me if I'd do it, my honest answer is, 'I don't know.' Would I be willing to sacrifice my children, my grand-children, I don't know. You don't know that until you are in that circumstance. I don't know how gutsy I am."

After the War

When the war ended Roman's father returned to Sosnowiec and, with Ro-man's mother, opened a bakery. But after several months of struggling with the business, and because Poland was under Communist rule, the Frajmans decided to leave Poland and move to Germany. There it was a hand-to-mouth existence, however. For instance, Bajla got some equipment to make and sell butter. When they got care packages from the Red Cross, they would take the cigarettes out of them and sell them one at a time. It was both an economic and an emotional struggle for his parents who, he said, "lost everything. They lost their families. My Mom lost a child."

After living in Eggenfelden, Germany, for several years, the Frajmans finally obtained visas to come either to Newark, New Jersey, or to Cleveland. They chose Cleveland because they knew people who lived there. They moved in September 1949 when Roman was eleven and a half years old.

When Roman finished high school he was uncertain about a career choice. So he went to Ohio State University and got a bachelor's degree in psychology. Then he did a stint in the military reserves and went to work for the Social Secur-ity Administration, which he served as an executive for more than forty years, retiring in 2006. His parents moved to the Cleveland area as well. His father lived until 1996 and his mother until 2003.

Roman and his wife, Elaine, have three children—two daughters, Laura and Julie, and a son, Michael—and four grandchildren. Roman has been an active member of The Temple-Tifereth Israel in Cleveland and has taught the youth there about the Holocaust for many years.

He has returned to Poland to see where he spent his early years, but he told us his major regret is that his parents did not stay in touch with Maria after they moved to Germany and then the United States. "My Mom was always very grateful to Maria. But the thing I feel guilty about today is that we never maintained a relationship while she was living. We never sent her any money. Maybe we didn't have any money to send her. So I have a lot of guilt feelings today." On Roman's last trip to Poland, he discovered where Maria's granddaughter—Czcziek's daughter—lives, but he was not able to see her in person. "I couldn't get in touch with her because she didn't want to be in touch with me. She's afraid. God knows why." Nonetheless, he said he has continued trying to make that connection. "I will connect with her one way or another."

Rose Gelbart

Sabina Grosman desperately wanted the job of housekeeper for a widower named Adam Zak. But Zak, a Warsaw banker with two children, left the choice up to his thirteen-year-old daughter, Hanna Barbara (called Hanka). Which of the two people sitting in Zak's office, facing the Warsaw Ghetto, would it be—Sabina or another woman who also had applied and who wanted to marry Zak?

Hanka did not hesitate. She pointed to Sabina. And in so doing, though no one could have known it at the time, she helped to save not only Sabina but also her little daughter, Rozia (now Rose Gelbart).

"The other woman was very angry and jealous," Rose told us when we interviewed her in her home in suburban Cleveland. So Zak took his daughter Hanka aside and said of Sabina, "But you know she's Jewish?" Hanka's response, Rose said, was "I don't care. I want her." As Rose explained, "My mother made a very good impression. She was a beautiful woman."

So Sabina worked in the Zak household off and on for several years, and Rose was hidden there whenever Sabina could not find other safe locations for her. Indeed, dozens of Polish non-Jews knew that Rose was Jewish, but—despite some threats to do so—none of them ever went to the Germans and turned her in. They either said nothing or they intentionally gave Sabina time to get Rose out of danger, even though the Germans were offering rewards to people who would turn in Jews.

Protecting Rose and her mother at times required extraordinary and unusual actions. For instance, after Hanka chose Sabina to be their housekeeper, her father worried that the woman who had failed to get the job would, in her anger, denounce Rose and Sabina as Jews. "So Adam Zak's son, Marian, who was twenty-one years old, married this woman who was ten years older, just to keep her quiet." Marian worked with the Polish underground and eventually was captured and sent to his death at Auschwitz. By then, Rose said, Marian's wife also was working in the anti-German underground and, thus, was not of a mind to turn Rose and Sabina over to German authorities.

Rose's circuitous path through the war began in Leszno, fifteen or twenty miles west of Warsaw. She was born there on January 3, 1935. When Rose was two, in 1937, her parents, Sabina (originally Sura) and Jozef Grosman, moved to Kalisz in west-central Poland, where Jozef manufactured children's and women's shoes. Sabina traveled around and sold them, along with merchandise from her

Rose Gelbart

Hanka Janczak

·Ostrołęka

Leszno· ·WARSAW

·Kalisz

·Warka
Jedlinsk· ·Kozienice
·Radom
·Lublin

·KRAKÓW ·Rzeszów

72

own textile business. "They did very well. My mother was a business entrepreneur." The Grosmans lived in a beautiful apartment in the newer part of the city, though most Jews at the time lived in what was called the Old City. In fact, of the six families in their apartment building, the Grosmans were the only Jews. They had a shoe store in Leszno and were preparing to move their manufacturing business from the back of their apartment and the basement of their apartment building to a factory. Rose's maternal grandparents (Henoch and Sisel Langner) as well as her mother's sisters and a brother all lived in the Old City in Kalisz.

Among her earliest Kalisz memories are the times she spent in a nearby park with her cousin Belusia, the daughter of her mother's sister Rozia. Their mothers would dress the two girls alike. Belusia was just a few months younger than Rose. Another memory is of Rose's fourth birthday, which the whole Langner family gathered to celebrate in 1939. But nine months later Germany invaded Poland.

"My first war memory was running away from Kalisz with hordes of people and horses and cars. Planes were overhead bombing and shooting at us. We were hiding in ditches, and my uncle covered me with his body to protect me."

The Polish army surrendered after a few weeks, and Rose and her family returned to Kalisz to rejoin family members. (Jozef's family lived in Łódź.) Kalisz was home then to about 15,300 Jews, which was roughly 30 percent of the city's total population.[32]

"As soon as we arrived there back at our apartment in Kalisz," Rose told us, "the Germans knocked on our door. They had asked if there were any Jews living in the building and someone told them there were." But when her mother opened the door, the Germans mistook them for non-Jews and went away. "Then they asked again, 'Where are the Jewish people?' And the people said, 'You had it right, the Grosmans.' So they came back and gave us about twenty minutes to pack up our belongings and leave. We didn't know where or what." The Grosmans' comfortable apartment was one the Germans wanted immediately.

The Germans told the Grosmans to gather with other Jews in a market area of the city. Each adult, Rose said, was allowed fifty zloty and fifty kilograms of baggage. "I remember that my father took me out of bed and carried me, still in my pajamas, in his arms to my grandparents' house in the Old City. That's one of only two memories I have of my father. It was still September and still a warm evening."

When Rose got to her grandparents' house, she found that her little cousin Belusia already was there. And they were happy to see each other. "We started jumping on the bed and we played."

But a few minutes later, in a repeat of the previous scene, there was a knock on the door, "and the Germans came in with their guns pointed at us and gave us fifteen to twenty minutes to pack up whatever we could carry. That was very frightening because they came pointing those great big guns at us. I remember everybody was in terror."

The family moved to the outdoor market area and stayed there all day and all night with other Jews while German soldiers plundered the goods the Jewish families had brought with them. The Germans separated families and sent them in different directions. Rose and her parents were told to board a crowded freight train for Warsaw while her grandparents and aunts and uncle were sent to Rzeszów in southeast Poland east of Tarnów.

So Sabina, Jozef, and Rose went to Warsaw, a journey that lasted three days without food or water. This was before the ghetto in Warsaw was formed, but Jews already were required to wear white armbands with a Star of David on them. Sabina was forced to work in a textile factory while Jozef had to go to work in a shoe factory. But in January 1940, Sabina asked a German resettlement officer if she and her family could travel to Rzeszów to rejoin the rest of the family, "and they gave her a permit to travel."

So they did, in fact, go to Rzeszów, which, when World War II broke out, had a Jewish population of about fifteen thousand, more than one-third of the city's total population.[33] There, Rose was thrilled to see her little cousin again. "In Rzeszów I was very happy. My cousin was like my sister." That cousin's father had run off to the Soviet Union when Jews were seeking safe havens after the German invasion, but he left his wife, Rozia, and daughter behind. So Rozia and Belusia lived with Balbina, another sister of Rose's mother, Sabina.

When Rose and her family arrived in Rzeszów, the ghetto there was not yet enclosed, but the whole family had to live together in a small space. That made for tense family relations. It was there that her grandparents died, of natural causes and surrounded by loving family members. However, things got worse when, in June 1941, the Germans moved Jews into what, six months later, would become a closed ghetto—divided into sections A and B—where people were starving and trying to survive a typhus epidemic.

The Germans registered Jews by trade, so Rose's father declared himself a shoemaker while her uncle Simon registered as a locksmith (that uncle survived the war and lived until his death in Cleveland in 1994). Rose said the two men worked for the Gestapo headquarters, one making locks, the other boots. Meanwhile, Rose's mother found road construction work outside the ghetto on what German authorities called the "Aryan" side of Rzeszów. And at night she helped to clean a German officers' quarters, but this meant she usually did not return home until midnight. As Sabina traveled to and from work, however, she was able to barter for extra food to sustain her family.

One of Rose's sharpest memories from this time (July 1942) was when all the Jews were forced into a gathering place (*Sammelplatz* in German) for the start of deportations to the Belzec death camp. An uncle, aunt, and their baby were among the first to be taken away. "I was crouching near my parents and the Germans would shoot at random, picking out people from the group to show how tough things are going to be by killing them in front of the family. The dogs would bark and it was just terribly chaotic. Bullets were flying and people were screaming and crying."

Families were crowded together in small apartments. Women, Rose said, were called to register to work. So Rose's mother, on her way to work outside the ghetto, asked her sister to take Rose with her while that sister went with her son to register. But without knowing it, Sabina's sister was headed for a women and children's train transport to Belzec. She told Sabina she had her hands full with her own child and a large bag of things, so she could not take Rose, too. "Had I gone with her I would not have come home," Rose told us. When Rose's uncle figured out where the train was going, she said, he ran after it but could not catch it.

After this first transport, when it was apparent that those sent away were not coming back, "there was panic," Rose said. "Whoever could run tried to escape." Sabina made a pledge to herself never to go on such a transport or to send Rose on one, so she found a woman outside the ghetto to keep Rose and she gave the woman some money to cover the extra costs of that. Then she put a little extra money in the lining of Rose's little green coat. When Sabina went through the gate in the early morning to go to work outside the ghetto, she asked the guard there if she could take Rose with her because she had nowhere else to keep her. Somehow, the man agreed.

So Sabina took Rose by the hand and marched out of the ghetto with other authorized workers. As soon as they were outside the ghetto, she pointed to a non-Jewish woman who was waiting at the curb and told Rose to go with her. "She let go of my hand and I ran over. Nobody saw me. The woman took my hand and took me to her apartment. She lived on a main floor of the apartment. I remember seeing her closing the jalousies and she told me to sit in the bedroom."

The woman, who was heading to work herself, told Rose she was going away but would return. "Well, that day I cried all day long and I wanted to go home. It was so sudden. Nobody prepared me for anything. When she came back in the evening I cried hard and said I want to go home."

Rose later marveled at the bravery of this woman, with whom she stayed for only one night. Even if it was done for money, Rose said, it was dangerous. "How many women would want to do that?"

This woman, responding to Rose's crying, took her back to the ghetto. "There was an opening under the wire and she pushed me through. And I came home. My father was lying in bed already, and when he saw me he stretched his arms out and I ran into his arms. He was so happy to see me. But when my mother came from work at midnight and saw me, she turned white because the next day all mothers and children had to report again to the *Sammelplatz*." From there they would be sent to their deaths. After this experience, Rose said, she did not cry any more. "It was like I learned my lesson because I saw how scared my mother was."

Sabina searched unsuccessfully all that night for a place to hide Rose. When that failed, she went before dawn again to the gate guard and got permission to take Rose to work again. They left hurriedly, without a chance to say farewell to Rose's father, whom she never saw again. Her father eventually perished at Belzec.

As soon as they were out of the ghetto that morning, Sabina took Rose by the hand and ran with her to a nearby Christian cemetery, where they hid behind some high headstones. From there they heard shots being fired at people trying to run away. Sabina was doing some work for a sympathetic *Volksdeutsch*, a man who had told her to come to his house if she ever needed help. Which is exactly what she did that morning before the sun rose. But Sabina was unable to rouse the sleeping man. So she and Rose waited for awhile in an outhouse on the balcony of the man's building.

But when other people in the building were getting ready for work, they began knocking on the outhouse door, so Rose and Sabina had to move. They returned to the apartment of the *Volksdeutsch* man and simply pushed open the door and woke him up. He told them to lie low there while he figured out what he could do. Eventually he returned with a Polish passport for Sabina. And he found a place for Rose to stay in Rzeszów. Sabina then went back to the ghetto to say goodbye to her husband and her sister. The sister asked Sabina to take her little girl with her, but she could not do it. "I don't even know if I can save one," she told her.

That's when Sabina went to Warsaw and got hired by Adam Zak, who arranged for her to have a *Kennkarte* (a Polish identity document). On her way, she took all the family photographs she had and destroyed them out of fear of being caught as a Jew. "So I don't even have a single picture of my father or my grandparents," Rose told us. Her grandparents both died while they were living in the Rzeszów Ghetto.

When Sabina brought little Rose from Rzeszów to Warsaw and the Zak home, she told Hanka that Rose was her niece. But Hanka quickly figured out they really were mother and daughter. One tip-off was that at times Hanka would hear little Rose call Sabina "Aunt" and at other times "Mother."

While staying at the Zak home, Rose was required to disappear whenever other people were around. "I couldn't understand why I had to be the one hiding and why my mother didn't have to hide. I probably thought they were after me, after the children. It's strange when you're that young and nobody tells you anything." The reality was that Sabina had false papers showing she was a Polish non-Jew married to Zak, but she had no papers that would identify Rose—who was given the false last name of Halinka—as her daughter.

Rose and Hanka got along famously. Hanka "was wonderful to me," Rose told us. "She would comb my hair, even when I had lice in my hair, and play with me. Even though I was Jewish, it didn't matter."

Still, Rose did not stay at the Zak home all the time. Rather, Sabina found a series of temporary hiding places "by word of mouth" so as not to put the Zaks in jeopardy—places in Warsaw, Ostrołęka, Radom, Jedlińsk, Kozienice, and other villages. But when there was no alternative, Rose came back to the Zaks. Over the course of almost three years, Rose was hidden in many places. She survived not only because people did not turn her in to German authorities but also because her mother helped her in many ways, because Adam Zak was compassionate, and because Hanka was resourceful and willing to put herself in danger to save Rose.

Among the many places Rose hid, early on, was a tiny farm where she stayed, between leaving Rzeszów and arriving at the Zak home for the first time. "I remember their mother passed away, and my mother kneeled by the bed and cried. I guess that was the only time she could cry. So she cried and held this woman's hand. She reminded her, probably, of her mother. And I was wondering: Why is my mother kneeling here and crying?"

At other times she stayed with a widow friend of her mother's named Mrs. Barbanilowa, who had a teenage son. "When my mother couldn't find a place, she would take me in and I would stay there with them." In fact, after the war, the woman came to Kalisz and wanted to match up her son with Rose. "It shows you how she felt about Jews," Rose said.

Another time Sabina left Rose with a family that had a little boy. When Sabina visited her there, Rose was instructed to call her mother "Mrs.," not "Aunt" or "Mother." The cover story was that Sabina was taking care of Rose because Rose's father was in the army, but Sabina needed help with child care so she could work. Rose, thus, stayed there, and sometimes she was left with the boy while his parents also worked. "There I remember my mother coming to me and kneeling by the little bed. She whispered a prayer in Jewish to me and told me to say the prayer every night before I went to sleep. I knew I had to say the prayer every single night after that."

Rose was told, there, never to look out the window, especially if she heard other children playing outside. "Well, as a child I tried to peek through the window. And they saw me. Someone must have told their parents." But, as would happen several times during the war, no one turned Rose over to the authorities. "They didn't give me away, but the people got a letter [from neighbors] saying that if they don't send me away they'll have to report me. So again it wasn't a long hiding place. At least they were nice enough to send a letter. That was my luck."

Once, her mother found a hiding place for Rose near the Warsaw Ghetto with a family that ran a stationery store. "It was a very nice family, and they were teaching me how to take Communion. So I was very excited because I'll be like one of them. So I was in the open, kind of. I was very happy there."

But one day the people hiding Rose notified Sabina to pick her up, because again, someone had told German authorities that the family was hiding a Jew. This time, in fact, the Germans came and took away the father of the family, because, Rose told us, they thought he was the Jew being hidden—"My luck!" By the time authorities checked out the man and verified he was not Jewish, Rose was gone.

Rose especially remembered a time when her mother had arranged for her to be picked up at one hiding place and moved to another. "We were walking through the fields in a blizzard. The snow was very deep and the wind was blowing like crazy. A stranger picked me up. I never knew who was going to pick me up. He was smuggling me from one place to another. I had a little red purse I'd had since before the war. It had a blue cornflower painting on it. All of a sudden I looked at my shoulder and the purse is gone. I cried, 'I want my purse back.' So he went back with me a short distance to look for it but we couldn't find it. The snow had covered it. Someone probably found it when the snow melted. But I never forgot my purse."

Rose did not remember being consistently hungry, nor did she remember being abused in any way. But she saw some terrible things, nonetheless.

Once, for instance, a man dropped her off "like a bundle" at a farm. A man was there with his mentally disabled sister. "He took a rope and tied her to the chair and started beating her. I crouched under the table thinking that I'm next. This was the most frightening episode." But she had no recollection of whether she stayed there overnight or what else happened there.

In all of these temporary shelters, Rose said, "I always thought my father was going to come to my rescue. I also knew that they were after the Jewish children because there was no one else hiding except me that I knew."

Rose said that her mother had little money, so the people who hid her were not doing it to get rich. Sabina, in fact, usually could give these families just enough to cover the cost of Rose's food. And all of these families knew it would be fatal for them if they were caught hiding a Jew, Rose said.

Eventually a time came when Sabina could not find a place to hide Rose and could not keep her at the Zak home for long. So Zak elected to take his daughter, Hanka, out of school and to send her and Rose to stay with a distant relative outside of Warsaw. While there, Hanka and Rose pretended to be sisters. This family had cats, Rose said, "and they would make me eat out of the same bowl as the cat. But they had a tree in the back, and when peaches fell down I would climb through the window and eat the peaches."

This family also took the girls to a nearby lake to swim, but Rose did not know how to swim and did not like the water. "So they said that if they didn't know I was Hanka's sister they would swear I'm Jewish because I'm afraid of water." Indeed, Rose later became convinced that the family knew she was Jewish all along.

"One day," while living with that family, she said, "they sent me for watermelon and I'm carrying this big watermelon. The children started running after me calling me 'Little Jew.' I was thinking that an adult was going to hear it, but if I start running I'll give myself away. Nobody tells you those things. It's just instinct. So I just walked with this watermelon right into the house." Another night, Rose recalled, German authorities came to the farm. People there thought they had come for Rose. But, in fact, a son in the family had been working with the Polish underground, and he was the one arrested. After that, in a repeat of what had already happened elsewhere, neighbors sent this family a note that threatened to expose Rose as a Jew if they did not send her away. "They knew that if they gave away the home where they were harboring a Jew, the whole family was going to get it, too. So I don't know whether they sent the letter to save me or Hanka or they did it to save the family."

When Rose and Hanka were sent away to hide together, Hanka's father had given her instructions to call her father if there were some emergency. So once that threatening letter arrived, Hanka and Rose ran away. "She took my hand, we took off our shoes and we were running and running and running until the spot where she called her father and they came to pick us up."

Rose expressed amazement at the pattern of her surviving, because non-Jews either hid her or chose not to tell authorities about her without a warning first. "There were so many places and so many people who did know I was Jewish but who didn't give me away. It had to be at least fifty, even more than fifty. I don't know if it was sheer luck or what." More than fifty people in at least a dozen different hiding places, almost never more than once in any hiding place except the Zak home, and the longest time in any of those places was a few weeks.

Rose remembered one time back at the Zak home in Warsaw when she and her mother heard a siren. "The custodian ran up to my mother to warn her, so it shows that he, too, knew I was Jewish. He ran up to her and said, 'The gendarmes are coming.' She took my hand and ran up to the fifth floor of the building. She was thinking that if they stop at that building she would jump with me so as not to endanger that family. But they didn't come in."

When the Warsaw Uprising occurred in August 1944, Rose, Sabina, and others escaped the city. "My mother, Hanka, and I were pushed toward some little towns."

At one point, Rose said, Sabina spoke to a German military officer and talked him into giving her, Rose, and Hanka a lift to another city on the man's horse and buggy. "Imagine the courage it took of my mother. Having Hanka with us helped but she was suffering with us through all those years. She didn't go to school. She was on the farm with us. She was with my mother in all those places. She even told us later that none of her family members knew it. She never told any of her aunts or uncles or anyone. That's how afraid you had to be that somebody will give us away. After the war she told them and they couldn't believe she didn't tell. And she was a child herself. She never went to school because of me."

When Rose, Sabina, and Hanka were on the road after the Warsaw Uprising, the girls would knock on doors seeking food, Rose said, "and the Poles would give it to us." Eventually they wound up in a house at the edge of a small village and witnessed a battle between the Germans and the Soviets.

"The bullets were flying over us and arms and legs were flying," Rose said. "We hid behind an upright piano trying to protect ourselves from the bullets and the cannons. We knew it was near the end of the war. The Russians liberated us but they didn't do anything to us. There was a lot of rape going on but we were lucky again."

Once things calmed down and Soviet troops had captured Warsaw from the Germans on January 17, 1945, Rose, Sabina, and Hanka returned there. But like nearly every building in Warsaw, the Zak apartment building had been destroyed. So they stayed with another family for a time. Adam Zak wanted to marry Sabina, Rose said, but she declined the offer.

Rose and Sabina did not stay long in Warsaw. Instead, they went back to Kalisz, and took Hanka with them. They got their apartment back there, and even some of their furniture. Not only that, but Rose's uncle returned, too. "My mother was happy to see him and I was happy to see him, but it was not my father."

On July 4, 1946, more than a year after the war ended, residents of Kielce murdered more than forty Jews there. The incident alarmed the few Jews remaining in Poland and many of them, including Sabina and Rose, packed up and left. Sabina took Rose and Hanka to a Polish-German border area controlled on one side by the Soviets and on the other by the Americans. From there Rose, Sabina, and Sabina's brother made it into the American zone, first staying at the Neu Freimann displaced persons camp and finally in Munich, where, for a time, Rose attended a religious school. Sabina wanted Hanka to go with them to Germany, for "she was like a sister to me and like a daughter to my mother," she said. But Hanka did not want to leave her father in Poland. Adam Zak eventually married another woman many years later and lived until the age of ninety, though he eventually went blind. Sabina and Rose gave Hanka all the furnishings of their old apartment in Kalisz, and she married. That marriage ended in divorce, though it produced two sons, and she later remarried. Rose has returned to Poland three times and visited Hanka.

After the War

Rose spent five years in Munich and attended school both there and in Switzerland. Her mother remarried, though she had no more children. In 1951, when Rose was sixteen, she and her mother got visas to come to the United States. That's when she came to Cleveland, where she graduated from Glenville High School in 1954.

"I said, 'This is America?' when I came to Cleveland. I mean New York was America." But she has stayed in Cleveland except for a few years when she and her husband, a Holocaust survivor named Arthur Gelbart whom she met in the United States in 1954, lived in Las Vegas. The Gelbarts were married in November 1955, and they operated a Cleveland store that sells flooring. They have two sons, Jerry and Michael, and four grandchildren.

Rose not only has been active in the World Federation of Jewish Child Survivors of the Holocaust but also has helped to create and run an organization of Holocaust survivors in the Cleveland area called Kol Israel. She has also helped to lead the Northeast Ohio Child Survivors of the Holocaust.

Our Visit with Hanka Janczak

When we met with Hanka and her son, Zbyszek Lewandowski, in Warsaw, we found a warm and engaging woman who still thought of Rose Gelbart as a sister. Here's how she explained, through a translator, the relationship between her father and Rose's mother. "My father and Rose's mother were kind of in love. They were much in love but they didn't make love."

Once the war ended and Rose and Sabina elected to leave Poland, Hanka said, "my father cried. For a long, long time he was single. All that time he thought about Sabina. He had Sabina in his mind. Then he married again when he was seventy years old." Hanka confirmed that she chose not to go with Rose and Sabina when they left Poland in 1946 "because I didn't want to leave my father alone."

Hanka described a time in the war when she and her father, along with Rose and her mother, left Warsaw and moved for a time to Warka, which is south of Warsaw and about halfway to Radom. Several times there, Hanka said, German authorities took her father in for questioning. To loosen him up the Germans served him vodka, and this began to worry Hanka, who thought he might slip and give away information that would lead to Rose and Sabina's true identity as Jews.

Once, Sabina, who could understand German well, learned that there was a good possibility of some kind of *Aktion* the next day, Hanka said. So that night the two girls left Warka and moved to Ostrołęka, which is north of Warsaw. There they stayed in an unused school building with homeless Poles. They were in Warka and Ostrołęka about a month each, Hanka said. After that, Hanka let her father know that things were too dangerous in Ostrołęka, so her father and Sabina came to get them and take them to Radom. From there they went to Jedliñsk, north of Radom, where they stayed for six months until liberation.

We asked her why she thought her family and other non-Jews risked their lives to save Jews. Her answer was that "the situation was very complicated. Some hid Jews for money, some because of being thoughtful people. Some cooperated with the German police—not because they wanted to cooperate but because they feared for their own lives. We did it just because it was the right thing to do. I did what I did out of human nature. The most important thing is that they lived."

When Rose and she have gotten together in recent years, she said, "we more weep than talk."

Felicia Graber

Felicia Graber is quick to acknowledge that she may be among the most fortunate of Holocaust survivors. Hers, after all, is a story of a child who was with her mother (and often her father, though she thought he was someone else) throughout the ordeal.

And yet it is also true that she did not know who her real father was until well after World War II, even though he lived with—and hid with—Felicia and her mother for about a year while the war raged. She thought he was a friend of the family whom she was told to call "Uncle," and that her real father was a missing Polish army soldier. And it's true that her mother trained the little girl to pretend to be Catholic. And, yes, Felicia lived in a ghetto, then in a small space in a building full of people desperately trying to make it through the war alive, and finally, with a poor Polish farm family who barely had enough to eat.

But in the end, with some help from Polish non-Jews, she made it. And her parents made it, too.

"I was unbelievably fortunate," she told us when we interviewed her in her St. Louis home with her husband, Rabbi Howard Graber, and her brother, Leon Bialecki. "One of the first pieces that I ever wrote was called 'Lucky Woman.' I'm not named Felicia for nothing."

Felicia eventually came to terms with her disrupted and precarious childhood. But to do that, she acknowledged, she "struggled with many issues without realizing that most had their roots in those early years. My feelings of insecurity, of being inadequate, of not being good enough for my bright, handsome, successful husband—my inability to understand and express my constant need for approval, acceptance, and reassurance—led to many heartaches but also propelled me to achieve more than I would have otherwise."[34]

Felicia was born on March 26, 1940, less than seven months after Germany invaded her native Poland. Her parents, Shlomo and Tosia Lederberger, lived in Tarnów in the Małopolska region of southeastern Poland. Tarnów was a city of more than fifty thousand people, almost half of whom were Jews. Her mother, in fact, seriously considered aborting this baby, given the likelihood of such a terrible and difficult childhood for a Jewish baby in German-occupied Europe. But Felicia's grandfather, "a very religious man, begged her not to," and her mother complied.[35]

Her parents had married on March 7, 1939. They had been raised Orthodox, but were members of what Felicia called a "left-wing Zionist organization," HaShomer HaTzair. "My father was a goldsmith by trade, and he worked with

Felicia Graber

Janina Glowacka

Sopot

Grodzisk· ·WARSAW

·Lublin

·KRAKÓW

·Iwonicz-Zdroj

his father, my grandfather," she told us. "He had a jewelry store on the main street in Tarnów. They were relatively well off."

Her mother, Tosia, had worked as a secretary before marrying, but she did not work at the jewelry store located at No. 4 Krakówska Street. Tosia had gone to Palestine in 1933 and was planning to live on a kibbutz there. But Tosia's mother, Felicia's grandmother, got sick back in Poland. So, after about a year in Palestine, Tosia came back to Poland to care for her mother, who died in 1934. And soon after that, Tosia's sister died in childbirth. Tosia also had a brother, a dentist in Tarnów, so she decided to stay in Poland with him.

In the first year of Felicia's life, things were getting progressively worse for Polish Jews. In 1941 her parents were forced to move, but not yet to a ghetto. Rather, they had to abandon their home on the city's main street. So they moved to a small house in what they thought would become the ghetto.

Jews were required at this time to give German authorities any furs they owned, but Felicia's father refused, preferring instead to burn them, she said. This act of defiance set the tone for her father's behavior throughout the war. Indeed, during the war, Shlomo Lederberger rose to the occasion in fearless and creative ways.

Relying on oral and audiotaped accounts by her father, Felicia told us that German soldiers would come into Shlomo's jewelry store in groups and steal merchandise. German authorities set jewelry retail prices, making it difficult to earn a profit. Felicia's grandfather soon quit coming to his store because he wore a beard, and Jews wearing beards were often singled out for brutal treatment. So, frustrated by conditions imposed by German authorities, he gave up his participation in the business.

One day German soldiers beat up Felicia's father because they discovered he was carrying five kilos of forbidden white flour. "Some woman came to the store and offered him some white flour and my father bought it. He happened to run

Felicia and her parents
(photo courtesy of Felicia Graber)

into a couple of [German soldiers] on the way home to his parents, and they wanted to know where he got it and he refused to tell them, so they beat him. They were going to shoot him but he said, 'If you shoot me, you're for sure not going to know where I got it.' And somehow he managed to convince them that 'If you let me go I'll find out'" the name of the person who was the source of the flour. He was given a deadline to come to the authorities with the information. In the meantime he warned the people who originally provided the flour. Then he sent his wife to talk to the authorities instead of going himself because he was bedridden as a result of the beating.

Eventually Shlomo lost the store. The Germans simply took it over, as they regularly did to businesses operated by Jews in Poland.

In June 1942 Felicia's family was forced to move into the ghetto and to live with another family, the Osterweils. It was a Bundist house "and was like a community center," Felicia told us. Felicia's family shared an upstairs room with the Osterweils, so they put a sheet in the middle "to have a little bit of privacy."

In this building, and the one next to it, Felicia's father established hiding places for many people as time went on. There were, in fact, two hiding places. One building had a slightly lower roofline than the other, and one hiding place was located just under that roof. The second hiding place was in the attic of the larger house.

Felicia's father did not tell German authorities he was a goldsmith for fear they would take any precious metals he had hidden. Rather, he said he was a metalworker. Her mother pretended to be a seamstress. Identification papers had to have the correct—but often changing—seal and documentation, and Felicia's father "somehow always managed to get the right one. He had all kinds of contacts. I don't know how he did it."

Shlomo Lederberger's actions in the war amazed both Felicia and her younger brother, Leon Bialecki, who was born in 1946, the year after the war ended, and who took as his own the last name Shlomo used for several years. That's because they knew their father, who lived until 1991, as an ordinary man without any obvious capacity for finding creative solutions to difficulties. And yet they learned much about the Holocaust from him because he spoke extensively and made audiotapes about it. And although "my mother couldn't speak of the Holocaust, my father couldn't stop," Felicia said.

"My father, by his own description, considered himself a very ordinary person before the war," Leon told us. "He was a guy who liked to play cards, liked to hang around his friends, liked to climb rocks. He was very athletic, apparently. He did not finish high school. He never considered himself very intellectual. He was just a nice guy but nothing extraordinary.

"But what is so extraordinary about our father is that it was during the war that he became a very extraordinary person by circumstances and rose to the occasion. It is only now that we grasp the absolutely mind-boggling guts he had. I mean, 98 or 99 percent of it was luck, but the 1 percent was his good sense and the courage to go against the stream."

The other aspect of their father that amazed both Leon and Felicia was that in the midst of terrible times, when he and his family were constantly at risk of losing their own lives, he "went out of his way to save other people," Leon said. "Which was insane. Totally insane."

"He himself said so," Felicia added.

"And interestingly enough," said Leon, "after the war, he again became just an ordinary person with his own problems, his own issues. He was just a regular guy. He was a fascinating personality."

In the second week of June 1942, Felicia and her parents moved to the ghetto. Her three surviving grandparents had been sent away in the first deportation earlier that month. Felicia's father paid someone to find out where the train carrying his parents was going and learned that it had gone to the Belzec death camp.[36] But witnesses reported that Felicia's grandfather was shot and killed even before the train left for Belzec "because he wasn't moving fast enough."

A second deportation from the Tarnów ghetto occurred early in the fall. Children were taken on this one, and Felicia's parents elected "to go with me rather than give me up," she told us. The night before the train was to leave, they were put in stables. But in the morning the Gestapo read off a list of Jews to be released before the deportation train left.

"Each German officer," Felicia explained, "had his own private little deals with some Jews. Like if somebody was a tailor, they would make suits for him or boots or something. And if the guy got deported, the suit wouldn't be ready, so they all asked for their little private Jews to be released."

In other words, these German soldiers were cheating the Nazi system for their own benefit?

"Oh, absolutely," Felicia said. It just meant that these few Jews would survive—but only until the next deportation.

"So somebody from the *Judenrät* [Jewish Council] managed to put my father's name on that list," she said. "Actually there were three of us on the list," including Felicia and her mother.

But her father had a cousin whose little girl was among those rounded up for the children's deportation. The girl's mother had asked Felicia's father to look after the child. When they called out the names of those to be spared from deportation to a death camp, her father took the little girl with him: "The Germans said, 'It says you have one child.' But he said, 'No, it's a mistake. I've got two.'"

Felicia said this situation petrified her mother because she "was very dark, and my father was also. And I was very dark with very dark hair. And yet here's the blonde, blue-eyed child. But somehow in the commotion they let us go."

Indeed, to get away with the extra child, Shlomo Lederberger put his jacket over the little girl so her blonde hair would not show, and—at least temporarily—he saved a child destined for the death camp. Eventually, however, the girl was murdered, Felicia said.

Felicia's father also took other chances to help his own family and to help others. When he was planning to escape from the ghetto, he had connections with someone who could provide him with transportation. A young man came to Shlomo saying he needed to leave the ghetto, and Shlomo gave him the name of his connection. The young man took several people with him, and eventually they got caught. When word of their arrest leaked back to Shlomo, he went into hiding in the ghetto because he feared that the people would reveal that they got the name of the contact from him.

After the children's deportation, Shlomo "decided that my mother and I needed false papers," Felicia said. But her mother did not want to leave the ghetto.

"We've heard this story over and over again," Felicia said. "She said, 'I want to die with you,' and he said, 'I want to live with you.'"

So, through his many contacts, Shlomo managed to get papers for Tosia and Felicia that identified them as non-Jews, and mother and daughter moved to a small resort town, which Felicia believes was Iwonicz-Zdroj, located southeast of Tarnów, while Shlomo stayed in the ghetto. He had a friend in Iwonicz-Zdroj who was living on false identification papers, too, and this friend helped Felicia and her mother get a room, pretending to be non-Jews. Well, that was the plan, but Felicia, who was only two years old, told the new landlady, when asked, that her missing father's name was Shlomo. That Jewish name, of course, told the landlady that this little girl and her mother were Jews.

The result, Felicia said, was that "the lady started to blackmail my mother, wanting more rent and this and that."

Felicia came to understand how brave her mother was through all this. "My mother had to fend for herself. She had to learn how to behave, what to say to whom. She had to invent a past that was foolproof, explain why she had to move away from her hometown with a young child. She had to watch her every word, every gesture, lest an eager Pole become suspicious and run to the Gestapo."[37]

Somehow, Felicia's father had money throughout the war, though she was not entirely clear how he did it. "My father always managed to have money," she said. Leon explained that his father had a secret jewelry pocket in his pants that nobody ever found, and there he was able to hide jewelry and cash. "The only time he almost ran out of money was about the time of liberation," Leon said.

Why didn't Shlomo leave the ghetto and go with his wife and daughter when they moved to Iwonicz-Zdroj? Felicia said she believed her father thought his wife and daughter had a better chance without him and that he had a better chance to survive and be flexible without a wife and child beside him, Leon said.

"I don't think that Dad did *not* want to leave the ghetto," Leon said to Felicia when we interviewed them. "He made several statements saying that he wanted to get you and Mother out, and he said, 'I, as a young thirty-year-old, have much more ability to take care of myself and survive without having a wife and child. I can join the underground, I can buy weapons, and if I join the underground I can jump out of a moving train.'" Later, when the ghetto was almost completely empty, he knew he had to get out—and did it, wearing the uniform of a train conductor.

Things were not going well in Iwonicz-Zdroj. Felicia's mother wanted to go back to the ghetto. "She became very despondent and at one point actually thought of turning herself in to the Gestapo," Felicia said.

Felicia's parents were using a non-Jewish friend named Marian Urban to take messages back and forth between them. Through Urban, Shlomo urged Tosia not to go to the German authorities but to move to the town of Milanowek, just southwest of Warsaw.

So they went to Milanowek, but once again Felicia said something she should not have said. "I supposedly told the landlady this time that I was Catholic but really Jewish." This is when Felicia's mother really began to work hard to turn her daughter into someone who could pass as a Catholic and not jeopardize the family in this way again.

Felicia and her mother left Milanowek and came to Warsaw, where, using their fake identity papers, they rented a room outside the ghetto. Indeed, they lived on the street where the Gestapo headquarters was located. Here Tosia tended to Felicia's Catholic education by taking her to church and teaching her the Lord's Prayer. "Don't ask me how she knew that," Felicia said. "I became a good Catholic girl. Before she trained me, I messed her up twice. In fact, by the time the war ended, I had truly forgotten my Jewishness. I did not know I was Jewish. They didn't tell me until we had left Poland in 1947."

So Felicia and her mother lived in Warsaw for about a year, starting near the end of 1942. During this time the Tarnów Ghetto, where Shlomo was living, finally was closed, except for a few hundred people assigned to sort out the deported Jews' belongings to be shipped to Germany. One of them was Shlomo, who—on purpose—did not know exactly where in Warsaw his wife and daughter were living. Only Marian Urban knew where to find Tosia and Felicia. Urban traveled between Tarnów and Warsaw about every two weeks. By not knowing where his family was, Shlomo was never in danger of revealing their whereabouts to authorities.

When authorities finally closed the Tarnów Ghetto, Felicia's father got help to get out. An officer—Felicia does not know if he was Polish or German, nor does she know what his motivation was—told Shlomo to go to the apartment downstairs and buy a train conductor uniform from the wife of the man who owned it. Shlomo also managed to get a bicycle. He escaped the ghetto and met Urban, who took him to Warsaw and reunited him with his wife and daughter. At which point, "my mother faced the double task of hiding him in her one-room apartment and redoubling her brainwashing effort [on Felicia] that nobody lived with me but my mother."[38]

But it was a precarious family reunion. For one thing, Shlomo had false identity papers under a different last name from Tosia and Felicia. Their last name became Slusarczyk, while his was Bialecki. So they couldn't live together as husband and wife. Indeed, Tosia had told neighbors that her husband was a Polish army soldier who was missing, and that Shlomo—known now as Andre Bialecki—was a friend of her husband who was going to help look after her and her daughter. Shlomo's fake papers indicated he was a silk merchant, even though he was wearing a train conductor's uniform when he showed up.

When Felicia's father stayed with them in Warsaw, "he played a game. He would come in with his uniform and talk to everybody and make sure everybody knew he was there. And then make sure everybody knew he was leaving. He'd wave goodbye and then he'd sneak back in."

Shlomo hid behind a closet in their room. Felicia was told that this man was a friend of her father, "and I was told to call him 'Uncle.' I assume I did not recognize him [as her father]. I also was trained not to mention to a soul that he was there. My mother tells me that she would wake me up at night and say, 'Who do you live with?' And I'd say, 'Only with my mother, only with my mother, nobody else. Let me go to sleep.'"

Felicia's memory of these things was quite sparse. Most of what she described came from what her parents later told her, though her memory did retain what she called "residues" of her early childhood: "Mobs . . . noise . . . shouts . . . screams . . . dusk . . . train fumes . . . a locomotive whistling . . . a steam engine hissing . . . people pushing, trying to get on the train . . . a woman standing on the tracks, halfway under the train, only her upper body showing—arms raised: 'Please take my child . . .'"

Indeed, sometimes Felicia wished she could remember. "When talking to older child survivors who remember their grandparents or happy scenes from their early childhood, I wish I could be hypnotized. I wish I could go back to the first months of my life to see my father's father, who, I am told, adored me and came to see me daily as long as he could. . . . I wish I could remember my father as a young man whose only worries concerned running his father's prosperous jewelry business."[39]

With Tosia and Shlomo living with Felicia in a tiny section of a Warsaw apartment, "My mother would say that all of our lives were in the hands of a four-year-old."

Felicia did remember a garden with trees in the courtyard of the apartment building in Warsaw, and she recalled going to that courtyard in the daytime to play with other children. In fact, she was taught that when she called up to her mother that she was hungry and wanted some bread and butter, she should never ask for butter because she should not reveal to others in the courtyard the fact that her mother sometimes had that luxury available.

When the Warsaw Uprising started on August 1, 1944, bombs began to fall, but Felicia's mother did not want to leave the room in which they lived to go to the basement because her husband was hiding in that room. "One of the neighbors said, 'Why don't you ask your friend Andre to come and stay with you in these terrible times?' So he all of a sudden showed up and was with us." Andre Bialecki, of course, was none other than Felicia's father, who was there in hiding all the time anyway. But now he had an excuse for his round-the-clock presence.

Toward the end of the uprising in the fall of 1944, Germans went from house to house in Warsaw to destroy any houses that were not already ruined. This implanted itself in Felicia's mind. "One of my earliest memories was walking out of the building and seeing a German soldier standing there. I was just tall enough to see his riding boots, and for years after that, whenever I'd see anyone with riding boots, I freaked."

Felicia and her family were taken with thousands of other Poles (or, like Felicia and her family, Jews pretending to be non-Jews) to the Pruszków detention camp near Warsaw, where people were sent after the failure of the uprising. There, the men were separated from the women and children. Felicia's father claimed he had hurt his hand and had his arm in a sling to avoid being taken to slave labor. It earned him a trip to the hospital.

Meanwhile, the Germans were releasing from Pruszków any women with children who were two and under. "And since I was quite short all my life, my mother told the guard that I was only two and he let us go. The amazing thing is that my father had sneaked out from the transport to the hospital, and my mother and I were let go. And by total luck, accident, we both entered the same train leaving Pruszków. My mother and I got on the train and at the next station my father walked in."

Once again, Felicia's father had beaten the system, this time feigning an injury. While her father was in the hospital, Felicia said, "there was a German officer who came to inspect the sick people, making sure there was nobody who was faking it. He stopped in front of my father and pointed at him and said, 'Now, this guy is really sick. You can see that.'" In fact, they took Shlomo's pulse, which was discovered to be racing—further proof of his illness, though in reality it was proof of his nervousness about being found out.

But now, free from Pruszków, the family once again had to look for shelter. Indeed, after the failed uprising, many Warsaw residents like Felicia and her family were sent out into the countryside to find a place to stay. After a few days, Felicia and her family found a farm near Grodzisk in the tiny village of Chyliczki.[40] The farm, just southwest of Warsaw, was the home of the Sieroczinski family—Piotr and Eleonora and their two daughters, Wladzia and Janina—who were living in two rooms with no running water. Felicia's family stayed with this family from October or November 1944 until February or March 1945, after that area was liberated by the Soviet Union on January 18, 1945.

There has been a debate in Felicia's family about whether the Sieroczinskis knew that Felicia and her parents were Jewish. Her parents told her that the family did not know. For a long time, that's also what Felicia thought. But she said that one of the daughters, Janina, has told her that they did know. Indeed, she said, Janina told Felicia that they knew all along and that their father swore them to secrecy. When we interviewed Janina in Poland, she said her parents knew they were Jewish, but that she did not know until after the war, though she said it's possible her parents may have told her older sister, who is now deceased.

One argument in favor of the Sieroczinskis' knowing that Felicia and her family were Jews had to do with the weekly communal bathing that happened in the house. "The men would wash and the women would be in the other room and then they would switch. Well, my father obviously could not do that because non-Jewish Polish men are not circumcised. But near the farm there was a river, and to this day they still talk about my father because he would go to the river and take a bath. In the winter time he would break the ice and take a bath under it."

Felicia has spoken about this to lots of people who know Poles and to some people who knew this Polish farmer who let them stay on his land. "And they say there was just no way they did not know or at least suspect it because, they said, my father would work in the fields with the men. All he had to do was just use a wrong word, use a Yiddish expression that would just come out."

Once someone asked Shlomo why he did not go to confession at the church. "My father . . . told them that he had been studying for the priesthood and had left it and did not feel right going to confession."

In 1994 Felicia returned to Poland and visited the farm with her husband, a rabbi, who that day wore a Greek fisherman's cap, not a yarmulke (a traditional Jewish skullcap). The older sister, Wladzia, was still living on the farm with her husband. "I actually wanted to tell her at that point that we were Jews. My husband wanted to know how they liked the new president of Poland, Lech Walesa. Her husband started yelling. He said, 'Lech Walesa is a traitor to Poland. He's selling Poland to the Jews.'"

At which point Felicia elected not to say anything about being Jewish. But Wladzia seemed embarrassed by the outburst, Felicia said, because she might well have been aware that Felicia and her husband were Jewish. Wladzia, in fact, tried to shush up her husband, Felicia said.

Wladzia died several years after that trip, but the other sister, Janina, kept in regular touch, "begging me to come back to Poland." Finally Felicia returned to Poland again in 2005, but not before deciding that, if she were to see Janina again, she wanted to know clearly that Janina knew she was Jewish. In a note ahead of the visit, Felicia told Janina about her busy summer, which included mention of her grandson's bar-mitzvah in Israel. This note was met by silence, which puzzled Felicia, but a priest friend encouraged her to write again. And the priest said that if Janina wanted to write to the priest so he could explain the situation, she could. Which she did. The priest explained to Janina that Felicia and her family were Jews. Janina, whose husband by then had died, responded to Felicia by letter, but she said nothing about the Jewish question, though she said she was happy about Felicia coming to Poland.

When Felicia and Janina met in Poland, this is what Felicia said to her: "'I've got to tell you something. I have to tell you that we are Jews.' And she looked at me and said, 'I know that. My father knew it.'" Janina said that her father told her and her sister that, if they ever saw German soldiers coming, they should run into the forest and hide.

Today, Felicia is willing to believe that the Sieroczinskis knew they were Jewish and gave them a place to stay anyway.

Felicia's memories of living on the farm were scant, but she recalled being put in charge of the family's one cow, "and I was told that you have to take the cow to pasture. But watch out because the cow should not go into the field where the corn was growing. I remember one day the cow started going into the field and I panicked. I did not know what to do. I took a stick and kept hitting the cow on the back. Of course, the more I hit the cow the more it went into the field. I ran crying into the farm."

When Felicia spoke with Janina on a visit to Poland in 2005, "she told me all kinds of stories that I really do not remember." Janina was eleven when Felicia lived with them. Wladzia, the older sister, was sixteen. Janina told her how, as a little girl, Felicia would "crawl into her bed whenever I was afraid. And they would comb my hair and braid my hair. I don't remember these things, but they told me. Janina considers me to this day her little sister."

After liberation, there was almost no food left for the Sieroczinski family to share with Felicia and her parents. In fact, Felicia told us, the farmer "told my father to go from farm to farm to beg for potatoes. So my parents knew that it was time we left the farm because there was no food."

But before Felicia and her family left Poland after the war, "my father went back to the farm and brought them all kinds of jewelry or money or whatever and said goodbye." While they lived with the family, "they did not demand any payment," Felicia said. But the farm family expected their guests to help with the farmwork. In fact, Felicia said, "my father offered to pay them but they refused."

Felicia said her father once told the story about life on the farm and described how, when it would get dark early, area farmers would get together and drink vodka and talk. In this story, one farmer described how another farmer "has Jewish pigs. My father's ears perked up and said, 'Jewish pigs? I thought Jews were not allowed to have pigs.' But the other man told him, 'You're a stupid Warsaw guy, a city person, so you don't understand. It was this Jewish family who came to this farmer and asked for shelter. He told them to go to the stable, and then he called the Gestapo. The Germans shot the family and had the farmer bury them. And now he digs up the corpses and feeds them to his pigs, so now he has Jewish pigs.' That," said Felicia, "was the kind of people who lived there, aside from the Sieroczinskis."

After the War

When the Soviet Union liberated the area of the farm on which Felicia and her parents were staying, her father went first to Lublin to find clothes and other necessities. Then he went to Łódź and found an empty goldsmith store to use, though he lacked any tools of the trade. But he heard he could find such tools in Gdansk, so he went there, but found nothing he needed amid the war damage. So he went to nearby Sopot and found goldsmith and watch repair tools. Giving up the idea of opening a store in Łódź, he hired an optician for a store he opened in Sopot, "and in two years he was a wealthy man," Felicia said.

But then the Communists came, and he found it impossible to continue in business. So he and his family, which now included their son, Leon, moved to Brussels. But even though Belgium granted the family political asylum, there were no work permits available. So Shlomo in effect commuted from Brussels to Germany, where he worked in the diamond business. Although Tosia at first refused to live in Germany, in 1951 she finally agreed to join her husband there so the family was together again all week long each week.

It was while they were living in Brussels that Felicia's parents told her she was Jewish. In fact, it was the day before she was to start second grade in a new school, "and it's a scene that is cast in my mind like cast iron," Felicia told us. "My father told me that I am a Jew and that he is one, too, as are my mother and my brother. He told me that his parents were Jews and so were my mother's parents. He also told me that he is my real father, not an uncle who married my mother—that I never had a father who was a Polish soldier and who was killed in the war as I had been told."[41]

Felicia said she's always asked how she took the news. "It's interesting," she told us. "I had a harder time accepting that he was my father than the fact that I was Jewish." Still, one of the first things she did on learning she was Jewish was to take a small Catholic hymnal or prayer book that her au pair had given her and tear it to pieces. "Now I'm sorry I did," she said. "I wish I still had it as a keepsake."

Felicia split her high school years among schools in Brussels, in Germany, and a boarding school in England. In 1957 the family tried to move to the United States, but the idea of starting life anew once more proved too much for her parents, and they ended up back in Frankfurt. She sought to attend Barnard College in New York, but her parents were reluctant to let an eighteen-year-old travel alone to the United States. So they offered her trips to Paris, Rome, Greece, and Israel if she would postpone her plans for a year. She got no farther down the wonderful travel list than Paris. When she returned from that trip, she met the man who was to be her husband. He was serving as a chaplain in the U.S. army in Germany in 1959. "America came to me. I didn't come to America," Felicia explained.

Felicia and Howard were married in December 1959. He was reassigned to the advanced chaplain school at Fort Hamilton, New York, in 1963. After several other moves, they came to St. Louis in 1972. There he became executive vice president of the Central Agency for Jewish Education, a position from which he retired in 1997. Felicia obtained a public school teaching certificate and, in addition to being a *rebbetzin* (a Yiddish term for the wife of a rabbi), taught for twenty-six years. In 1999 she founded the Hidden Child/Child Survivor Group of St. Louis. She is also a driving force in the effort to restart a group for children and grandchildren of Holocaust survivors and victims. In addition, she serves as a docent and speaker for the St. Louis Holocaust Museum and Learning Center. The Grabers have a daughter, a son, and eight grandchildren.

Felicia said that she wrote to Yad Vashem, seeking to have Janina and her family honored as "righteous," but the agency "refused because I was too young to be a witness, and there are no other witnesses to testify as to whether her parents knew that we were Jews and not just refugees from Warsaw."

Our Visit with Janina Glowacka

When we visited Janina, she lived alone in a modest apartment in a building in Grodzisk, about twenty miles southwest of Warsaw. Among the most important questions we wanted to ask her was whether she could clear up any remaining confusion about whether she and her family knew Felicia and her family were Jews when they lived together at the farm, located a little over three miles from Janina's apartment.

"In the beginning," she told us through a translator, "my father did not know they were Jews, but he figured it out. When Andre—the name by which Felicia's father, Shlomo, was going—continually went to the fields, maybe my father asked him or maybe Andre decided to tell him. I don't know. My father eventually told my mother that they were Jewish. But my sister and I didn't know. My father told my mother: 'For God's sake don't tell the children.'"

And yet Janina acknowledged the possibility that, because her sister was six years older than she was, her parents might have trusted Wladzia's judgment enough to confide in her that Felicia and her parents were Jewish. Janina said she simply did not know.

After the war ended and Felicia and her parents had left the Sieroczinskis' farm, Felicia's father returned "to thank us," Janina said, "and he told everything about their family." That meant not just that they were Jewish but also that he was really Felicia's father, not her uncle, and was really married to Tosia.

While Felicia and her family were living with the Sieroczinskis, Janina said, she "had an uncle who was suspicious that something wasn't 100 percent. But he decided it wasn't his place to know. My father turned it into a joke: 'What are you talking about? Jew or not Jew? What difference does it make?' he would say."

Janina confirmed that "there was a stream not far from there and Andre used to bathe himself in it because he didn't want anyone to see he was circumcised."

Her memories of having what she thought of as a younger sister around were warm and clear. "We loved Felicia. I was already ten years old and my sister was sixteen and she was about six. So we loved her as a child. She had beautiful braids. We had one room with a large kitchen. In the wintertime we all stayed together. In the summertime it was hot and the people would go sleep in the barn or the field."

Still, she remembered a sense of fear and uncertainty. "Our father told us that whenever we see Germans approaching the house or when you see anyone in a car or a motorcycle approaching, you should hide in the wheat fields or the barn." She knew from personal experience how brutal the German soldiers could be. "When the people were being driven out of Warsaw, I had a cousin who was seventeen and they were going out to meet people to give them bread and an SS man killed my seventeen-year-old cousin. I saw the blood coming out of my cousin and I fainted. I saw it with my own eyes." In addition, her twenty-year-old brother was taken to Germany for forced labor in an ammunitions factory, but then her family received word that he had perished there.

When Janina was young, she said, she and her family "attended church from time to time," and she believes that her parents' religious beliefs were influential in their decision to help Felicia's family. "My mother always said that Jesus Christ was saving people, and it was our responsibility to save people." Janina said their priest did not know they were hiding Jews until the war was over and they told him. He thought they simply were housing non-Jews who had been driven from Warsaw by the uprising.

Immediately after the war, Janina's family and Felicia's family remained in contact, but once Felicia and her parents moved to the United States, they lost contact until, in the 1990s, Felicia decided to return to Poland to find the places where she and her family had survived. After that, Felicia and Janina, as well as Janina's sister until her death, remained in regular contact and reestablished their long-ago friendship.

Janina accompanied us to the farm where Felicia and her family stayed. When we visited it, it belonged to Janina's nephew. The small gray brick and stucco house was surrounded by an imposing metal fence and had a red metal roof. An old refrigerator sat to one side of the front door next to a wooden stool. The house was at the end of a couple of rural roads (paths, really), almost as isolated as it had been during the war.

The wooden barn in which Felicia and her family sometimes slept still was on the property, though when we saw it, it leaned and slumped precariously and showed no evidence of ever having been painted. A ten-rung handmade wooden ladder, its feet resting on weeds and dirt, leaned against that building the day we were there.

Janina said that "as long as my sister was alive, the farm was well taken care of. But now the son has sort of neglected it." Then she looked around the property and remembered the war. "The most important thing is that everyone here survived," she said.

Feliks Karpman

When Marianna Konarzewska's family hid Wolf [now Feliks] Karpman from the Germans, the two teenagers fell in love. They married on January 6, 1946, less than a year after the war ended, and were in their sixty-second year of marriage when we interviewed them in their home in Góra Kalwaria, southeast of Warsaw.[42] "We were two stupid kids," Feliks said, laughing as we sat at the dining-room table of the couple's home. "We went to school together and knew each other but we weren't falling in love then. All my other family died in the camps. So after that, I had her. Where else am I going to go look for someone? Just after the war, I was twenty and she was eighteen. We knew each other and liked each other and we promised each other that we would get married. So we got married and now I'm over 80 and we still love each other a lot." Feliks was born on November 29, 1926, and Marianna was born on January 2, 1928, both in Góra Kalwaria.

We asked Feliks if he felt some sense of obligation to marry Marianna after she and her family saved him from death.

"No, no," he said. "I could have taken another girl. What's the problem?" At which point, Marianna laughed and added, "And we got used to each other."

Feliks has had many reasons to love Marianna—beyond the fact that she and her family saved his life. They have had a fruitful life together that produced two children, four grandchildren, and three great-grandchildren. Marianna's family members were not the only non-Jews who came to Feliks's aid in the war, but he said that, without Marianna, her brother Edward Konarzewski, and her mother, he may not have survived.

The odds against Feliks surviving the war to marry anyone were high. At the start of the war, at least three thousand of Góra Kalwaria's seven thousand residents were Jews, according to Feliks's memory.[43] When we interviewed Marianna and Feliks in August 2007, he was one of just two Jews left in town. The other one was a man in his nineties.

Feliks's father was a butcher and operated two stores that sold beef. Marianna's parents were farmers. The Germans took her father to Germany to be a forced laborer. Her mother was left behind and struggled to make a living on the small farm. After the war, Marianna's father obtained some land in Germany and stayed there. Marianna's siblings moved there and lived with him until he died. But Marianna and her mother stayed in Góra Kalwaria.

Marianna's and Feliks's families knew each other before the war. In fact Marianna's mother, Helena Konarzewska, often bought milk from Feliks's parents,

Marianna Konarzewska Karpman and Feliks Karpman

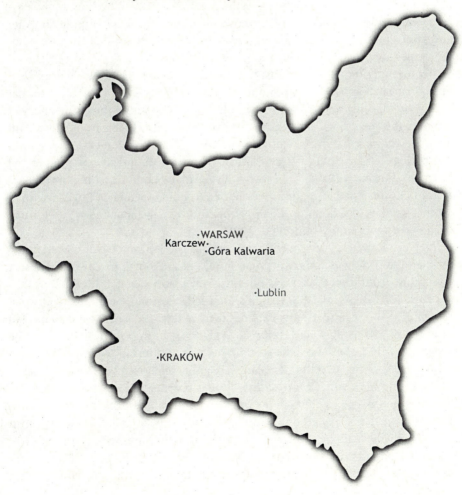
·WARSAW
Karczew·
·Góra Kalwaria

·Lublin

·KRAKÓW

and when she came for that purpose Marianna's mother would set out tea and challah (a braided bread Jews traditionally eat on holidays and on the Sabbath). The two women would talk as old friends.

But soon after the Germans took control of Góra Kalwaria, they established a ghetto. The ghetto lasted until 1941, when most of Góra Kalwaria's Jews were transported to the Warsaw Ghetto. From Warsaw, many of them were deported to Treblinka, where they were murdered.

"Just before the Germans took Jews from the ghetto here in Góra Kalwaria," Feliks told us, "my family was left with two cows. We sold them to Jews in Otwock. So one Jew and one Pole came at night to get the cows. But one of the local people saw the cows and began to yell, 'Jews! Jews!' So he took the cows to his place. He stole those cows, and we didn't know where they were. Later, the mother-in-law of the man who stole the cows was walking by Marianna's parents' house, and she told them, 'The cows are at our place.' So I and my brother and father ran over there and took the cows. We told them that they were not their cows, that they stole them and we're taking them back."

Because of later developments, the cow-theft incident came to figure in Feliks's survival, because at one point in the war, Feliks told us, "I had to go to that family and tell them not to tell that I'm hiding here because they were angry at me over the cows. So I said, 'Listen, what's in the past, let's leave it there. And after the war, if I survive, I will give you four cows. Just don't betray me that I'm hiding in Marianna's family's house.' The man didn't say anything to the Germans, but his wife did. That's why the Germans came searching for me. Afterward, I threatened to go and shoot her. I was going to kill her. But Marianna's mother said, 'Feliks, don't go. You're going to leave this area and we'll be stuck dealing with this family, so don't do that.'"

As Góra Kalwaria's Jews were being sent to the Warsaw Ghetto, Marianna's brother, Edward, helped the Karpman family escape north to Otwock, a resort community southeast of Warsaw. But their stay in Otwock did not last long.

"In 1942," Feliks said, "the Germans rounded us up and took us from Otwock to a forced labor camp at Karczew, not far from Otwock. There were about 350 of us there." His parents, however, managed to stay in the Otwock Ghetto, while Feliks and his brother Mordkhe (or Morris) went to the labor camp. One night the brothers learned that the Germans were going to destroy the Otwock Ghetto, so Feliks and his brother came and took their parents to a tiny town called Sobiene, then returned to their labor camp, which was not especially well guarded. "It was not too hard to go out through the gate," Feliks said. That labor camp was where Feliks said he lived from late 1942 until the summer of 1943.[44]

Feliks's parents did not last long in Sobiene. In December 1942, some six months after Treblinka had started operating, they were transported there and gassed.

In early April 1943, Feliks told us, his brother, Morris, came down with ty-phus and was evacuated to Warsaw. When Feliks somehow left the camp to go to Warsaw to check on his brother, he arrived on a momentous date, April 19, 1943, the very day the ghetto uprising started. Feliks said he used a twenty-dollar gold coin to buy a hard-to-obtain weapon from someone (though he no longer remembered who sold it to him), and he joined the fighting.[45] In the group with which he was fighting, he said, "I was the only one who had a gun. The others were fighting with whatever they had, even empty bottles." Feliks said he fought in the uprising for about two weeks and in the process managed to kill some Germans.

Feliks had been to Warsaw often before and had been in danger in Warsaw before, too. Earlier, in 1941, he and others were delivering leather goods to the Warsaw Ghetto from Góra Kalwaria. But police caught them and took them to prison. A neighbor of Feliks's father found out about the arrest and arranged to bribe someone at the police station to let Feliks go. But he was not released until after he was beaten several times. Finally he was told that authorities knew he was Jewish but were going to let him go anyway.

After the Warsaw Ghetto uprising, Feliks escaped the ravaged city—but with-out his brother, with whom he never made contact in Warsaw—and returned first to Karczew, then to Góra Kalwaria, where he was hidden first by a family named Szymanski. "Before the war, my family and the Szymanski family were very close," Feliks said. "We worked together and did everything together."

The family hid Feliks on—or at times just under—the roof of a building on their property. Family members would send food up to him through a hole in the roof. But one time as food was about to be sent up to him, some German au-thorities came around and began yelling at the family, accusing them of hiding Jews.

The Szymanskis and Feliks had a deal, he said. "I had a gun," the weapon he had acquired in Warsaw, "and if I get cornered I can shoot the Nazi and they will bury him somewhere." But this time the Szymanskis convinced the Germans that there were no Jews there, so they left.

From the summer of 1943 through July 1944, Feliks hid both with the Szy-manski family and with a family named Orlik—Michal Orlik, the father, and Kazimierz Orlik, his son. At the Orliks, Feliks and his brother hid in a cowshed most of the time.

While Feliks was staying with the Szymanskis, a grandfather in that family died, and Feliks insisted on attending the funeral, though being in the open put him at considerable risk. Morris also put himself at risk one day while staying with the Orliks. He left his hiding place for a bit just to experience the small pleasure of standing in front of the house and watching life go by. Some Ger-mans saw him there and came over and demanded to know if Morris was Jewish.

Feliks said the Orliks answered this way: "No, he's crazy." Somehow it worked, and they left him alone.

Such experiences made Feliks and his brother know that "we had to escape the Szymanski place because the Germans were coming and looking all over through the city and taking out whoever was left." So they were glad when their friend Edward Konarzewski came to investigate after he learned that two Jews were hiding somewhere in Góra Kalwaria.

The day Edward came to investigate this rumor, the Karpman brothers were lying in some bushes about three hundred meters from the Szymanski house. Edward discovered them there and thus also discovered that the boys were his friends. So he took them to hide on his family's farm just outside Góra Kalwaria. We asked Feliks how he knew to trust the Konarzewski family. His answer: "Marianna's family was not antisemitic. I knew which family I could trust."

Once they got to the Konarzewski farm, Morris hid in an outbuilding while Feliks often stayed in the family house but moved from place to place both inside and outside the house. One time German soldiers came to check things out and make sure no Jews were hidden at the Konarzewski farm. They did not discover Morris, but they saw Feliks, who pretended to be a non-Jewish hired hand.

"My mother told them he was hired to work in the fields," Marianna told us. "We lied to them and they bought it. The Germans returned the next day but by then Feliks had escaped. The Germans said to us, 'We knew that he was Jewish and we should shoot all of you but you are too young and we feel sorry for you.'"

In fact, Marianna's mother more than once was put in a position of having to convince German authorities that Feliks was not Jewish. "Many times Marianna's mother was in the situation where members of the Gestapo put a gun to her head and said, 'Tell us who this guy is,' and she would say, 'He's a Pole working in the fields.'"

While Feliks was staying with Marianna's family, there often was little or nothing to eat. "All they had were some potatoes once. So her brother Edward took me to the city, and he had a gun. He said, 'Let's go find some flour or whatever we can.' While we were in the city we met someone I knew from before the war and he said, 'Oh, my God. You are alive?' And I had to take out Edward's gun and say, 'Yes, I'm alive, but you won't tell anyone.' The father of this guy was in good relations with Germans. I had to do that to protect my life."

Though Feliks worked hard to protect his life, he needed help from several non-Jewish families. But he was proud of using his own ingenuity and wits to survive, too. "To hear all my stories," Feliks told us, "you'd have to sit with me for a month." We did not have a month with him or with Marianna on our visit to Poland, but we recognized that their story is rare not only because Feliks survived at all but because he married into the family that saved him. That's not unheard of, but in our research for this book we learned of only two stories in which that was the case.

After the War

When the war ended, Feliks's brother, Morris, moved to the United States. He died of cancer in 1961. Feliks took up the butcher profession that his father had followed, and he worked for the Polish government in that capacity. "I worked hard all my life. Now I'm getting a pension of just $200 a month from the government." Marianna was a retail clerk for thirty-seven years.

Marianna did not hesitate to marry Feliks, but she said she knew that some people would look down on her for having a Jewish husband. So, she told us, "I preferred to tell people the story, even before we got married, so there would be no problems later when they learned about us. They should know there is a Jew in the family so there won't be any surprises later."

To which Feliks added, "Yes, we don't deny who we are."

In his retirement years, Feliks kept the keys to the old Góra Kalwaria synagogue, which gets used occasionally as a learning center when Hasidic visitors come to the town. He also was the keeper of the keys to the old Jewish cemetery, and he has tried to restore it, including directing the rebuilding of the *ohel* (*ohel* means house or tent but is, in effect, a burial monument) where previous Gerer *rebbes* are buried. The cemetery, with many headstones crumbling or purposely destroyed in the war, is located just across the street from a well-maintained Catholic cemetery.

Feliks told us the story of a woman in Góra Kalwaria who died in 1979 and was buried in that Catholic cemetery. But Feliks and the few Jews left in town knew that the woman, though widely thought to be a Catholic, was really Jewish. And she was a prominent artist of whom the Jews were proud. So, Feliks said, he bribed the guard of the Catholic cemetery to look the other way as Feliks and others simply dug up the woman's casket at night and reburied it across the street in the Jewish cemetery, where it remains to this day.

Before we left the Karpman home, we asked Marianna what led her and her family to save Feliks and his brother. She answered, "It was impossible for my family to think that innocent people were being killed. And we knew them before the war. It was impossible for us not to help. Not hiding them was not an option."

In recent years, Feliks said, because he survived the Holocaust he has become distraught over what he called a renewal of antisemitism in Poland. "It's happening right now on Radio Maryja. Why?" Radio Maryja, operated by a Catholic priest, spreads a distinctly antisemitic message in Poland. It has gained millions of listeners but has been reprimanded by Pope Benedict XVI.[46]

Though Yad Vashem has honored Helena Konarzewska, Edward Konarzewski, Marianna Konarzewska Karpman, and Michal and Kazimierz Orlik, Feliks told us that even though members of the Szymanski family all were dead, he was considering asking Yad Vashem to honor them posthumously.

Jerry Koenig

There would have been room for this newborn girl with the eleven other Jews hiding in a bunker under a barn floor in northeastern Poland—except for one thing. She did what all babies do. "She was crying," Jerry Koenig, one of those eleven, told us. "And, really, she had a very good reason to cry because she was being eaten alive by the pests—the lice and bedbugs—that we had in the bunker. Of course, eleven souls depended on maintaining silence."

So to try to save the eleven from the Germans, the child was fed a poison to silence her cries forever. Feiga's daughter died so that Jerry Koenig might improve his chances of living—and not just Jerry, but also his brother, Michael, their parents, Isadore and Mary Koenigstein (later Koenig), and seven others, including Feiga herself. They were all hiding in a barn owned by Jan Góral and his wife.

The people in the bunker thought about giving the infant to the Górals' daughter-in-law, Kasia, to rear as her own. But when Kasia gave birth a few days earlier to a baby boy who died almost instantly, that birth was attended by a midwife from the nearby village of Kosów Lacki. The swapping option "wouldn't fly because the midwife was involved [and, thus, other villagers would know]. So the decision was reached that the little girl was going to have to die. The farmer's wife came up with the method" of poisoning her using opium from poppy seed pods, and "the little baby went to sleep, never to wake up."

This death "had a terrible effect on the people in the bunker," Jerry told us when we interviewed him at his home in Chesterfield, Missouri, a suburb of St. Louis. "We really thought after this happened that somehow or another we're not going to make it. But we did."

The death of the baby, however, was not the only traumatic decision about life and death that had to be made in the twenty months Koenig and the others spent in the bunker, from the winter of 1942–1943 to the late summer of 1944. Well into that time, a Jewish family named Zylberman, who earlier had provided life-saving shelter for the Koenigs, was told to leave their own hiding place by farmers who lost their courage to continue offering them a safe place. Desperate, the Zylbermans hid in the woods for a time but made their way to the Góral farm, somehow having guessed correctly that the Koenigs were hiding there.

"Mr. Góral came down to the bunker," Jerry told us, "and said that, while he was out in the woods, he came across a Jewish family. The father of that family said he wanted to talk to my dad. It was the Zylbermans. They were hoping,

Jerry Koenig

·Kosów Lacki

Pruszków· ·WARSAW

·Lublin

·KRAKÓW

of course, that they could be given shelter with us. But Mr. Góral said to them, 'Look, I don't know how much longer this is going to drag on. And I don't know how I'm going to feed you. I've got eleven people here already. And I cannot take you in,' knowing full well that if they're caught they could give us away. So he turned them away. And I don't hold it against him in any way at all. But you can just imagine how my parents felt."

A prime reason for his parents' anguish was that, after the Koenigs had escaped the Warsaw Ghetto, it was David Zylberman and his wife and children who took them in and let them live with them on their small farm in Kosów, near the Koenigs' own much larger farm, which had already been commandeered by the Germans.

Just a few days after saying no to the Zylbermans, Mr. Góral came again to the bunker and reported that all four members of the Zylberman family—father, mother, son, and daughter—had been found murdered in the woods. All the evidence pointed to death not at the hands of Germans but, rather, local people who did it for a reward given to people who turned in or killed Jews.

"When that happened," Jerry said, "we really thought we were goners." The people in the bunker guessed that, under terrible pressure, the Zylbermans might have revealed that Jews were hiding at the Góral farm. But, in fact, the Zylbermans "didn't give us away," Jerry said. "So we owe it to them twice."

The fact that the Koenigs were able to find any hiding place at all was due mostly to the family's healthy economic status. "My family was middle-class, fairly well off by Polish standards," Jerry said. In their hometown of Pruszków, just a few miles southwest of Warsaw, Jerry's father managed a slaughterhouse and an apartment building that his own father had acquired. Besides that, nearly one hundred miles away, at Kosów, the Koenigs owned a sixty-acre farm run by a hired hand. Jerry's father made periodic trips to the farm to oversee the production of rye, wheat, potatoes, and other crops. When it became apparent to the Koenigs that they were facing death at Treblinka, Jerry's father made a deal with the Górals. If they would hide the Koenigs and the two brothers who made the initial contact with the Górals, the Górals would get title to the Koenigs' farm when the war ended.

"In the beginning," Jerry said, "it was strictly a business deal." And, in fact, the Górals did wind up owning the farm, though Jerry said he does not know what happened to it once that area came under Soviet control and its economy became communistic. But as the twenty months of hiding dragged on, Jerry said, the Górals and the Koenigs became fast friends.

"If we had not had the farm," Jerry said, "most likely we would never have found anyone willing to risk hiding the family. If a neighbor of yours or a friend of yours found out what you were doing, the reward was tempting enough that you would be denounced and turned in."

When Jerry was a boy in Pruszków he never could have imagined that life would take so many dangerous and deadly turns. Jerry's father, an only child, became manager of his own father's businesses when the older man began to retire and devote more of his time to religious interests. Jerry's paternal grandmother had died when he was three years old, but Jerry's maternal grandparents lived across the street from them in Pruszków and ran a small general store there.[47]

When vacation time came, the Koenigs would go to the farm at Kosów and stay for a few weeks, and on one of these trips the farm came under gunfire. His family believed the attack came from people seeking to drive Jews out of the area, Jerry said. Indeed, as a public school student Jerry had experienced antisemitism such as boys throwing rocks at him and calling him a "dirty Jew" as he walked to school each day. In addition, he'd often heard such children yell, "Jews, go to Palestine." Some of these children, Jerry said, "were exposed to this stuff [antisemitic thinking] all the time and took it seriously." Jerry's parents had both Jews and non-Jews as friends, and Jerry insisted that not all Polish non-Jews in the 1930s were hostile toward Jews.

Jerry was almost ten years old when the war began. His family, he said, knew quite well the pressure Jews were under in Germany and, thus, were not surprised when the Germans put anti-Jewish measures into effect once they controlled Poland. In fact, one German Jewish refugee family came to Pruszków before the war and became friends with the Koenigs.

When Germany invaded Poland, the Koenig family tried to escape to the east using a horse-drawn wagon. They and others thought it would not take long either for the Polish army to drive back the Germans or for Poland's allies Britain and France to join the battle to turn them back. They thought that, when that happened, they would return to the Warsaw area. But Warsaw surrendered to the Germans a few weeks after the start of the war.

Beyond that, German military airplanes were strafing the roads that the Koenigs and many other families were using to flee to the east. "So after a week or so on the road, we decided to go back. Somebody gave my dad some 'good' advice. He said, 'Look. Warsaw is the capital of the country. It's going to be defended until the allies come to our aid. And the thing to do is to stay in Warsaw for a few days.' That was probably the worst bit of advice we got from anybody. We almost died there." When Warsaw surrendered, the Koenigs simply returned to Pruszków, where a ghetto was established.

The Koenig family was crowded into a small apartment with several other families in the Pruszków Ghetto. Almost everything they owned, including furniture, had to be left behind. All they were able to take with them was "anything that was small, anything that would retain its value. If you had jewelry, dollar bills, foreign currency, gold . . . you took that."

After more than a year in the ghetto in Pruszków, the family was forced to move to the Warsaw Ghetto in the winter of 1940–1941. The Germans lined up people outside in the cold and made them wait for trucks to take them there. "I ended up with frostbite on my toes," Jerry said.

Jerry's whole extended family ended up in the Warsaw Ghetto. "My grandfather, who lived with us, my grandparents on my mother's side, aunts, uncles, cousins, and so on." They were split up in Warsaw. After the Koenigs escaped to Kosów, though, they remained in some mail contact with extended family left in the ghetto. The Germans had murdered most of Koenig's family before the war ended.

Conditions in the Warsaw Ghetto grew worse as time went on. Jerry said that when his father mentioned in a letter to the Zylbermans "how miserable the situation was," they said that things in Kosów were still just fine. Oh, now and then Germans would press local Kosów residents into work forces, but they returned each evening, and life was continuing pretty much as usual. Jerry said that the Zylbermans also made this generous offer in a letter to the Koenigs. "If you can get out of that hellhole, come and live with us. Our house is your house."

So Jerry's father found a man who made a dangerous living smuggling people out of the ghetto. At the man's direction, the Koenigs used the streetcar line that ran through the ghetto, because Jews who could afford the fare were allowed to ride the streetcar when it was within the boundaries of the ghetto. When it reached the last stop in the ghetto, however, Jews were required to exit. But as the smuggler knew, bribes could cause various authorities to look the other way. So, "bribing a lot of people, we got out of the Warsaw Ghetto" in shifts, Jerry said. By "we" he meant himself, his brother, his parents, and his paternal grandfather.

To reach Kosów the family took the train and a horse-drawn wagon and also walked part of the way. When they showed up at the Zylberman farm, "the surprise was unbelievable." Things seemed to be just as the Zylbermans had described them. "All of a sudden I had the freedom to move around. There was no hunger. People were going to work." So, to the Koenigs, life in Kosów seemed comparatively normal. They were told that a big part of the reason was that Kosów was providing slave laborers for various German needs, including at what they eventually learned was the Treblinka death camp, and the Germans were not anxious to do away with this source of workers.

For a time, then, things were close to normal on the Zylberman farm. "I was out in the pasture with the cows and the sheep. I was helping with the harvest," Jerry said. And although there was no school for Jerry and his brother to attend, their father arranged for Jerry to learn a little woodworking from a Jewish carpenter. The Koenigs could not, however, go to their own considerably larger farm because it had been taken over almost immediately by the Germans, who installed their own administrator there.

In the Zylberman house things were crowded. Mr. and Mrs. Zylberman had two children—a son, Buma, and a daughter, Mala. The Zylberman and Koenig children all slept in one bed, alternating head-to-toe and toe-to-head. In addition, there was a Zylberman grandfather. So to the five Zylbermans were added the five Koenigs, including Jerry's grandfather, all jammed into a small farmhouse barely big enough for one family.

Jerry's memories of the time spent with the Zylbermans were quite clear, perhaps because he was near puberty and discovering aspects of life he had not known about before. "Buma, who was about a year older than I was, enjoyed showing us younger kids his maturity and masculinity. Mala Zylberman was a pretty girl, probably three years younger than Buma but with a permanently disfigured face because as a youngster she had dumped a kerosene lamp on her and suffered severe burns to her face and arm."

The Zylbermans, Jerry said, "were probably the best friends our family ever had."

As the Koenigs and Zylbermans lived together, word came of worsening conditions in Warsaw, and eventually correspondence between the ghetto and the Zylberman farm was cut off. But there was another source of news about the fate of Jews: people who escaped from the trains that were taking them to Treblinka, just a few kilometers from Kosów. "So we knew what was going on," Jerry said. "And by this time there were tremendous odors, if the wind was blowing in the right direction." They were smelling Treblinka, where the gassing of Jews began in late July 1942.

Earlier, in June 1941, the Germans attacked Soviet-held territory, including areas not far from Kosów. Quickly the streets of Kosów filled with Soviet prisoners of war. German soldiers with fixed bayonets made sure local residents did not feed them or give them water. "Several weeks later, trucks loaded with dead bodies were seen going through town."

If Russian POWs were being treated in this barbaric way, Jews had no hope of anything more humane, Jerry's father, Isadore, concluded. So he began to search for an alternative to staying on the Zylberman farm and eventually getting deported to Treblinka, the purpose of which now became much clearer to the Koenigs. "All of a sudden it became clear to everybody what Treblinka represented and what was in store for the Jews confined to the ghettos of Poland."

Isadore found two Jewish brothers, Abram and Mendel Rzepka, ages eighteen and twenty-two respectively, who were willing to help find a solution—one that would include them. Jerry's father told them that if they could find a farmer willing to hide both of them along with the Koenig family, the farmer would get the Koenig's sixty-acre farm when the war ended.

The brothers located a man willing to take the risk—Jan Góral. He had a farm of about five acres that he managed by himself with his wife, whose first name Jerry had forgotten. Also living at the farm were the Górals' married son, Stanislaw, and that son's wife, Kasia, and three daughters, Celina, Lucyna, and Cesia. The idea of owning sixty more acres (a large farm at the time in Poland) intrigued him enough to put the lives of his whole family on the line.

When the four Koenigs moved to the Góral farm near the end of 1942 (Jerry's paternal grandfather had died of natural causes while they were living with the Zylbermans), "it was extremely cold and the ground was covered with snow," Jerry said. At first the whole family stayed in a room in the farmhouse because the bunker under the barn wasn't yet ready. It was being built stealthily at night by Jan Góral and his son along with Isadore Koenig and the Rzepka brothers. In fact, the first night the Koenigs arrived at the farm, Jerry's father and the two Rzepka brothers went back to town for some additional supplies while Jerry, his brother, and mother stayed at the farmhouse. Suddenly they heard gunfire quite near them, and "the Górals were convinced that the Germans or Polish police were coming after us and told us to leave the farmhouse and get into the nearby woods."

So Jerry, his brother, and mother fled into the cold woods. "Despite the fear of being detected, Mom kept falling asleep," Jerry said. "Even I knew that in this subfreezing temperature this could be deadly, so we desperately tried to keep her awake."

Eventually the firing stopped, and then they heard steps and short whistles. "It turned out to be Dad and the Rzepka brothers looking for us. Later we found out that a German airplane made an emergency landing in a nearby field, and part of the crew went into Kosów to get help and drinks. On the way back they got lost and were firing their guns to pinpoint the location of the plane. Nobody was after us, but we almost froze to death in the woods."

Soon, however, work on the bunker was finished, and "we all became permanent residents, along with the lice, fleas, and bedbugs." The bunker, located under the Górals' grain barn (as opposed to their animal barn) was about twenty-four feet long, six-plus feet wide, and a little over four feet high. There was just enough room for eleven people to lie down at night and sleep shoulder to shoulder.

At first the bunker contained just six people—the four Koenigs and the two Rzepka brothers. But before long, five others joined them. There was a woman named Gitla along with her pregnant daughter, Feiga, plus three men who had escaped from Treblinka—a man from Warsaw whose name Jerry no longer could recall, Berek, and Szymon, who was a wagon driver. A fourth man, Feiga's husband, had been with those three but did not survive the escape. These other five people also made whatever payments they could afford to the Górals from any valuables they had managed to keep out of German hands.

Using those valuables the Górals "had to buy a lot of things when feeding eleven other people," Jerry said. "And keep in mind that things were so tightly controlled. If your cow had a calf, you had to immediately report it to the authorities. An official would come out and put a tag on the calf's ear." Jerry said he does not know in detail how the Górals were able to acquire food enough for eleven extra people without arousing suspicions in the community.

Life in the straw-lined bunker was miserable. "We had no way to wash and no change of clothes," Jerry said. For occasional light, the residents had a kerosene lamp and a carbide lamp. The light was insufficient, just enough to read the newspaper. Jerry, using paper and pencils provided by the Górals, used to do a lot of drawings. A favorite hobby was to copy political cartoons found in the papers, "which were, of course, nothing more than German propaganda."

The bathroom for the people in the bunker was a chicken coop just outside the barn. But using it required the greatest caution to make sure no one except the Górals was aware of them. "You had to lift up the trapdoor, walk up into the barn, walk the full length of the barn, and go to the chicken coop." That exercise and occasional chances to walk around in the barn, Jerry said, prevented muscle atrophy, a common affliction for Jews in cramped hiding places. Other common bathroom functions, such as showers and baths, were unavailable.

The Górals delivered food to the people in the bunker once a day—either in the morning or the evening, depending on when it was possible to do so without anyone noticing. The meal was always the same, a pot of soup and a loaf of bread.

Jerry said that people in the bunker got along with each other remarkably well. "When you put that many people in such close quarters, you're going to have friction, you're going to have problems, but everybody realized that if we did, this whole thing would blow up immediately. People upstairs were risking their lives, and if we had any kind of disagreements or problems down below, they'd kick us out, that's all."

Despite their taking care to be invisible, there were some close calls, particularly during the harvest, when neighbors would come to the farm—and especially to the grain barn—to help. "The barn would be a beehive of activity," Jerry said.

Other close calls involved the three Góral girls, who were of dating age. When boys would come to the farm, "where would you take a girl to have a little privacy?" Jerry asked. "To the barn. They were discouraging it, but when they came into the barn, they would sing and joke around and make a lot of noises to let us know they were coming in. At that point, we stopped living."

One of the most traumatic times in hiding, of course, was when the decision was made to put Feiga's child to death. That and other experiences in the bunker took a heavy toll. "People's spirit was broken. And you were hungry and miserable for so long," Jerry said.

In the summer of 1944 Soviet troops were driving the Germans back from east to west, and "we heard the front lines approaching," Jerry said. "You could hear artillery and later on rifle fire. So you knew the lines were coming closer and closer."

One day, as the front line neared the farm, the people in the bunker peered through the knotholes in the barn and saw a German soldier sitting, tired and dejected, outside the barn. "His helmet was on the ground and his rifle was next to him. He was just sitting there by himself wiping his brow. So we said, 'What should we do? Try to kill him?' What if somebody coughs? So we let him sit there, waiting him out. And he left."

Soon, however, "the sounds of war started coming from the other direction. That's when Mr. Góral stuck his head in and said, simply, 'They're gone.'"

So they were free. All eleven of them survived until liberation because of Jan Góral and his family. In their time of hiding, however, "the relationship between the people in the bunker and the people in the farmhouse really developed," Jerry said. "There were twenty months for that to happen. Mr. Góral would pay us a visit every day. He would go into town and buy a newspaper. That was our entertainment for the day. We read the paper from front to back and over again. Many times he would just sit down with us—even though the place was full of lice and bedbugs—and talk. So the relationship really developed into something a lot deeper than a business transaction."

When the Koenigs left the bunker for good, they stayed in the Kosów area at the family farm they were giving to the Górals, waiting until Warsaw was liberated in mid-January 1945. In that time, one of the eleven Góral bunker survivors was shot to death on the streets of his Polish hometown.

After the War

The family returned to Pruszków with plans to start life anew. But on July 4, 1946, more than a year after the end of the war, a pogrom in Kielce resulted in the murder of forty-two Jewish survivors, terrifying the few Jews who remained in Poland.

In response to that, Jerry said, "Dad decided there really was no future for us in Pruszków or in Poland." So that summer the family escaped to Czechoslovakia, then to Austria, and eventually to the American zone in Germany, where they lived in a displaced persons' camp. Jerry returned to school and graduated from a Munich engineering institution in 1951, at which point the family got the necessary approval to emigrate to the United States. The Jewish community in Davenport, Iowa, sponsored the Koenigs. In September 1951 Jerry was drafted into the U.S. army. Most of his two years in the military were served back in Germany.

In 1954 Jerry moved to St. Louis to take a job as an engineer with Sachs Electric and then with Laclede Gas Company. He worked for the gas company for thirty-five years before his retirement. He and his second wife, Linda, are members of Temple Israel. Jerry has two daughters by a prior marriage, Laurie and Lynn, who live in Kansas City along with Jerry's three grandchildren. He is past president of a B'nai B'rith lodge and has been active in various ways in support of Israel, where his brother, Michael, and his family live.

The experiences of the Holocaust left deep marks on the Koenig family. "My dad left Poland with a chip on his shoulder," Jerry told us. "He was very patriotic and it was his country. He was born there, raised there, and he loved the country. He felt that either the population in general was very antagonistic toward the Jewish population, or they didn't care, or they were simply collaborating with the Germans. And many of them ended up with bits of property that belonged to Jewish people."

Jerry himself since then has lived with what he called a siege mentality. "I sort of inherited my mom's pessimistic view of life rather than the opposite view of life that my father had." Indeed, when things were really bad after the Germans occupied Poland, Jerry said, his mother thought they would all be better off committing suicide, but her husband disagreed. "To this day I feel like I'm under the gun, even though there's no reason for me to feel that way. On the other hand, many of the misfortunes that everybody has in life are a lot easier for me to cope with because I can always look back and say I've been through worse. But Linda will frequently say to me, 'You worry about little things,' and I do."

Beyond that, Jerry said, "Every time I talk to a group the old wound is not allowed to heal. It just isn't easy." And, as Jerry told us, "the Holocaust certainly killed whatever little religion I had." Although he became an active member of a synagogue, he said that was more to belong to a community than for any religious reasons.

Our Visit to Kosów

In the summer of 2007 we went to Kosów Lacki, a town of about twenty-one hundred people, to see if we could find any traces of the Góral family and to hear this story from their perspective.

Because Jerry and his brother had no contact with the Góral family and, thus, no address or other information to give us, we first stopped at the city hall to see if there were records that might lead us to the Górals. Despite help from several employees there, we were unable to locate anyone by that name in Kosów.

But a city employee told us there was a Góral family living in nearby Dybow. Before going there, we stopped at the large Catholic church in Kosów to see if—as often is the case in Poland—records there might be more helpful than governmental records. But there was no one at the church at all.

So we drove to Dybow and found the small house where a Góral family was supposed to be living. An elderly woman watched us through the front window as we waited in our car for a downpour to abate. When it finally did, she answered the door, along with a man in cutoff blue jeans who appeared to be in his fifties. But they said they were not related to Jan Góral, of whom they had never heard. Instead, this was the Kazimierz Góral family.

Andre Nowacki

When Andre Nowacki thought back to the two years he hid in the Warsaw apartment of the Kwiecinski family, these were the painful words he spoke: "I did not exist. I did not exist. Officially I did not exist."

Making the outside world believe that Andre did not exist was, in fact, his mother's goal. It was her way of making sure the Germans never discovered he was living with a non-Jewish family. So he stayed away from apartment windows to avoid being seen, he hid in a crawl space when strangers entered the building, and he spent his long days reading books, playing cards, and wondering what it might be like to have children his own age to play with.

His mother, Helena (originally Haya) Tejblum, was remarkably resourceful. After her husband—Andre's father, Henryk (originally Haim) Tejblum—was caught because he was staying illegally outside the Warsaw Ghetto and was sent off to a concentration camp, never to be heard from again, Helena showed enormous resourcefulness and creativity as she fought to keep herself and her only child alive.

Andre was born on June 5, 1936, in Warsaw and was named Salomon. He gave up this name when his father arranged for him to have false papers showing him to be a Polish non-Jew named Andre Nowacki. Andre's parents had a small textile factory in Warsaw named Serena, where they made bathing suits and other articles of clothing.

The Tejblum family lived on Nalewki Street, which was in the northeast part of what would become the Warsaw Ghetto. When the Germans established the ghetto in late 1940, Andre's aunt (his mother's sister) moved into the Tejblum residence, too. But before the ghetto was completely enclosed by a wall, Henryk Tejblum transferred the location of his business to a location outside the ghetto and turned over purported ownership of it to a trustworthy Polish friend with the last name of Woznica. The man's first name was lost to Andre's memory, though he said his father had known the man since his youth. Although papers showed that the plant was in Woznica's name, he continued to respect Henryk's direction. Later, when Henryk was gone, Woznica continued to make monthly payments to Helena so she could help support herself. On the same equipment that the factory used to make bathing suits, the ten or twenty factory workers also made sweaters, socks, and other articles of clothing for the German army.

Andre's parents were able to leave the ghetto each day and work in the factory, taking their boy with them. And the plant stayed in business until the Warsaw

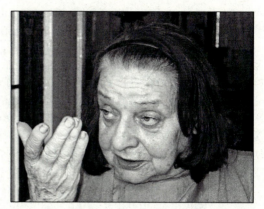

Andre Nowacki   Hanna Morawiecka

Uprising of August 1944. Andre's father and mother were observant Jews, he said, "but the minute you went outside the ghetto, you tried to be as Polish as possible." For that reason Andre's parents did not teach him Yiddish.

One day Andre's father was caught outside the ghetto when he should have been inside. "He was taken to a concentration camp—I don't know which one— and he disappeared out of our life," Andre told us when we interviewed him at the New York City offices of the Jewish Foundation for the Righteous.

When Andre's father disappeared, "the only support we had was the Polish friend who was running the factory," Andre told us. This man, Woznica, suggested that Andre and his mother not return to the ghetto but, rather, move to the small resort town of Otwock a little southeast of Warsaw and settle there, using false identification papers. Andre explained that the documents were not fake, merely false. That is, "they were original Polish documents that Poles were helping to make." Woznica told Helena that in Otwock she and Andre could live in more safety using the monthly money he was paying her from the factory's revenues.

So Andre and his mother slipped out of the ghetto and moved to Otwock. "It was easy to escape, but once they caught you, that's it."

They moved into a resort hotel that was busy and quite full. "But my mother felt a little bit uncomfortable there because people were asking questions—'What is this little boy doing here?' 'Why is he not going to school?' So we transferred to another place, which was like a compound, with little cottages. It was quiet and private." The new location was just a short walk through the forest behind the hotel.

Helena spent time there teaching Andre how to pass as a non-Jew. She took him to church often, "but going to church had one purpose—meeting other Jewish people. We would sit together. We would open the books. We would participate in some ways so people wouldn't come from behind and ask, 'Hey, Jews, what are you doing here?' You had to know how to pray the Our Father. I had to be prepared for it."

Andre and his mother stayed at the new location for several months and developed a routine of walking in the forest and going into the village to shop for groceries. But mostly they tried to stay out of sight. One day they realized they were being followed by a man on a bicycle. "And my mother was afraid to go back home. So we spent some time in a restaurant. We sat and had lunch, and he was waiting outside for us on the street. Wherever we went, he went. And then she had a very good idea. We went to the big hotel where we stayed at first, and through that hotel we went through a back exit straight to our cottage. She put everything into one suitcase in a matter of minutes. The concern was not to leave any pictures or any documents so that somebody could find them and later follow us."[48]

Andre and his mother got on a nearby train and returned to Warsaw, some forty-five minutes away, to see Woznica and get his help to decide what to do next. After speaking with him, they moved to a village named Milosna, just northwest of Warsaw. There they found a small hut near some railroad tracks, owned by a farmer who let them move in. Andre told us that while they were there he and his mother did "as little as possible to show ourselves." By then it was the fall of 1942, and it was far from clear when the war would end or who would emerge victorious.

Railroad tracks naturally attract adventuresome boys. That certainly was true of the tracks close to the hut where Andre and his mother were living in Milosna. Groups of non-Jewish teenage boys would hang around those tracks and steal coal from trains as they slowed for a curvature of the tracks there. "Those boys were jumping on the train, throwing the coal off to the side, jumping off the train, and then selling the coal to whoever was close." Among their potential customers, the boys believed, were Andre and his mother, "And this is where the problem started."

The boys, Andre said, suspected he was Jewish. Fifteen or twenty of them gathered outside the small dwelling where Andre and his mother were staying, and they demanded to check Andre to see if they were right. If they had been allowed to examine him, of course, they would have discovered that Andre was circumcised. So Helena had to think fast. She picked out the oldest boy from the group and invited him to come inside the house as the representative of the others. "So he came to the house, and she said, 'Look. I don't want problems with you. I will pay you. Just tell me how much you want. But you have to tell the others that you checked him, and he's all right. Then chase them away and come back here, and I'll give you the money.'"

That, in fact, is what the boy did, telling his friends that Helena was a Polish woman and the boy was, too. But Helena was not yet through using the boy to survive. While she packed up their belongings, she told him that she wanted him to walk with her and Andre to the next station so that the other boys would not become a problem again. "He was paid—even more than he imagined—only when we got on the train back to Warsaw."

When Andre and Helena returned and saw Woznica again, she told him it was too dangerous for her and Andre to continue to live on the run. Woznica had connections with Zegota, the underground aid agency for Jews in Poland. He said he would try to place them in what he called a "safe house" supported by Zegota.

As Andre was telling us this story, we asked him whether, at the end of the war, Woznica managed to keep the business or whether there was even a business to keep. Andre choked up, his eyes became teary, and he said, simply, "He did not survive."

The safe house that Woznica found for them, it turned out, was not very safe. The Kwiecinski family, who provided living space to Andre and his mother, suspected that the Polish concierge of the building was an informant aiding the Germans. So after a few days, that family—as well as Andre and Helena—all moved to a home at the end of Alberta Street by a park, Saxony Gardens. It did not face a busy street, and better yet, all the windows in the building looked out on the park, not the street. It was, thus, at least partly secluded.

The move gave Andre and his mother a home with the Kwiecinski family for about two years, until the Warsaw Uprising of August 1944. Janina Kwiecinska, the mother, was an actress. She had three school-age daughters—Hanna, whom we interviewed in her apartment in Warsaw, and twins, Janina and Marysia, both of whom now are dead. Janina was married, but her husband, a member of a Polish agency similar to the American FBI, spent the war on the run from the Germans, and only once came to the Kwiecinski house when Andre and his mother lived there, though Andre said the man never saw him. The Germans' search for the man frequently brought them to the Kwiecinski home to see if he was there. And that, of course, put Andre at more risk.

Indeed, whenever any outsiders came to the house, Andre hid in a crawl space above a door. The only way to reach it was by a stepladder, which he then would pull up into the hiding space with him. "It would look very innocent," he said. The rest of the time he would be in the unusually large five-bedroom apartment, though not near windows. Once, however, Germans came into the building before Andre had a chance to hide in his crawl space. "I was with the girls on the big sofa and they threw a blanket over the sofa and they sat on me." It was a narrow escape. As Hanna recalled the story when we spoke with her in Warsaw, she happened to be away from the house, and it was just Janina who sat on and hid Andre.

Helena was not working while they were hiding, though at times she pretended to work at the Serena factory. Andre said his mother contributed what money she could to cover grocery costs, but the Kwiecinskis were not hiding them to make money. In fact, Helena was paying as much as she could afford just to cover the cost of food, which at least was enough to keep Andre from being hungry. "In the morning my mother would pretend she was going to work and she would take the streetcar. She would go to someplace where farmers were selling food. And then later in the afternoon she would come back and carry something with her. And sometimes in the afternoon she would go again because there were other Jewish people hiding in our apartment." These other Jews were hidden there for only a few days at a time, but they, too, needed to be fed. A more permanent Jewish resident was an electrical engineer, whom Andre identified as Anthony Kelner. A Yad Vashem account about Janina Kwiecinska identified him as Zygmunt Keller. "He was really the only man there I could relate to. Nearly all the rest were women. And he was really a very nice person."[49]

Another person living in the same dwelling was the boyfriend of the mother, Janina Kwiecinska, whose husband (who also had girlfriends, Andre said) was on the run. Andre said this boyfriend would leave the house each day to go to work, too. "It was a house where there were a lot of people coming and going." Janina Kwiecinska, in fact, allowed several Jewish theater friends to hide in her home until more permanent arrangements could be located for them.

For roughly two years, Andre hid here and played with Janina Kwiecinska's three daughters. "They were like my sisters." They would bring library books for him to read, "but I didn't have anyone in my age group and I had nothing to do so I was reading books." Andre also said he was "good at following orders. They told me to shut up, do not open your mouth, don't speak up, don't answer questions, just smile."

There were fairly regular bombing raids at night, and people sought to protect themselves by going to shelters. "We did not go to the shelter because we were afraid. We were less afraid of the bombs than of the neighbors. The most frightening thing was that there were anti-airplane guns, German guns, in the park. And they were shooting. So what made it really frightening was that we were so close to where the action was. And if someone who was flying way up high in the middle of the night wanted to get even, then he would go for those guns. Was I terrified?" Andre shrugged at his own question and then added, "You don't know how long you have. Is it going to be this bomb or the next one?"

But aside from a small fire, the building in which Andre hid was never seriously damaged by the war action then. Later both this house and nearly all of Warsaw were reduced to rubble. When the Warsaw Uprising broke out in 1944, Andre and the others managed to stay in their building for about two weeks. "Then our streets were so-called liberated by the Germans, reoccupied by the Germans. And they assembled a big group of people from all surrounding streets. We were marched to Pruszków," site of a detention camp southwest of Warsaw. Before they were marched off, however, the men were separated from the women and children and taken to be workers in Germany. Among those forced to go to Germany was Janina's boyfriend.

"We were marching through a main street," Andre told us, "and buildings on the left and right were burning. It was like going through hell. Of course, nobody knew where we were going and what was going to happen to us."

When we interviewed Hanna in Warsaw, her memories of that time were quite vivid. "The whole town was burning and they were separating the men from the women. We were praying to God that they shouldn't take the children. There was a very narrow street and both sides of the street were burning. We thought they were trying to push us into the fire. People started running away. My mother said, 'Let's keep together. Let's keep together.' There were dead people everywhere. My mother said, 'We can't possibly go to the Pruszków camp because we will lose Andre and maybe lose one of our own children.'"

With the Warsaw Uprising, the Serena factory was destroyed, and Woznica, the plant manager, was taken to Germany, too. He never returned.

As Andre and others from his apartment were being marched to Pruszków, they stopped at a place outside Warsaw to rest and to get a drink. They saw a kiosk at that spot, "and we went into that kiosk and closed the door from the inside." It was crowded. There was Andre and his mother, Janina and her three daughters, and a woman who helped around the Kwiecinski house, along with her daughter. The eight of them hid there, waiting for everyone else to leave. Then they ran into nearby farm fields. They ended up in a farmer's barn and slept there, Andre said.

Hanna recalled that a woman named Pogonowska let them stay in her house in a Warsaw suburb. "Mrs. Pogonowska didn't know that Andre and his mother were Jewish. My mother dyed her hair gray to look like she was an old lady so she wouldn't be attacked by the guards. And Andre was hidden. And my sister was hidden in a tree. My older sister was beginning to look womanly and we were afraid they were going to rape her, so she had to hide. After the war we went to thank the woman who saved us, but she didn't remember whom she had allowed into the house."

Then Mrs. Pogonowska made them leave because she learned that neighbors had heard she was hiding people and she feared being caught. "We were walking from village to village, from barn to barn, from farmer to farmer," Andre said. "At times they would give you some food. At times you worked in the field and got some food and someplace to sleep."

Throughout all this movement, they remained quite close to Warsaw, and they hoped and prayed that the Soviets would come soon to drive out the Germans. "But you know what they did? They froze the front just some miles away from the Vistula River." This allowed the Germans to finish crushing the uprising and regain control of Warsaw.

By this time, Andre said, fall was coming on, everyone was hungry, and all of them were being "eaten alive by lice." Finally, as winter arrived, Janina found a connection in the village of Rylsk Wielki. "We ended up with a farmer who was like the head of the village." Today this village is known as Rylsk Duzy. It is southwest of Warsaw and east of Łódź. They shared a room with eight beds and a fireplace. The farmer gave them one meal a day, though they were penniless and, thus, could not help pay for their board. Farmers by then were so overwhelmed by refugees from the Warsaw Uprising that it was hard to find any accommodations. "We got so lucky that we ended up in a house," Andre said.

They spent part of the winter of 1944–1945 there until the Soviets finally liberated the area.

After the War

Once the Soviets were in control, Andre and his mother went with Janina Kwiecinska and her daughters to a home in the village of Koluszki, east of Łódź. They stayed there several weeks, but Helena wanted to return to her native village, so she and Andre separated from the Kwiecinskis. "We were wandering around Poland from *shtetl* to *shtetl* for a long time." Among other places, they went to Mordy and Biała Podlaska, both east of Warsaw.

Finally they ended up in Łódź. There Helena found a Jewish woman with two daughters. Helena and the woman became business partners in a small clothing store for about five years. Then Andre and his mother left Poland and moved to Israel, where he stayed for twelve years, finishing high school and serving in the Israeli air force. After that he moved to the United States. Helena remarried in 1956 and lived in Tel Aviv until her death in 1988.

As Andre considered the people who saved him and his mother by providing a hiding place, he said he was unable to explain their motives fully, but "this was the right thing to do, regardless of the risk and the consequence." He described the Kwiecinski family as "independent thinkers, very brave, cool, and fast thinkers." Janina Kwiecinska was this way, he said, "and why was she so good [as a rescuer]? Because she was an actress. She opens the door and now she plays her role. This woman was fantastic."

Still, in thinking about what it took for a Jew to survive outside the Warsaw Ghetto, he expressed special gratitude for the older Kwiecinski daughter, also named Janina. "She was a mature person at the age of fifteen or sixteen. She kept her sisters [in line] with an iron fist. This kind of discipline was necessary in the war."

For many years after the war, Andre told us, he did not talk about the war. When he later wanted to reconnect with Kwiecinski family members, he had considerable difficulty finding them. Finally, in 1987, a Polish man came to work for him. Andre requested that this man ask his father back in Poland to locate the Kwiecinskis. A week later, the father found them. Through this connection Andre learned that the older daughter, Janina, was a physician and quite well-off. Hanna was a clothing and set designer in the movie industry, but he did not learn much about Marysia. After reestablishing contact with them, Andre bought a plane ticket for Janina to come to the United States to visit her son in Chicago. And since then he has helped support Hanna in Poland, as has the Jewish Foundation for the Righteous.[50]

Andre spent his career as a food chemist, and even into his seventies did consulting work in this field in many countries. He and his wife, Eve, have two grown daughters, Daliah and Alexandra, and one granddaughter, Maya. He remained friends with the surviving Kwiecinski daughter, Hanna Morawiecka, with whom he was reunited in New York in 2004, thanks to the Jewish Foundation for the Righteous. Hanna told us this: "I thought I would faint when I saw him again because I only remembered him in torn up pants." Hanna and Andre shared a Thanksgiving meal that year, and when they met at Kennedy International Airport in New York with journalists covering the reunion story, Andre said to them, "Please meet my little sister. She tells me I haven't changed since I was nine years old."

Our Visit with Hanna Morawiecka

We journeyed to Hanna's small apartment in Warsaw and found a gracious and energetic woman in a wheelchair. It was immediately clear that she was proud of her late mother. In fact, almost the first thing she told us, through a translator, was this: "My mother didn't do this for any money. She did it because it was morally correct. She was always trying to help others. I was raised by my mother to help people. I didn't know the difference between a Jew and anyone else. I only knew it was the right thing to do. I was a child, and when I played with other people I had no idea of any differences."

But even as a ten-year-old Hanna knew the likely consequences for the family if her mother's generosity and hospitality were ever discovered by the Germans. "I learned as a child from this Jewish man who stayed with us that if we'd been caught we would have been shot. And I was always living in fear knowing this. But my mother didn't think about it. There were three of us and she just didn't think about it."

We asked her if she would do it again if given the chance. "Yes," she said. "I would take the risk because that's how I was raised."

When we asked her why her family took the risk of saving Jews, she first argued that many Polish non-Jews did the same. "A lot of people helped. But these people are not around now." Then she acknowledged, "it's true that in relation to the total population there weren't many because there were placards everywhere warning you that if you helped you'd be immediately executed. And after the war, people who saved Jews did not come forward as heroes because neighbors would criticize them for that." But Hanna said she never heard such criticism of her own family.

Hanna said she had thought a lot about what it might take to rid the world of hatred. Finally, however, she acknowledged this: "I don't know how we can heal the world."

Anna Schiff

One bitterly cold night Anna Lubich left the hiding place that a non-Jewish woman had provided for her and slipped back to the Grodno Ghetto. She went to find her husband, Ephraim Lubich, and their one-year-old son, Izydor, so they could join her.

Anna moved quietly and quickly through the frosty deserted streets toward the house in which she had left them. She had told Ephraim to hide in the attic if the ghetto was closed—as, indeed, it had been—while she was gone. Suddenly she saw a German soldier who, because it was so cold, was noisily clapping his hands and arms to keep warm. Anna slipped into a doorway to hide and took off her shoes to avoid making noise. She held her breath. The man did not notice her, and she thought, "This is a miracle."

Eventually she left the doorway and walked to the house where she hoped Ephraim and little Izydor were hiding. But when she searched the dwelling, it was empty. She was too late—by just a few days. In fact Anna would never see Ephraim or Izydor again.

She later learned that, soon after she left the ghetto to find a hiding place, the Germans had rounded up all the remaining Jews there—except for a handful still hiding successfully or who were forced to work directly for the Gestapo—and sent them to the ghetto in Białystok. As Ephraim and Izydor were being moved with this group, a lawyer with whom Ephraim had worked recognized him and shouted at him, "Lubich, leave the child and run away." But Ephraim would not abandon his son. Soon there were shots, and Ephraim and Izydor lay dead.

Those murders left Anna Schiff forever bereft. "Something is always missing," she told us. What has been missing is her large, close, loving family. The Germans took all of this away. They murdered not just her husband and her son but also her father, sisters, nephews, nieces, aunts, uncles, cousins, and more—some sixty relatives in all.

"Ever since then I never could laugh completely with all my heart," she said. She could not even enjoy those times when friends came over for a party. She would look at the people in the room and silently ask herself why her young husband, her son, and the family in which she grew up were not there: "Where are they?"

Anna Schiff almost died several times herself in those tumultuous years—once when she intended to commit suicide. But she survived, with help from family and friends, with her own wits and bravery, and with help from several non-Jews.

Anna Schiff

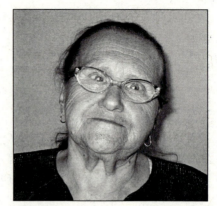

Wanda Cherpatuk

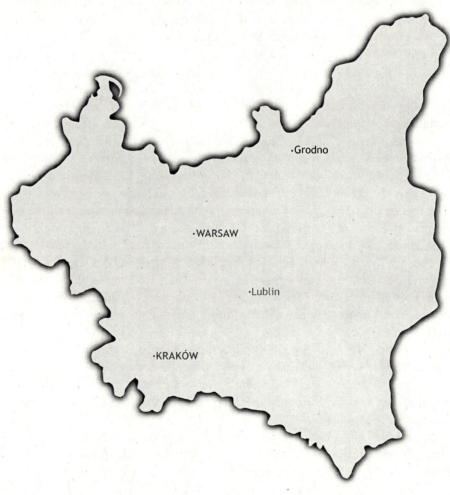

·Grodno

·WARSAW

·Lublin

·KRAKÓW

Nevertheless, "I miss a family; I lost my family," she said in an interview in her apartment in suburban Kansas City, where she moved in late 2006 from California to be near her daughter, Irene Weiner, and her daughter's family. In addition to a granddaughter in the Kansas City area, Anna has a grandson in California. Irene is the daughter for whom Anna always felt sorry, because "she didn't have any aunts, any grandparents. I was thinking how much love she would have for my sisters and for my father."

After World War II, Anna said, she thought through her experiences and decided that, despite her terrible losses, "I have to live because the genes that my father gave me I can pass on farther and farther." When she thought of her destroyed family, including her first husband and their son, she said, "We had each other. We were together." And she said she considered the time when she and her extended family all lived in close proximity in the ghetto as one of the best times of her life.

Anna was born on July 15, 1918, in Grodno, as World War I was winding down.[51] Named Chaya Klempner (but called by the diminutive Cheyele), she had five older sisters, Luba, Cyla, Liza, Pola, and Fania. Their father, Yitzhak Klempner, ran a family hardware store that his father had started. Anna's mother, Ida, died at age thirty-nine, when Anna was only about three years old. Yitzhak might have remarried to have help rearing six bright and active daughters, but Anna said he did not want to have to referee between a new wife and his children. So he remained single, later helping to take care of two grandchildren in a Grodno ghetto when the children's mother, his daughter Luba, died.

"He gave us so much love and devotion," Anna said, so she rarely felt she was missing a mother. It helped, too, that an older sister became something of a surrogate parent. "Cyla was like a mother for us. Every child was like her child." It also helped that they had a devoted housekeeper, a Russian named Nadia, who was not Jewish.

Anna said her father was not very religious, but he had great reverence for Jewish traditions and almost always could be found at the synagogue in Grodno on the Sabbath. In that way, he was like many Jews in Grodno who were raising families that were becoming more secular. Members of such families often spoke Polish as much as or more than Yiddish, and they began to give up traditions that were particularly Jewish. In other words, they were acculturating, though that process varied from family to family.

Yitzhak Klempner loved his daughters with his whole heart, Anna said, and did everything he could to give them good Jewish values and a good life. Anna remembered, for instance, that in the middle of cold winter nights when her toes were cold in bed, her father would get up from his own bed and fix a hot water bottle for her. "He was a wonderful, devoted father."

Anna's loving attachment to her father and sisters remained deep and profound. She said she tried not to remember all the details of the Holocaust but "only remember my family. And for me they're still alive. That's the way I survived. That's how I found the strength to survive." She just imagined that they were somewhere else, temporarily beyond contact with her. Even as an elderly woman, she said, she still felt her father was taking care of her. "I feel that when I have to decide what to do I ask him."

In the summers when Anna was a girl, her family often would rent a cottage in the woods near Grodno from a woman named Mrs. Koslowska. She was to prove a fortunate acquaintance for Anna. Indeed, it is doubtful that Anna would have survived without Mrs. Koslowska's help.

As Yitzhak's daughters grew up, they began to give up their Yiddish names in favor of more popular names. "My sisters all changed [their] names," Anna said. "And I didn't want mine, either." But her father wouldn't let her change her name because it had been his mother's name. Only later, in the midst of war, did she become Anna, sometimes going by the diminutive, Ania, which is the name Felix Zandman, another Grodno Jewish survivor and the subject of another chapter in this book, called her.

Life was good for the Klempner family as they lived among many other Jews.[52] Grodno then was an intellectually, culturally, and politically active Jewish center. The Klempner family lived in a comfortable home inherited from Yitzhak's parents. "It was a large house with enough room for everybody," Anna said. Three of the daughters shared a bedroom, but "we were very happy. We never felt deprived."

The home had an everyday dining room as well as what Anna called "the better dining room." On Friday nights and Saturdays they would eat in the fancier room. On Friday nights their housekeeper, Nadia, prepared a Sabbath dinner while Yitzhak went to services at the synagogue. Anna's sisters would light the Sabbath candles, often placed in beautiful silver candlesticks, and they all would eat gefilte fish, chicken soup, an apple dish, and other traditional foods.

The warm and loving atmosphere was made more so by frequent visits from various relatives in the area. "Everybody used to come to our house for Rosh Hashanah," Anna said. And most other family celebrations took place in Anna's childhood home, too.

The Klempner sisters were close. "My sister Pola was the beauty," Anna said. "My father used to say that she is a Greek goddess." When Pola got invited to a dance to which her sisters were not invited, all the sisters would help her get dressed. "And we were so happy for her. We would wait for her date like it was our date. That's how we were."

As she grew older, Anna was aware of some restrictions on Jews in Grodno, but, she said, she rarely encountered acts of antisemitism "because we were among other Jews all the time." But when she ran into antisemitism, it was hurtful. In the summers, for instance, near a cottage her family would rent, they would take boat rides. And when they would pass Poles on the riverbanks, sometimes those Poles would throw stones at them and shout, "You Jews, go back from here," Anna said.

One difficulty for Jewish children was that there was a strict—and very small—limit on the number of them allowed in public schools. Thus, Anna said, paying for private school for six daughters was her father's biggest expense.

After Anna finished school in 1936, at age eighteen, she went north to Vilna, which today is Vilnius in Lithuania but then was part of Poland, to go to a university, hoping to become a pharmacist. But there was a tight quota on the number of Jews allowed into medical or pharmacy school. So while she sought ways around those restrictions, she chose to major in German. "My father thought that German was a good language to know," in addition to the Polish, Yiddish, Russian, and a little Hebrew she already spoke.

But rumblings of war and other concerns brought Anna back to Grodno after only a year of college work. That's when Anna accepted a marriage proposal from Ephraim Lubich, whom she had known from childhood. He was studying as an apprentice to a lawyer and seemed to have a bright professional future. "I was very proud of him, too. Not only was he very brilliant but also a very noble person. And he gave me so much love," Anna said.

They were wed on May 18, 1938. Just over a year later, on June 6, 1939, less than three months before the start of World War II, Anna gave birth to a son, Izydor, named for Anna's mother, Ida. She and Ephraim then rented a cottage for the summer in nearby Losossna. On the last day of August, Anna, Ephraim, and baby Izydor went for a walk with neighbors and were talking about whether and when war might come.

"We knew what was going on in Germany," Anna said, "but we felt it was temporary. We didn't realize." That night, as Anna and Ephraim were preparing to go to bed, Anna broke a lamp. "I said, 'This is a bad omen.'" She was right. Before dawn the next morning, Germany invaded Poland.

"In the middle of the night [of August 31/September 1]," Anna once told interviewer Sophia Felsenfeld of the Survivors of the Shoah Visual History Foundation, "we heard some booms and we knew that the war [had] started. I could see that in Grodno everything was in flames. We were only three kilometers from Grodno. I wanted to go see what had happened to my sisters, my father. But my husband was against it. But I had a very strong will at this time." So she went to Grodno alone. But recognizing the need for families to stick together in such a crisis, she quickly returned to Ephraim and brought him and Izydor to Grodno.[53]

Soviet troops soon took over the eastern area of Poland. When the Soviet army came in, Anna was pleased because she knew she and other Jews were much safer under the Soviets than they would have been under German occupation. Indeed many Jews from German-occupied areas farther west tried to escape to areas controlled by the Soviets. The Soviets sent some people to Siberia, and Anna said, "I wish they had sent us to Siberia so my husband and my child would be alive."

But by late spring of 1941, Germany had turned on the Soviets and had begun to drive them out of eastern Poland. On June 23 of that year, German troops took control of Grodno. November 1, 1941, was the deadline for Jews in Grodno to be living inside a ghetto. Eventually Grodno had two ghettos, about two kilometers apart from each other. One was the old Jewish Quarter, where Jews had lived since the Middle Ages. It was known as the fish market. The second, the one to which Anna and her family moved, was known as Slobodka. Some fifteen thousand Jews were crowded into the first ghetto and about ten thousand into the second.[54]

On moving day Anna made numerous trips back and forth from her previous dwelling place to her new quarters in the ghetto, trying to save as many items as possible from her home. Each time she would return to her home she would find her non-Jewish neighbors looting what they could. However, one non-Jew, Pawel Harmuszko, helped carry Anna's heaviest items, such as her son's crib, to her new location. Later Harmuszko would save much more than Anna's goods. He would save her life.

Just after moving to the ghetto, Anna's oldest sister, Luba, died from a stroke, leaving behind two young children. Anna's father took care of those grandchildren. Indeed, he later sheltered those children in his arms as they were forced to board a transport for Białystok and then to the death camp at Majdanek near Lublin. Another sister, Fania, died of heart disease before Anna went to the ghetto.

Because of severely crowded conditions, it was impossible for all of Anna's close relatives to live together in the same house or apartment in the ghetto. So they split up. Anna and her baby lived with her father and two sisters, Pola and Cyla, and their families. Another sister, Liza, lived with her husband in another house in the ghetto. In fact, they lived with her sister Luba, because Luba was quite ill. Before the ghettos were created, Anna's husband hid in the attic of an old woman's house to avoid being rounded up by the Germans, who were seeking to eliminate the Jewish intelligentsia. Eventually Ephraim joined Anna and their son inside the ghetto, though he was hidden there, too.

The Germans' search for the Jewish intelligentsia resulted in the death of Pola's husband. "We didn't think they would take him, but they took him," Anna said. "She got back his wedding ring and other belongings. So she knew he was dead."

Life inside the ghetto was appalling, and Anna, like others, chafed under it. "I used to walk around in the ghetto and look at cats and think, 'Here's a cat or a dog. They have the right to live. I don't have the right to live.'"

But at least Anna's family did not starve, partly because her father managed to buy food that had been smuggled into the ghetto. Without that, hunger would have been a constant companion. So life in the ghetto was harsh and tenuous. Jews were required at first to wear white-and-blue armbands and later yellow stars on their clothes, both front and back. "We were not allowed to walk on the sidewalks," Anna said. Instead, they had to walk on the streets with the horses.

There were acts of major oppression but also small indignities, and sometimes the latter stuck in Anna's memory. For instance, when they went to the ghetto they were not allowed to have any fur coats, so Anna and her sisters left their fur coats with non-Jewish friends. But the coat Anna brought to the ghetto nonetheless had a small bit of decorative fur left on the collar. "I had to take off the fur from my coat and I was very mad."

Eventually the Slobodka Ghetto, or Ghetto Two, was closed. At this point Anna moved to the other ghetto. In all, she remained confined to one or the other ghetto until March 11, 1943, when she left to find a place to hide. Starting in November 1942, the Germans deported Jews from the Grodno Ghetto to Auschwitz-Birkenau and then to Treblinka. By the middle of February 1943, only about one thousand Jews remained in the Grodno Ghetto.

In the house in which Anna was living at the time, there was a big attic where she and others could hide when people were being rounded up for the transports to death camps or labor camps. By hiding there, Anna, Ephraim, and Izydor survived the roundups for those transports. But one of her sisters, Pola, and Pola's baby were taken on the first transport to Treblinka. She hoped she would be reunited with her husband, who previously had been taken to Treblinka.

On the second transport, another sister, Cyla, and her two children were deported to Treblinka. Cyla's husband avoided the transport as did an older son with whom he was hiding. By March 1943 Anna's family in the ghetto had shrunk considerably. Anna was growing more and more restless and unwilling simply to wait until death claimed her or even more members of her family.

"I was all the time telling my father that I want to get out," Anna said. "I want to talk to my gentile friends. Maybe they can help us." Anna also had encouragement to get out from, of all people, a German soldier, who noticed the attractive young woman with her baby and told her, "Try to get out of here. You're not going to last long here." The man also gave Izydor a piece of chocolate. That small gesture of kindness led Anna to conclude she was more afraid of the Poles than of the Germans.

When Anna told her father and husband she was going to seek help outside the ghetto, they said they had lost so much already they were reluctant to let her go. Still, this strong-willed young woman was insistent on trying to make contact with Mrs. Koslowska, the kind woman from whom they used to rent a summer cottage. "She was the first one I thought would help me," said Anna.

But, of course, Jews could not simply come and go from the ghetto at will. So Anna had to concoct a plan. She got a friend, who was a physician, to tell ghetto officials that she was sick and needed to go to the hospital. From the hospital in Grodno, Anna said, it was easier to get to the world outside the ghetto. So on March 11, 1943, with this physician's help, Anna left the ghetto and checked into the nearby hospital.

Before she pulled off this ruse, however, her nephew came to her and told her wistfully that he wished he could live as long as she had lived—so far not quite twenty-five years. The nephew was just thirteen. "He gave me his wallet and told me to take it. 'You'll have something to remember me.'" She kept that wallet the rest of her life and showed it to us when we interviewed her. And just before heading to the hospital she found that the shoelaces on her baby's boots needed changing. When she got to the hospital, she realized she still was holding one of the old shoestrings, so she put it in the wallet and kept that, too.

And she did one other thing before leaving the ghetto to seek help. She told her husband that if the Germans were to close the ghetto and move everyone out of it while she was gone, he and their son should hide in the attic of the house, and she would return as soon as she could and take him to the hiding place she was sure Mrs. Koslowska would provide. "I said goodbye to my husband, to my child, and to my father. My father told me, 'Oh, my child. We have lost too much in our life ever to be happy.' And in a second he told me, 'Oh, but you are young. Go. God bless you.'"

On the way to Losossna to find Mrs. Koslowska, Anna said, "Some Polish people recognized me and they started to ask for money and they wanted to take me right to the Gestapo." They took her to a house and stole her money and jewelry. They also demanded to know where Jews were hidden. She said she did not know any place. Early the next morning she was allowed to leave.

Anna found Mrs. Koslowska who, as she hoped, assured her she would take not only Anna but any members of her family who could get out of ghetto and come to her large rural property. So Anna was anxious to go back to get her remaining family from the Grodno Ghetto, and though Mrs. Koslowska was reluctant to let her go, she eventually did just that. By then, however, Ephraim and Izydor were dead, though Anna would not have confirmation of their deaths until the war ended.

When she realized, back in the empty ghetto, that her husband and child were gone—and maybe dead—she was devastated. "I didn't care any more. There wasn't anything to care about." She returned to Mrs. Koslowska and wrote a letter to her family in the Białystok Ghetto saying she wanted to join them there. They might get murdered, she reasoned, but "at least we'd be together."

Anna had hit bottom. "I thought, well, I will go out and I will kill myself. I told Mrs. Koslowska that I didn't want to live. There was no use for me to live. In the middle of the night I would go out and find a truck and let them run over me."

But Mrs. Koslowska would have none of that.

"No," she told Anna, "you're not going. First of all, why should you do Hitler this favor? He wants to kill all the Jews. Why do you have to help him? And second, life is very precious."

Mrs. Koslowska meant not just Anna's life but also the lives of her own family—her husband, Jan, and their daughter, Jadwiga (called Junia) whom she had put in jeopardy by helping Jews. She told Anna that if she went out to kill herself, some German would find her first and demand to know where she had been staying since the ghetto was destroyed. "And," Mrs. Koslowska told her, "you'll mention my name, and I and my husband and my daughter are going to be killed, too. So do you want to kill us, too? Maybe another miracle can happen. Why can't you wait?"

As Anna thought back to that traumatic time and to Mrs. Koslowska's wise counsel, she said, "She was a very good woman and she was righteous."

Anna had hidden clothing and other goods with non-Jewish friends. Not having any money to help pay for the food she would eat while staying with Mrs. Koslowska, she retrieved a fur coat and some other clothes and gave them to Mrs. Koslowska. But Mrs. Koslowska, Anna said, did a foolish thing and started dressing up in these beautiful clothes. It made women in and around the village start talking about whether this meant she was hiding Jews.

Anna promised Mrs. Koslowska that if she survived she would pay her for her expenses and her trouble, but when we asked Anna if she thought Mrs. Koslowska hid her for money, she replied, "She was very much against Germans. And, besides, she liked me, too. Sympathy."

At first Anna stayed right in Mrs. Koslowska's house. The only times she had to hide in a closet was when people came to visit, so "it was almost a normal life." But after a time, especially as other women began to suspect her of hiding Jews, Mrs. Koslowska began to get uneasy about hiding Anna in her home. So she made a double wall in a barn where she kept a pig. This is where Anna hid all day, though at night Mrs. Koslowska let Anna come into the house.

Before the war Mrs. Koslowska's husband had been a corporal in the Polish army. He, too, was kind to Anna, and she asked him if he could take her to be with the partisans. Anna thought she might be safer with them. But he declined, saying, "The partisans look for people like you Jews to kill."

Although Mrs. Koslowska was glad to help, she became increasingly uneasy about hiding Anna. In the meantime Anna learned that a young woman friend, Halinka Schiff (the sister of the man who would become Anna's second husband), was hidden in a place not far from Losossna. So Anna contacted the man who was hiding that woman and several other people, Pawel Harmuszko. He wound up saving not only Anna's life but the lives of many.[55]

Not far away from Mrs. Koslowska's property, Harmuszko owned several villas as well as a barn he co-owned with Jozef and Stefania Gawronik. Anna went to Harmuszko's house to talk with him. Because Harmuszko's wife was so frightened by the presence of a Jew in her home, Harmuszko quickly took Anna to one of his nearby villas—unused at the time—that he rented out in the summer. "He put me under a porch," Anna said. "He brought me a piece of bread and told me he's going to come and pick me up later."

As Anna lay there, she heard children near the house playing ball. Soon a ball fell under the porch right by Anna, and a little girl, perhaps three or four years old, came to retrieve it. The child saw Anna, and Anna was terrified that she might run and tell her mother what she had seen—and that, in turn, the mother would denounce her to the Germans. But the girl grabbed the ball and almost immediately other excited children grabbed the ball from her "and she forgot to tell them and they kept on playing and they didn't come. So, talk about miracles. Each survivor's life is a miracle. Here is another miracle, too, that the child forgot and I was alive."

That night Harmuszko came back to Anna, put her in a wagon, covered her with straw, and took her to a barn a couple of miles outside a nearby village called Novosiolki. It was the barn Harmuszko and the Gawroniks owned together. When they arrived Anna found that other people were hiding there, too, including people she knew. "They were happy to see me," she said.

Indeed, Anna discovered there her family's physician, Dr. Grigory Woroshylsky, an obstetrician who had delivered all the children in her family. With him were his wife and his three children (daughters, Rita and Cesia, and son, Viktor) as well as the man who would become Anna's second husband, Bolek (or Boris, later Blake), Schiff, and his sister, Halinka, who was Anna's friend.

Gawronik and his wife and children lived next to the barn and let Harmuszko hide Jews in it "because they were friends," Anna said. "Mrs. Gawronik would cook the food for us. Pawel took care of us."

The only hidden person in the barn who had any money was Dr. Woroshylsky. So he provided the wherewithal to buy what the people in the barn needed to survive. Harmuszko, Anna said, "wouldn't take a penny for himself. Pawel is a wonderful man. Really. He was a good man. He understood that it wasn't fair to kill people just because they were Jewish."

Before the war Anna's friend Halinka would talk to her about her brother, Blake Schiff. "She would tell me that she has a brother who is very bright and very intelligent and very smart. She would talk about her brother like he was a god."[56]

But when Anna got to the barn, she saw a pale, hungry man, weak from being hidden in a cold dark place.

"This," Anna thought to herself, "is the god? This is the Apollo?"

Life in the barn for the eight people hiding was dirty—they could never bathe there. It also was tedious, monotonous, and dangerous. They never knew if or when Germans might come in and search for hidden Jews. While they worried, they tried not to be eaten by lice.

But the Gawronik family provided bread and water. And almost every night Wanda Gawronik, a daughter who still lives today in Grodno and whom we interviewed in Warsaw, would bring them something warm to eat, usually soup. The Gawronik family, however, could not buy all the extra food they needed for the people in the barn in one place. That would have aroused suspicion about hiding Jews. So they would spread their grocery purchases among other nearby villages. Sometimes the people in the barn got onions that they would put on their bread. "That," Anna said, "was a feast."

To pass the time, the people in the barn would talk a lot. The doctor and his son, Viktor, as well as Blake were quite well read, and "we had very intelligent discussions." Although the light was terrible, they also would read books and newspapers that Harmuszko would bring to them. The papers always were several days old, but they allowed Anna and the others to have a fairly good sense of how the war was going.

When asked whether conditions in the barn led to bad relations and fights, Anna said, "Oh, no, no, no, no. As a matter of fact, Dr. Woroshylsky's daughter, Cesia, she loved me. She just took to me. And I loved her very much. We were all very close."

They had a little straw to sleep on at night, but the flies and lice were chewing them up. Their bodies were bloody from scratching, Anna said. Years later Anna's daughter asked about the circumstances of her parents getting to know each other, and Anna explained, "He was killing the lice. That's how I was dating your father." As Anna told us, "Everybody likes a little warmth in the barn, and Blake started to show me that. I liked it. So little by little I got used to him."

Blake Schiff became the main lice killer. Which meant everyone—men and women—had to take off their shirts so he could find the lice. If that was a stark reminder that no one had any privacy, so was the presence of a bucket in their common area for bathroom needs.

Anna hid in the barn for more than a year, until Soviet troops liberated that area on June 23, 1944. When Anna and the seven others emerged from hiding, they quickly wanted to go to Grodno, about twenty-five miles away, to see what had happened and who might have survived. After such a long time in the barn, however, "we could hardly walk," Anna said. But there was no other way for them to get to Grodno. So they took off and eventually made it.

"On the way to Grodno, we met a Polish lady," Anna said, "and when she saw us she spit and said, 'Oh, my God, we have Jews again.'"

"When we reached Grodno," Anna said, "we looked for a place to live." Anna moved in with a woman who had watched Anna's first husband and their son get shot. The two women had known each other before the war, "and I knew she lived alone in an apartment. So I asked her to take us. So she took us in."

When they arrived back in Grodno, they realized how few Jews from there had survived. Two who did were her previous boyfriend, Sender Frejdowicz, and his nephew, Felix Zandman, whose story we tell also in this book. Anna found a trunk containing household goods that her father had buried before the war, and in it found two comforters, one of which she gave to Felix. He remembered and mentioned her generosity when we interviewed him.

Even before Anna left her hiding place in the barn, however, she had decided to marry Blake Schiff because she assumed her husband, Ephraim, had perished. After they were liberated, and Ephraim's death was confirmed, she stuck with her decision. She said, "I grew to love him. He was very good and very devoted."

Indeed, she married him not once but four different times. On the way from the barn to Grodno, they celebrated by performing a ritual of marriage using straw for rings. Dr. Woroshylsky served as a fill-in rabbi because no real rabbi was available. Later a rabbi married them. Then they had a civil marriage, but that happened in territory controlled by the Soviet Union, so later, when they needed a Polish passport to leave the country, they had to be married again in Łódź, Poland. That marriage happened after their daughter, Irene, was born, so Blake had to adopt his own daughter to make everything legal.

After Anna returned to Grodno from her hiding place, she went to a mill that once had employed her briefly before the war, and she got a job for a time.

After the War

The end of the war did not mean the end of danger to Jews in Poland. "There were still pogroms, and we were still afraid of the Poles," Anna said. Before long Anna and Blake moved to Łódź, along with some other Jews who had survived. They lived there as non-Jews under the names Stephan and Anna Podolski, and on July 21, 1946, Irene was born.

They kept the Podolski name when, in 1947, they were able to leave Poland and move to Sweden for two years. Departing Sweden later, Anna was reminded of how much she had lost in the Holocaust. "When we left Sweden, and we were standing on the boat, there were so many people waving goodbye, goodbye, goodbye, and I saw my father waving to me and telling me goodbye. 'My child, God bless you.' I saw it. I saw it. And I feel that my father is taking care of me."

Podolski continued to be Anna and Blake's last name when, after that, they got visas through family connections that let them move to Mexico for four years. For quite a long time Irene's parents did not reveal to her or anyone that in fact their background was Jewish. But Anna finally had to explain to her, "Yes, we are Jews. But we're not bad people, we're good people."

When the Schiffs finally got a chance to move to Texas so Blake could take a job there, they got new passports, and this time, for the first time, they used their real names. "When I got my passport and saw my own name, I kissed my passport. I was so happy that I wasn't Anna Podolska any more."[57]

Throughout all of this, and even for decades afterward, Anna Schiff struggled to make sense of her survival. She said she recognized how good God had been to her, but at the same time, whenever she thought about her family killed by the Germans, she concluded, "To tell you the truth, very often I wish I went with them. I cannot forget the cruelty. I will never forget. And the injustice I will never forget. And I want the world to remember it and not to forget the cruelty. But I was trying to believe that there are good people, too, in life."

After living in Poland, Sweden, and Mexico, in 1952 Anna, Blake, and Irene moved to a suburb of Houston, Texas. Blake worked in the oil industry and went to school at night, eventually finishing a degree, while Anna worked as an accountant for a grocery store. In 1960 Blake was transferred to the Los Angeles area by his employer, Occidental Petroleum, and in 1968 Occidental moved him to Sydney, Australia. Anna, who held various accounting jobs prior to the move to Australia, followed him there after Irene was married that year. Anna went to work in Blake's Sydney office, and they remained in Sydney for eight years.

When they returned to Los Angeles, Blake left Occidental and established a consulting firm, eventually even doing some work for Vishay Intertechnology, the electronic components giant created by another Grodno Jewish survivor, Felix Zandman, whose uncle Sender Frejdowicz (who survived with Zandman) was Anna's first boyfriend.

Blake Schiff died in 2006, and Anna moved from California to suburban Kansas City.

In the mid-1960s Heinz Errelis, the head of the Grodno post of the German Security Services (or SD) in the Białystok district, and Kurt Wiese, who served under Errelis, were finally arrested and brought to trial in Cologne, West Germany. Both Anna and Zandman went to Cologne to testify against them. Anna told us that when she came into the courtroom and saw Wiese, "I started to scream, 'You buried my child!' I wanted to go out, and I wanted to choke him." A woman from the Red Cross eventually calmed her down.[58]

Twenty years after the end of the war, Anna's daughter, Irene Weiner, visited Harmuszko in Warsaw. In his wallet he still carried a small, folded, yellowing piece of paper that was a note from Irene's aunt Halinka, her father's sister whom Harmuszko had helped to save.

Our Visit with Wanda Cherpatuk

We arranged for the Gawroniks' daughter, Wanda Cherpatuk, to come from Grodno to see us in Warsaw for an interview. She was accompanied by her daughter, Nadja Kocniewa, also of Grodno. At the start of our time together, we opened a laptop computer and showed Wanda a photo of Anna we had taken some months earlier. She grasped the screen and kissed Anna's image several times.

Wanda was about thirteen years old when she met Anna, so her memory of those war years is quite clear. Indeed, she told us this, through a translator: "I can close my eyes and see everything."

The question we always wanted members of rescuer families to answer is Why? What drove Wanda's parents to help Jews?

"A neighbor, Harmuszko, brought Anna and the others to us," Wanda said. "And they were just people. We couldn't turn them away because to us they were just people."

What her family understood of the Jews they helped to save, she said, was that "they were fine people and neighbors." In fact, members of Wanda's family were regular patients of Dr. Woroshylsky, one of the people hiding in the barn. "My parents weren't thinking about the consequences," Wanda told us. "They loved them. What will be will be."

Still, Wanda remembered being worried as a teenager whose life was at risk because of the hidden Jews. "When I was a young girl, I would sit before the religious painting of the Madonna and pray not to be discovered. Our parents may not have had the right to risk our lives, but they loved these people and they did it anyway."

The "first action" of her mother each day, she said, "was to take care of the eight people. They were fed three times a day. In the morning they had some bread and butter. In the afternoon they usually had soup. And from time to time we would slaughter a pig and they'd have meat."

Wanda said her family fully understood what would happen to them if they were found helping Jews. "Death. Nothing else." So Wanda "never told the priest about what we were doing because . . . to save people was not a sin. Quite often, the German Hitlerites would come on motorcycles. We never knew whether they were coming to search or just coming to the village. Quite often we were scared to death. There were people who came to our property because they suspected us, but fortunately no one among the hidden Jews was coughing or sneezing when they came in."[59]

After the war, she said, "A lot of people came to our family and screamed at us, 'You risked the whole village. You risked all of our lives by doing this.' Our parents said that this was our business and our right to do and they paid no attention to what they said."

Wanda and Anna Schiff stayed in touch over the years through letters and phone calls. In fact, the first time we interviewed Anna, she had just received a letter from Wanda. And when Wanda kissed the photo of Anna on the computer screen, it was evident how much the friendship has meant to her.

Barbara Turkeltaub

It was still dark when the clip-clop clip-clop of horse hooves awakened Barbara Gurwicz and her little sister, Leah, near the brick kiln where they had found rest and warmth. Barbara looked up and saw a priest driving a buggy. He slowed and gazed at the girls, and they at him, but then he drove on. So not knowing what else to do, Barbara (called Basha) and Leah went back to sleep. They were scared children who, to avoid being turned in to the Germans, had slipped away earlier that night from a farmhouse where they were hiding near Vilna (today Vilnius).[60]

An hour or so later the priest returned. "This time he looked at us, and he stopped," Barbara told us when we interviewed her in her home in Canton, Ohio. The priest asked the girls if they were Jews. Barbara's father had prepared this little girl well for exactly this question. No, she lied. Bombs had fallen on their family's house, she told him, and she and her sister did not know where anyone else was. They were lost. That was the story she had rehearsed and rehearsed. And she thought she told it well.

The priest nodded and smiled. Barbara later decided that the man knew right then and there that the girls were, in fact, Jews. "Would you like to come with me to a safer place?" he asked. Barbara, speaking for herself and for her younger sister, said yes.

So the priest loaded them in his buggy, hid them under some blankets, and took them to a nearby convent run by Benedictine nuns on a farm not far outside Vilna. The priest, known to Barbara only as Father Jan (she never knew his last name) took them to safety, to survival, to a future that many times in the war before then had nearly been cut off.

He was not the only non-Jew who helped Barbara, her sister, her brother, and her mother survive the Holocaust (her father and two other sisters perished), but to Barbara he was the most important. "When I look back I'll tell you the truth: I am alive today because of one person, Father Jan, who was ready to sacrifice his life."

To be sure, her survival required the willingness of Father Jan to pluck these two little girls from danger and carry them to relative safety. But without Barbara's own ingenuity, her mother's careful preparations, the warm embrace of nuns, the police chief of Vilna who was a family friend, and a farmer willing to risk the life of his family by hiding Barbara and Leah at least for a time (though only in exchange for money), Barbara Gurwicz would not have survived. She

140

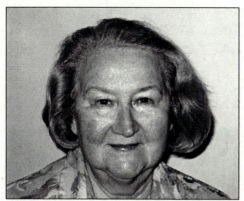

Barbara Turkeltaub

never would have gotten to Israel, then to the United States, and never would have become a nurse, a wife, a mother, a grandmother.

Barbara was born in Vilna, probably in 1934 and possibly in October, though she is not sure of the exact date. Her parents, Mina Gimpel Gurwicz and Moses (called Moishe) Gurwicz, already had two daughters, Mira and Hannah. About two years after Barbara was born, Mina gave birth to Luczia (or Leah) in 1936. Then in 1943 Barbara's brother, Henry, was born. Barbara's father and her two older sisters were killed near the end of the war by retreating German soldiers.

Barbara's early years were full of good family times. Her father was an accountant with the Vilna city government, and her mother ran a profitable seamstress business out of their house, located near the Vilia River not far from a synagogue. Her father came from an assimilated Jewish family while her mother's family was Orthodox. Mina, a native of Kovno, kept a kosher house that, because she was running a business, required help. So she hired a non-Jewish nanny named Anastazia Boyar (called Nastia) and an Orthodox Jewish cook named Dobcia. "It was a happy household," Barbara said, located in a city often called the "Jerusalem of Lithuania" because of its large Jewish presence and Jewish scholarship. Vilna—and Lithuania as a whole—had a substantial Jewish population then. Nastia, in fact, sought to help Barbara's family after they were sent to the Vilna Ghetto and, for her troubles, was beaten by a German soldier. She even rejoined the family for a time after the war.

When World War II started, the Soviets quickly assumed control of the city and ruled it until June 1941, when the Germans drove them out. German planes were sent to bomb the vital infrastructure of Vilna to force the Soviets to surrender the city, and they did, on June 26. So the bridge near the Gurwicz home was a natural target, and the day the bombs began to fall, Barbara, not quite seven years old, happened to be playing near that bridge with some other children. One of them sent a ball flying into a ditch, and Barbara went in to retrieve it just as the shrieking sound of bombs falling from the sky made people run for cover. "I think maybe a guardian angel was watching over me," she said, "because the ball fell in the ditch and that's where I was when the bomb fell on the playground. Then I didn't hear any more kids, any voices, nothing. There was a lot of debris falling all over the place and it became dark. I was petrified. I was clutching the ball. When I emerged from the ditch I couldn't see what was going on. From far away I could hear a voice calling me, and then my father grabbed me and carried me away from there. Later we found out that most of the kids who were there were killed."

Back at the Gurwicz home, window coverings quickly went up to keep the indoor lights from being seen by passing bombers. Mina, Moishe, and the neighbors spoke together, using words such as "Germans," "Nazis," "Bolsheviks," and other terms that did not make any sense to little Barbara, though she could tell that things were bad and likely to get worse.

Barbara told us that her father feared the Soviets more than the Germans, and he declared, "I will take my chances with the Germans." When the Germans captured Vilna, things got much more difficult for the city's Jews, however, because the same kind of oppressive restrictions they had experienced elsewhere were put in place. As Barbara described it in 1996, in a video interview done for the Survivors of the Shoah Visual History Foundation, "It was a campaign to humiliate, belittle, and demean."[61]

One of Barbara's sharpest memories from this early period in Vilna was seeing German troops goose-stepping through the streets, singing words to the tune of "The Happy Wanderer." All through her life after that she has shuddered when she hears this tune. She also recalled being forced to march into the area designated as the ghetto. "We were allowed to take only those things we could carry."

One of Moishe Gurwicz's friends was the city's police chief, whose last name Barbara remembered as Sandra. The Sandras tried to help the Gurwiczes in many ways. "My parents constantly had conferences with them," Barbara said. Chief Sandra even was able to delay the Gurwicz family's move to the ghetto. But not for long. Eventually the family was forced to crowd into half a room—divided from neighbors by a curtain—in a three-story apartment building. They had no running water and no electricity. Barbara told us she had no idea how her parents even cooked meals. But, she said, they got so hungry for meat that one day her father found a stray cat and slammed a door on it until it was dead. Then her mother cooked it, but Barbara could not force herself to eat it, hungry as she was.

By the time the Gurwicz family moved to the ghetto, Barbara's older sisters were in high school, though the war soon interrupted their schooling. One day, Barbara said, the Germans rounded up the high school students and took them to the nearby Ponary forest to be massacred.[62] The Germans killed thousands of Jews as well as many others at Ponary, and later Barbara herself would witness German troops murdering Jewish women there. Barbara said she does not know why her sisters Mira and Hannah were not among the high school students killed that day. She just knows that somehow they avoided it.

Things were no better for younger children. Barbara said she and Leah went each day to a children's center in the ghetto to be with teachers and caretakers while their parents worked outside the ghetto. Not much happened there except a little singing, Barbara said. One day she saw several vehicles she described as buses—their windows covered so that no one could see in or out—pull up across the street from the center.

"Two German officers came out," she told us, "and talked to the two ladies who were supposed to take care of us." Barbara watched as one of the women covered her face with her hands in a gesture of shock at what the Germans told them. Then Barbara heard one of the women say to the other, "Don't tell them," meaning the children.

Knowing this could mean nothing but trouble, Barbara grabbed Leah and hid in some bushes behind the center. From there she watched as dozens of children came out of the center as each one's name was called and got on the buses. The vehicles sat there with the engines running, idling, for quite a long time, going nowhere. Eventually, however, the buses departed bearing away all the children. When word got out in the ghetto that children had been taken away, panicked parents came running to find out what had happened. Needless to say, Barbara and Leah never returned to the children's center.

After this incident with the buses, Barbara's father sat her down and explained as much as he could about the realities of war for her Jewish family. "My father put me on a little stool and lowered himself to the same level and said, 'Basha, there is a terrible war going on. In order for us to survive we need to separate. You will go with your sister to a farmer. Mother is going to stay in the ghetto and there's a special place where she's going to hide.' She was expecting a baby then. My father and two older sisters were going to the partisans. He told me, 'Never admit that you speak Yiddish and never say your last name. Say a bomb fell on your house and you don't know where everyone is and you're lost. And you are always to take care of your sister.'" As Barbara's father said all this, her mother was standing next to her, crying, and "I was clutching to her dress and she was holding my sister and she was praying."

So Moishe and Mina made arrangements with a farmer whom Barbara and Leah were taught to call "Uncle," but whose last name may have been Switzky. The family knew him because he made regular deliveries of milk to them before there was a ghetto. Switzky put them in his wagon, covered them up with hay, and slipped them past bribed ghetto guards. "We were lucky. Sometimes the Nazis would stick bayonets into wagons like this but they didn't do that this time." They went to his home in the nearby village of Wierszuliszki. The Gurwiczes gave the farmer and his wife some money or jewelry to cover the costs of extra mouths to feed, and Barbara said the Switzky family probably did this more for the money than for any altruistic reason. But, she said, Switzky "wasn't a bad person."

The Switzky family "had a whole bunch of children, like five or six kids," Barbara said, though none of them knew that she and her sister were Jews. "If they had known, I know we would not have survived. The parents just told them that we were to spend vacation time there."

Mrs. Switzky was a nervous woman, Barbara said, who "was afraid for her own family." It was clear to Barbara that the woman was not happy with her husband's decision to hide Jewish children, and she did not hide her angst well. "From time to time she would call us brats."

Barbara and Leah stayed with the Switzky family for just four or five months, during which time they never saw their own parents. Only later did they learn that their mother, hiding then in the sewers of Vilna as the Germans were destroying the ghetto, had given birth there to their brother, Henry, whom Mina had tried—but failed—to abort.

Then one evening at the farm Barbara overheard Mrs. Switzky tell her husband that the next day he must go to the German authorities and turn in these Jewish children to receive the award being offered—some sugar.

"So I was afraid to wait until the morning," Barbara said. As her sister slept that night, Barbara sneaked into the pantry and cut off some bread from a large loaf. While in the pantry, she saw some jars of what she took to be honey on the shelf. So she slathered some on a piece of bread and went to wake up Leah, who always seemed to be hungry.

Barbara held the honeyed bread right in front of Leah's face so that when she shook her awake she would go right for the food and not cry out. But it turned out that what Barbara had unintentionally put on the bread was not honey at all. Rather, it was some kind of soap or cleaning substance, and as Leah chewed the bread, bubbles began coming out of her nose and mouth. But the smaller child refused to quit eating or to give up the treat. So Barbara let her have the bread, despite her fears that it would make her sick.

After Barbara got Leah dressed, they slipped out of the house and took off quickly down the road in the dark. "I didn't know where to go, just down the road," Barbara said.

The girls were cold and tired, and Leah was not happy to be running in the dark. So eventually they located the brick kiln where Father Jan found them and from which he took them to the Benedictine convent. When Father Jan drove up to the convent with the girls in his buggy, nuns quickly emerged and rushed them inside. They were fed, bathed, and given a warm bed. In a few days they were into a routine, rising early in the morning, attending Mass, then having breakfast, after which came quiet time. Nuns began to teach them basic reading and math, and the girls had some housekeeping chores to do, too. The nuns also helped to heal an infected wound inflicted on Leah's head. It happened at the Switzky farm when she had too eagerly grabbed for food before grace was said at one meal, and the upset father had tossed his knife her way, wounding her scalp. Barbara said the nuns used hot tar and linen to dress and heal the wound, which left a permanent scar on her sister's head and a permanent image in Barbara's memory of her sister screaming when the nuns would pull off the dressing and change it.

But rarely did they have anyone to talk with except themselves. The nuns generally spoke little, except when leading the girls in their lessons. None of them, for instance, ever asked the girls if they were Jewish. Rather, they simply taught them as if they were Catholic, instructing them in traditional practices. Barbara and Leah neither saw nor heard any other children at this convent, so it was a lonely existence, but not an unhappy one—especially for Barbara, who enjoyed the peace, the security, the rhythm of life, the tender care of the nuns, and the chance to draw pictures, read, and write poetry. Barbara, in effect, created her own tightly ordered world and became attached to the convent's structured pattern of life. She was baptized, took Communion, and learned to be an obedient Catholic. She believed the theology she was learning "very, very much," she told us.

There were, of course, special rules for the children—whom the nuns knew were Jewish. "We were told not to venture from the house by ourselves. I usually was a very good girl and listened."

Usually. But not always. One day Barbara wandered into the forest adjacent to the convent. As she did so, she began to hear what she described as popping sounds in the woods. Curious, she moved toward them. "I stayed behind a tree," she said. "Then I saw a group of people undressed by a huge ditch. I began to hear voices. I saw a group of women undressed. Some were holding babies in their arms. The Germans were shooting randomly and the women and babies were falling. I was so stunned I couldn't move. I was like hypnotized. Very soon afterward, somebody grabbed me and carried me from there. It was one of the older nuns."

Barbara later learned that she had inadvertently wandered into the Ponary killing fields and watched Germans murdering Jews. The memory never left her, even though she "was told not to mention that. Forget about it. Erase it from my mind."

The nuns decided Barbara and Leah could not stay there any more. So they fetched Father Jan again, and that same day he took them to the main convent in Vilna. Again they hid under hay in his buggy. When they got there, nuns quickly took the girls inside, fed them, bathed them, and gave them their list of rules, including an important prohibition against going beyond the small area to which they were assigned inside the building. This time, Barbara listened and obeyed. While at this convent, she occasionally heard the voices of other children but almost never saw them. It was, she decided later, a way of making sure hidden children did not give away other hidden children if pressured by the German authorities.

At this convent, Barbara and Leah fell into the rhythm of cloistered life. Nuns continued to teach them school subjects as well as prayers and other religious practices. But the girls' contact with the outside world was so limited that news of the end of the war did not reach them until 1947, two years after the fighting stopped. That was when their mother, who had been searching for them the whole time, finally found them. She had gone door-to-door, asking people if they had seen her two girls, one blonde, one with dark hair. Finally a woman told her that she may have seen at least the blonde girl singing in the choir at a worship service at the convent.

Mina went to Mass to see for herself. And there she saw two girls she was sure were her own. She asked to speak to the priest who celebrated Mass there, Father Jan, to tell him of her search and to ask to meet with the girls.

"He came to me," Barbara told us, "and said there is a woman who lost her children—he didn't tell me she was Jewish or anything—and is looking for them. She thinks that maybe you might be one of her children. Right away I was on guard. Everything in my background I had put away, far, far away. I never forgot my parents. I never forgot my grandmother. But I thought that being a Jew must be something really, really bad if people are killing them and doing all those awful things. And I was scared to think about it."

So Barbara did not want to see the woman who might be her own mother. She had found comfort and security in a Catholic convent and was loathe to lose it. "But then Father Jan came again and again. I think what an angel he was. He told me the lady is crying and looking for her children, so 'would you please reassure her that you'll help her to look for them?' So that's how I said OK."

But the woman Barbara then met with did not match the image of her mother in her memory. That image was of a tall, strikingly beautiful woman with black shiny hair and shiny eyes. By contrast, this woman was "bent down," wore glasses, and had a babushka over her gray hair. "I did not recognize her. But I started to talk to her and I said, 'Don't cry. You will find your children.' And she said, 'My daughter, Basha. I'm your mother.' And I recognized the voice. But then I ran away. Isn't that something? I was so scared. I just ran to the door. And they let me run."

A few days later Father Jan came again and asked Barbara if she was ready to see her again. "I said yes. She was sitting there smiling. I remembered her smile. And she said, 'My daughter, my daughter.'"

Leah reunited with her mother first. Somehow she was more ready than Barbara to reconnect. "She probably forgot my mom. But by their second or third meeting she just went to her like you wouldn't believe. My mother hugged her and kissed her and Leah was sitting on her lap. I thought to myself, how could she do that and I could not? I had so many questions I wanted to ask her. I was angry with her. Why did she leave us? Why did we separate? There was so much emotion. Where was our father? There was anger about that. But she didn't want to tell us everything."

Out of this anger and this questioning, Barbara made an extraordinary demand of her mother. "When the time came for us to leave, my mother had to promise me that she would come to the church and she would convert and she would be coming to the Mass."

Her mother, in turn, indicated to Barbara that she would do that, but in fact that was just a way of gaining custody of her daughter. Her mother never did convert, and Barbara, after a time, became an observant Jew again.

When Barbara considered all of this later in her life, she realized that "separation is very painful for any child in any circumstance. For me, on top of the separation, we were also scared." In fact, when Barbara had a son and a daughter of her own, she never insisted that they go to summer camps. "If they didn't want to go, that was fine with me. I didn't want to send them anyplace."

After the War

When Barbara and Leah left the convent, they moved into what Barbara described as a lovely apartment that their mother had managed to obtain in Vilna, not far from a big Catholic church. There they joined their younger brother after Mina had reacquired him in a long and complicated legal struggle with the non-Jewish family to whom she had entrusted him, uncircumcised, when he was nine days old. But the strains on Mina's family were enormous. Little Henry wanted to go back to the family that had reared him, and Barbara longed for the convent. Mina decided the only way to re-create a new family foundation was to move to Łódź, where many surviving Jews had congregated after the war ended.

She did this with the advice and help of a Soviet Jewish soldier named Blumkin, who had taken a shine to Mina and helped her in many ways, Barbara said, including during the legal battle for Henry. In Łódź, the tight housing situation required another family separation, though this one was comparatively minor. At first all of them shared a room with another couple, but that proved impossible. So, with the help of a Jewish aid organization, Barbara and her siblings moved to a children's home just down the street from where their mother lived.

Eventually even Łódź was not a satisfactory place to build a new life. Even there, Barbara spent time trying to contact the nuns and Father Jan at the convent in Vilna. Mina began to make secret plans to get her children out of there and take them to live in Israel. Just a few days before they left Łódź in 1951 or 1952, Barbara said, her mother "told us that we're going to Israel. Then we went to Italy on a train and from Italy we took a boat to Israel."

Arriving in Israel turned out to be "a very traumatic experience for us," she told us. "In Israel we couldn't be integrated into the society right away. We had to be in a camp, Sharalea in Haifa. We're in a camp with thousands of people, different looking, different speaking, different cultures. It's like a tower of Babel. We were behind barbed wire and couldn't go out. And I thought to myself, 'What's happening?'"

Mina's task, once they reached Israel, was to help her girls remove the trauma of the Holocaust from their memories. "She did absolutely everything she could for us to try to forget, not to remember people—good, bad, or indifferent, just to start a new life."

Eventually Mina was able to rent an apartment in Tivon near Haifa. Barbara then spent about a year in the Merchavia kibbutz in Afula before entering nursing school in Haifa. In all, Barbara lived in Israel for two and a half years before coming to the United States in 1954. But before leaving Israel, Barbara met Joseph Turkeltaub, a Holocaust survivor and native of Stopnica, Poland, who had come to Israel to visit his sister. She and Joseph were married for fifty years until his death. The couple had two children, Mark and Esther, and three grandchildren, Matthew, Evan, and Aaron. Barbara's sister in Israel, Leah, also married a Holocaust survivor, but she remained in Israel.

Mina never remarried, "though she had many opportunities," and stayed in Israel for many years before coming to the United States to live near Barbara until her death in 1987. Barbara's brother, Henry, also came to the United States and lives in the Cleveland area.

Barbara never made an effort to be in touch with the Switzky family, because she believed they helped mostly for mercenary reasons. She tried unsuccessfully, though, to be in touch with Father Jan after the war.

Having experienced the Holocaust, as well as the kindness of people who risked their lives for her, Barbara finally was able to "see the balance of things. I see that there is good in every person, and it can escalate when it's needed. There is also the opposite sometimes, and unfortunately we experience that. But there is potential for good in every person. The miracle was that among so many bad there were some good people."

Barbara, who spent decades as a nurse in Canton, Ohio, returned to Israel periodically. She told us that such trips have served as a way of restoring her soul. But she never returned to the Vilna area. "There is nothing for me there. There is an emptiness over there and sorrow and nothing."

Father Romuald Jakub Weksler-Waszkinel

Batia Weksler and her husband, Jakub, were frantic. Already they had given away one son, Samuel, to save him from the Germans. They had sent Samuel to live with a Lithuanian family in their town of Stare Swieciany, just northeast of Vilna.[63] And now she was ready to deliver another Jewish child who would need to be hidden, too.

But just before the second son's birth, the people taking care of Samuel brought him back to the Weksler home in the ghetto. These people went back on their word to keep the child, but they returned none of the valuables the Wekslers had given them to cover the cost of hiding, feeding, and housing him. When Samuel's brother was born, Batia decided to try to find a non-Jewish family who would at least take Samuel's brother and bring him up as their own. The Wekslers elected, at least for now, to keep Samuel and hope for the best. So Batia spoke to a couple she knew through contacts at Jakub's thriving tailor shop, Emilia and Piotr Waszkinel. Piotr was a metalworker.

Emilia Waszkinel
(photos of mothers courtesy of Fr. Weksler-Waszkinel)

150

Reverend Romuald
Jakub Weksler-Waszkinel
(photo by Jacek Pokrzycka)

Batia Weksler

Sister Klara Jaroszynski

·Stare
Swieciany

·Pasłęk

·Łosiniec

·WARSAW

·Lublin

·KRAKÓW

Batia knew she had to be convincing. Romuald said that his adoptive mother later told him Batia looked her in the eyes and said, "You believe in Jesus Christ. You told me you believe in God. You know Jesus Christ was a Jew, so please save my Jewish child because you believe in Jesus Christ. Please take care of this child." Then she suggested to Emilia that when Romuald grew up, he could become a priest.

As frightened as Emilia was to say yes, she agreed.

Today that baby is the Reverend Romuald Jakub Weksler-Waszkinel, a Catholic priest who teaches philosophy at Catholic University in Lublin. We interviewed him, using a translator, at his Lublin apartment, in the same room where he finally learned the truth about his Jewish background. He has been a priest since the 1960s and a teacher for much of that time. So his Jewish mother's prophesy came true, though of course she had no way of knowing the remarkable path this man would travel to get from being a Jewish baby to being a Catholic priest who did not learn about his Jewish background until twelve years after his ordination. The story of that journey involves a nun, whom we interviewed near Warsaw on her ninety-sixth birthday in 2007, the late Pope John Paul II, and countless other people whose lives intersected with Romuald's as he sought to discover the mysteries of his origin.

Romuald refers to Jesus as "my rabbi," and when he met Pope Benedict XVI at Auschwitz in May 2006, he knelt before him wearing both a priest's collar and a yarmulke. So he has sought to use the discovery of his Jewish background and the reality of his priestly calling to be a bridge between two related religions that often have been at odds. He reminds Christians that their faith "started with Judaism."

For Romuald himself, everything started with Germany's persecution of the Jews and what it would mean for his life. Romuald said he was not sure just when he was born, though he believes it may have been February 28, 1943. In 1978, when Romuald finally got Emilia Waszkinel to tell him the facts about his birth, she said this to him: "You had a wonderful, good, wise mother. I was afraid, so afraid. The punishment for saving Jews, even infants like yourself, was death. As you know, we didn't have our own apartment. We rented a room. I explained all of this to your mother. . . . She listened, but didn't seem to hear. She looked at me, and her sad eyes—you have your mother's eyes—said more than words."[64]

Romuald told us that his Catholic "mother eventually said to me, 'I was not able to say I didn't want you because if I did say that I would be saying I don't believe in Jesus Christ.'" So the Waszkinels took him in, pretending to their neighbors that someone had simply abandoned the baby on the balcony of the house where Emilia and Piotr lived.[65] In the meantime, on April 7, 1943, the Germans transported Romuald's biological parents and his brother, Samuel, along with other Jews living in Swieciany to Vilna. He said he believes his family members were murdered either in the Vilna Ghetto or in Ponary, a Vilna suburb where, starting in the summer of 1941, Germans massacred Jews, Poles, and Soviet prisoners of war.

Once the Waszkinels brought the baby into their home, they did their best to keep his existence a secret. "Nobody knew about me," Romuald told us. "Even the sister of my [Catholic] mother didn't know." His memories from early childhood are few. One is a memory of tripping and falling into some boiling water in their kitchen. But he said he does not remember moving with his parents at the end of the war back to Poland from Swieciany, which had become part of the Soviet Union. The Waszkinels got off the train in Białystok and moved to a small town named Łosiniec, north of Białystok, which was the town Emilia had left when she was eighteen, heading for France to find work. Romuald has described himself at that age as "dark-haired, stuttering, and tearful."[66]

After the War

So the war was over, and Romuald had been successfully rescued from the Holocaust, but he still had no idea about his background. This would require a quest, not for survival this time but, rather, a search for identity so that he could make sense of who he was and the path he traveled to get there.[67] By the summer of 1946, the Waszkinels had moved to Pasłęk (sometimes Pasłęka), east-southeast of Gdansk in northern Poland. There Romuald grew up, "afraid of everything."[68] He was especially afraid of airplanes flying overhead, imagining that they were coming again to drop the bombs he had heard fall earlier in his young life.

Both in his early childhood when he was always at risk of being found to be Jewish and then in the early postwar years, he picked up what he later understood were small clues about his Jewish roots. When he was four or five years old, he heard two drunken men shout "Jew, Jew, Jew bastard" at him. When he told his mother about this, she simply told him that wise people would never call him such names and that he should avoid such fools. Later in primary school, children occasionally would taunt him with the label of Jew. But mostly he just thought that was because children sometimes are cruel to each other.

Despite the profound love he received from Emilia and Piotr, Romuald was bothered when "children asked whether I looked like my mother or my father," he told us. "It was a very important question to me because I didn't look like my parents. Then, when I was nine years old, my sister was born and she didn't look like me, either." Romuald developed a theory: Somehow in the war his mother had been raped, and though he was her child, he was not his father's child. But he kept this terrible—and inaccurate—secret to himself. In fact, when he asked his father once about whom he resembled, Piotr replied, "Look in the mirror. Don't you see? You look like yourself."[69]

When he was nine or ten years old, he stood in front of a mirror in his room and combed his black curly hair in such a way that he thought he finally resembled his father. He called to his mother to have a look, asking, "I look quite like Daddy, don't I?" When Emilia hesitated before answering him, his doubts and insecurities boiled to the surface, and he shouted at her, "Because, if I'm Jewish, then just you wait and see what I'll do to myself."[70] He felt almost immediate remorse at his words but later acknowledged that they expressed his true fear of discovering he was Jewish.

When Romuald was twelve or thirteen, he went with his father to visit his father's home village, Wejszyszka, in the Vilna area. While they were there, an old man pointed to the boy and asked Piotr, "Where did you conjure up this little Jew?" Piotr called the man a pig and a fascist, then he hugged Romuald and took him away from the man. "I didn't ask any questions and my father didn't explain anything," he said.[71]

After that, Romuald experienced essentially no more hints of his Jewish roots for a long time. His high school years flew by, and he was an excellent student. Then in February 1960, in his senior year, he blurted out to a catechism teacher that he wanted to enter seminary and become a Catholic priest. "I myself was shocked at what I'd just said, but I had said it, and I felt I must keep my word." His shock was rooted in the doubts about faith he was experiencing then. Piotr was not happy to learn of Romuald's seminary intentions, and because his parents were deeply religious, this negative reaction surprised the boy. His mother, he said, did not try to affirm his decision or dissuade him, though she was upset by his decision.

Determined to show his father that he was wrong to oppose his son's desire to become a priest, Romuald entered the seminary in Olsztyn that fall. Soon his father came to visit him there—and Romuald knows today that Piotr wanted to talk him out of becoming a priest because he was Jewish. But Piotr could not get those words out.

"My father came to see me at the seminary," Romuald told us, "but he just cried in the chapel. I didn't know why. I asked why he was crying. 'Is there something bad about my becoming a priest?' And he just said, 'This is not your path. This is your life and your faith, but don't regret anything.'" Then he left, not having revealed anything of Romuald's background to him. That was a Sunday. The next Thursday, Piotr died of a heart attack at age fifty-two. Romuald's first reaction was to decide he should leave seminary, but both his mother and the seminary rector talked him out of that. And eventually he swore that in response to his father's concerns he would become the best priest he could be. "I thought to myself that, if my father thought that I would be such a bad priest, I would prove to him that I would be a great one because I loved my father very much."[72]

Before he could be ordained, however, seminary officials questioned whether he had ever been baptized, and Romuald again wondered if this meant he had been born a Jew. But Romuald's godmother was still alive, and she testified she had been an eyewitness at his baptism in 1943, so the matter was put to rest. Romuald said he gave himself to Jesus Christ and, because of that, told himself that it would be wonderful to discover that he was as Jewish as Jesus. Romuald was ordained in June 1966 and worked as a parish priest for a year before entering Catholic University in Lublin for additional study. He received a graduate degree in philosophy in 1970 and began teaching in the philosophy department the next year.

In 1975 Emilia sold her home in Pasłęk and moved to Lublin to live with her son. By this time, Romuald had read a lot and learned a great deal about the Holocaust, including stories about non-Jews who had helped to save Jews. But he noticed that his mother always avoided any talk about the Holocaust. He once read to her something about how the Jews had suffered in World War II, and he noticed her wiping away tears, so he simply asked her, "Mother, why are you crying? Am I Jewish?" Her only response was, "Do you think I don't love you?" And then she broke down in tears. At this, Romuald told us, he was convinced he had been born a Jew.

But after that, on February 23, 1978, which Romuald now considers his second birthday, he and his mother were talking about their old town of Swieciany and the various kinds of people who lived there. Emilia mentioned Poles and Lithuanians, Russians and Tartars. "And I asked her, 'Jews? You didn't know any Jews in Swieciany?' And mother started to cry. I kissed her hands and asked her to tell the truth because I deserve to know the truth. Then she told me, 'You had wonderful parents. They loved you very, very much. They were Jews. I only rescued you.'"

So there it was—finally the facts about who he was, which took thirty-five years to uncover. "For thirty-five years, I felt that I was only half alive," he once said.[73] But there were so many more questions: "I asked her, 'What is my name?' Mother said, 'I don't know.' I was nervous and emotional and I shouted, 'Mother, you killed me. You treated me as if you killed me, because you don't know my family's name.' Mother cried. And she said, 'It was not your last name that was important. It was you that was important.'"

Emilia explained to him that she purposefully tried not to remember his last name so that she never would give it away under pressure. "So," Romuald told us, "I was quiet. And mother told me then about meeting with my Jewish mother, who was a very wise woman because she decided to tell her about Jesus Christ. And that persuaded her to take me."

For several nights after learning he had been born a Jew, Romuald could not sleep. He had discovered his origin, but "I didn't know anything about Jewish life and history. On the other hand, I felt deeply connected and, what was worse to me, I was not able to tell anyone about it because I was afraid."

So he wrote a letter about all of this new information to his old professor from the university in Lublin, a teacher who by now was Pope John Paul II. And Romuald asked the pope to keep his background a secret. "I received an answer, a letter from the pope. It started, 'Beloved Brother,' and he wrote that he would pray for my Polish Catholic and Jewish parents."

Even though Romuald now knew he had Jewish parents, it took another fourteen years before he discovered his family's name. It was 1992, and by this time his Catholic mother had been dead for three years. Romuald, as part of his priestly duties, once heard the confession of a nun, Sister Klara Jaroszynski, "and I told her that if you are with God there is nothing to worry about because I myself was rescued at five minutes before twelve, or midnight." This common Polish phrase struck a chord with the nun, who, with her parents, saved several Jewish children.

"After this confession," Romuald told us, "this sister wrote me a letter and said that if I could tell her more, probably she could help."

So Romuald went to see Sister Klara to ask how she thought she could help. "She said, 'You are a Jew, aren't you? What else could it mean that you were rescued at five minutes before twelve for someone of your age?' I started to cry and said, 'Yes, I am a Jew. So how could you help me?'"

Sister Klara asked him what he knew about his family. All he knew, he told her, was that he was born in Swieciany, that his father was an excellent tailor, and that he had a brother named Samuel. With just that much information, Klara started to write letters of inquiry to people she knew in Israel. But ten years passed with no new information. Finally, in 1992, Sister Klara went to Israel and met with Holocaust survivors from Swieciany. "When the sister said there is the son of a tailor, everybody shouted, 'It's Weksler.' They had a book with a picture of my mother." Klara returned from Israel and gave the photo to Romuald.

"All my life," he told us, "I wanted to find someone who looked like me. My mother's face was my face when I was fifteen."

We spoke to Sister Klara at her convent in Laski, near Warsaw, where the nuns have long operated a home for the blind. With help from a colleague, Sister Rut Wosiek, and through a translator, Klara recounted essentially the story that Romuald had told us. But then she added this: "He looked like he was lost. He didn't know if he was Jewish or Catholic, so I decided to help him find out."

Sister Klara connected Romuald to his father's brother and sister who were living in Israel, and Romuald traveled to Israel that same year to meet his aunt Rachel (also known as Rose) Sargowicz, whose maiden name was Weksler, and his uncle Tzvi (or Cwi) Weksler. When Romuald arrived in Israel, he told us, "My uncle asked me at the airport how I can bring in myself nineteen centuries of antisemitism against Jews. I told him I haven't been around nineteen centuries."

His uncle, an Orthodox Jew, "wanted me to be with him in the synagogue and was happy when we went. He was unhappy when I told him I want to go to the church, too." But his uncle found a way to make room in his heart for this nephew who had become a priest. "My uncle said that the most important thing in your life is to listen to your soul: 'If your soul tells you different from me, you have to listen to your soul.'"

Romuald has spoken out against the anti-Jewish sentiments expressed officially and unofficially by the Christian church across many centuries and insists that Christians must honor their Jewish roots.[74] Romuald Waszkinel has added his father's name to his to become Romuald Jakub Weksler-Waszkinel, but the only physical remnants he has left of his own Jewish roots today are the down coverlet in which he was wrapped as a baby and a samovar and hand scales that once belonged to his Jewish parents and that his Catholic mother saved. He keeps them on display on top of a bookshelf in his apartment.

"Today," Romuald has written, "I know that I have my mother's eyes, my father's mouth, and the fear and tears of my brother. I carry in me the love of my parents"—both sets.[75]

Felix Zandman

Felix Zandman's Grandma Tema once did Anna Puchalska a big favor that Anna never forgot. Tema Frejdowicz helped Anna through a childbirth at a difficult time in her life. So years later, when Felix knocked on Anna's door and asked for a single night's shelter to hide from the Germans, Anna took him in, glad for a chance to do something for a member of his Grandma Tema's family. Anna told Felix, "God sent you." And Anna let Felix stay more than one night. In fact, by the time Soviet troops liberated the area around Grodno, where Felix had grown up and where Anna and her family lived, he had survived for seventeen months hidden with at least four and sometimes as many as six other people in a small, dark, fetid pit under Anna's home, a pit so crowded that the people hiding there had to take two-hour turns lying down and one person always had to sit on the waste bucket.

Felix Zandman later would get his Ph.D. in physics from the Sorbonne in Paris. He went on to found what became a huge international electronics company, Vishay Intertechnology Inc. But it was Anna Puchalska who gave him a chance just to survive.

Felix was born in 1927 in Grodno, then in Poland, now in Belarus. About thirty thousand of Grodno's approximately fifty-seven thousand residents at the time were Jewish.[76] Nearly all of those thirty thousand Jews perished in the Holocaust. In fact, only ninety-seven Grodno Jews showed up there again after the Soviets liberated the city. There is a Jewish community again today in Grodno, but it is made up almost entirely of immigrants from Russia. Felix told us that only one Jew, Gregory Hosid, survived the ghetto and still lives in Grodno.

Like many Jews in prewar Grodno, Felix was part of a large close family. That family's active engagement with political, religious, and social ideas was a microcosm of Grodno itself, which was an active Jewish intellectual center. Young Felix, his sister, Mira, and his parents, Aaron and Genia Zandman, lived in one of four apartments in a big house at 28 Brygidzka Street. His married uncle Grishka Frejdowicz had a second apartment there with his wife, Tania. His uncle Sender and his wife, Sarah, lived in a third apartment, while a large fourth unit on the second floor was occupied by his maternal grandparents, Nahum and Tema Frejdowicz, and their still unmarried children, Kushka, Fania, and Lisa.

Felix's father, a chemistry scholar with a Ph.D., had married into the Frejdowicz family, which operated a construction and building supply company. But Felix said Aaron Zandman was not allowed to teach chemistry in Poland because

Felix Zandman
(photo courtesy of Felix Zandman)

Krystyna Maciejewska and Sabina Kazimierczyk

159

he was Jewish, so he joined the Frejdowicz business as a salesman. Felix's paternal grandparents, Berl and Rifka Zandman, also were a big part of his young life. Rifka was the daughter of a famous nineteenth-century holy man, an itinerant Jewish preacher known as the Kelmer Maggid, and this lineage was a source of family pride. Rifka's husband, Felix's grandfather Berl, was a rabbi.

Although Jews made up much of the Grodno population of Felix's boyhood, he frequently experienced antisemitic behavior. Often, he said, boys from the Catholic school he had to pass when he walked to his school would beat him up merely because he was a Jew. Still, he told us, he had lots of wonderful memories of his pre-Holocaust life in Grodno. "I remember the Friday evening dinners at my grandparents'. I remember going to the synagogue, which was very nice. I remember how my grandfather, on holidays, would invite everybody from the synagogue to have some schnapps. I remember our vacations. We had a summer house where this Janova [the woman who later hid him] was the caretaker.[77] I remember with fondness how she would take me to drink milk from the goat. I still remember the odor of that milk. I remember playing there, playing volleyball there, swimming in the Niemen River. All of my past life I remember," including school and the political debates he and his peers had about Zionism and other subjects.

Memories of his Grandma Tema stayed good and strong, too. And it was her generosity toward others in need that formed a crucial part of the story of Felix Zandman's survival. Felix came to understand that Grandma Tema's act of mercy toward Anna led her to hide Felix and several other people, including his uncle Sender.

Not that Anna Puchalska was the first, last, or only person Tema had ever helped. Far from it. In fact, Felix described Tema as "a charitable institution all by herself." But the seed of obligation was planted in Anna when she was pregnant with her second daughter, Sabina. As Felix told the story, one night Anna's husband came home very sick and could not help his wife, who was just about to have a baby. At that time most babies were delivered at home. Without any money and nowhere else to go, she walked to Grodno and showed up at Tema's doorstep. Tema took her in, arranged for her to deliver her baby in Grodno's Jewish hospital, and gave her some money. "It was just one of the thousands of Tema's good deeds," Felix once wrote, "none of which she ever mentioned to anybody."[78]

Before Felix showed up penniless and desperate at Anna's house, he and his family discussed various options, including moving to the United States, where one branch of Tema's family had gone decades earlier. But the family decision to move never came about. When Germany invaded Poland in 1939, bombs fell on Grodno. As the defense by the Polish army soon collapsed, Felix's family, fearing that Grodno would be occupied by the Germans, evacuated to the east on September 5. They went to Lida, where various Zandman relatives lived.

The Germans began the war by attacking western and central Poland, but on September 17, the Soviets attacked eastern Poland, where Grodno is located. After Soviet troops took over eastern Poland, Felix's family moved back to Grodno, and for a time, life under Soviet domination was tolerable. In fact, in some ways it was an improvement. For twelve-year-old Felix, it felt as if he had never been so free because he experienced no more attacks from Catholic children.

But soon Jews in Grodno began to learn how fragile life had become in areas of Poland under German occupation. Felix's family considered leaving Grodno for the United States via Lithuania, which was not yet occupied by the Soviets. In fact, a business associate of Grandpa Frejdowicz fled to Grodno and urged Felix's family to escape because, he predicted, the Germans eventually would kill all the Jews. But the Frejdowicz and Zandman families did not leave even then, though later some family members moved around to avoid being exiled to Siberia.

When the Soviets confiscated Grandpa Frejdowicz's business and home, he and his wife fled seventy miles southeast to the village of Slonim. So Felix's family was oppressed, scattered, and anxious. But at least the Soviets were not rounding them up and murdering them and other Jews.

That minimal sense of security would soon change, however. In mid-June 1941, the Germans began to drive the Soviets out of eastern Poland. Felix was visiting his grandparents in Slonim when bombs from this action set the mostly wooden village aflame. With fire everywhere, they fled—with thousands of others—to a nearby river.

"We instinctively went to the river, knowing that a river can't burn," Felix told us. When the fires died out, Felix found that his grandparents' rented home was reduced to ashes, so they found space in one of the few houses still standing, as neighbors took in neighbors.

In a matter of days, the Germans arrived and took over. When they began rounding up the Jewish men in Slonim, Grandma Tema made Felix and his grandfather get in bed together and cover up. Soon a German officer came into the house, but Tema insisted her husband was paralyzed in bed and that her grandson was sick with a fever. The German simply left. Tema's subterfuge had worked. Outside the bedroom window Felix saw Germans beating Jews and forcing them into trucks. "I knew we were in the hands of savages," he said.[79] He was right. The Germans had taken the men outside of town, lined them up, and shot them. Felix said that local peasants saw it and reported the terrible news. (Such actions were carried out by the *Einsatzgruppen*, special mobile units assigned the task of shooting Jews.)

Some days later, Felix's aunt Lina, who by then was married to his uncle Kushka, came to Slonim and managed to get Felix's grandparents on a train back to Grodno. There being no room on the train for Felix and Lina, they walked back as far as Białystok and then caught a train for the final fifty or so miles to Grodno. When they arrived then learned of a roundup of Jewish men the night before. Felix's uncles Kushka and Sender had hidden, but Felix's father had been taken (though later he was released). Half of the approximately two hundred people rounded up were murdered. Felix said his uncle Grishka, who at the time was living in Lida, had been shot there by the *Einsatzgruppen*.

Like other Jews in Grodno, Felix and his family first had to wear white-and-blue armbands and then yellow stars. And they began to think in great detail about how they were going to survive. Felix's uncle Sender, an engineer, decided the family needed to build a false wall in the basement of their home and hide whatever paintings, furs, carpets, gold, and other valuables they had removed from their business properties before the Soviets confiscated things. They managed to get that done before the Germans ordered all Jews in Grodno to move into one of two ghettos by November 1, 1941. At age fourteen, Felix moved into an apartment of a cousin in the first ghetto. In one room were Felix, his sister, his parents, and his Zandman grandparents. His uncle Sender's family and Sender's wife's family were located in another room. Other family members were assigned to the second ghetto, called Slobodka. At the insistence of Felix's father, who did not want to be seen as a collaborator in any way with the Germans, no Zandman or Frejdowicz family members joined the Jewish police.

To survive, Felix and his mother both began to smuggle food into the ghetto. More than once Felix was caught and beaten. Felix also devised—or joined in— other ways of making a little money to be able to buy food or to pay the *Judenrät* when its members were forced to raise funds to bribe the German authorities in charge of the ghetto.

To raise more money, Felix's Grandpa Frejdowicz sent his sons Sender and Kushka out of the ghetto to retrieve merchandise hidden behind the false wall in their old house. But when they broke the wall to get access to the hiding place, they found to their shock that the hiding place had been cleaned out. Someone had broken through the outside wall and entered. That someone turned out to be the very person they had paid to build the false wall. This disaster, however, eventually turned out to have a good result.

A year after moving to the ghetto, Felix and his family learned that the Germans were going to start deporting Jews. No one quite knew where they would go, but there were rumors about both labor camps and death camps. The deportation news required a quick family decision about whether to stay or to try to escape and hide. After much anguish, Felix's father elected to stay behind in the ghetto with his aging parents. Felix, his mother, his sister, and his aunt and uncle Sarah and

Sender, with their small children, Haim and Abrasha, slipped out of the ghetto and went to their old house on Brygidzka Street, which had been taken over by a company that occupied it in the daytime, using it as an office and warehouse. Almost immediately after arriving there, Sender left with his two children and delivered them to their former nanny, who had previously agreed to help out in this way if needed. When he returned, the five of them went to the attic to hide.

Several days later, when it seemed to Sender that the attic was no longer safe, they moved to the storage attic of a nearby warehouse. But a non-Jew soon discovered them there and yelled for someone to get the Germans to deal with these runaway Jews. Sender quickly found a way out through a trapdoor, and the five of them ran to their old house and down to the cellar, where the false wall had been built. They got through that fake wall by using the hole Sender and Kushka had made in it when they came to retrieve the family's possessions, and they escaped through the hole in the outside wall that the thieves had made. With the German soldiers chasing them and quickly closing in on them, they surely would have died there had that hole in the outside wall not existed, Felix said. The five of them escaped via that fortunate route and ran through the next-door garden and out to a sidewalk. Quickly they made their way to the home of a non-Jewish friend of Sender's and barged in, temporarily safe from their German pursuers.

Decades later, when Felix thought about their escape through the hole made by thieves, he remained almost incredulous. "Extraordinary, extraordinary," he told us. "Somebody doing so much harm to us, everything is gone, and it saved our life because of it."

Having escaped their German pursuers, Felix and his family survived for a few days outside the ghetto by hiding with people they knew. But Felix's mother was frantic, wondering what had happened to her husband in one ghetto and to her own parents in the other ghetto. When Felix insisted he wanted to try to survive by staying outside the ghetto, she and Felix's seven-year-old sister, Mira, left him to survive any way he could, and they went back to the ghetto. Within a few days, however, Felix, uncertain what to do, returned to the ghetto, too—and there found his mother, sister, father, and grandparents, as well as Sender and Sarah, all still alive.

Soon authorities closed Ghetto Two (Slobodka). Some residents there who had family in the other ghetto and who paid off some policemen were allowed to change ghettos before that happened. So Felix's Frejdowicz grandparents, his uncle Kushka and aunt Lina, his aunt Fania and uncle Berko with their infant son, Haim, and his aunt Lisa and uncle Mula with their three children, all crowded in with their family that was already there.

The remaining Ghetto Two residents were taken to Auschwitz-Birkenau.[80] Meanwhile Felix, along with many others in the remaining ghetto, was put to work for the Germans. Felix was bringing home a little food for his family, at least, but he thought continually about how to escape and improve his survival chances. Felix's father refused to work, not wanting to help the Germans in any way. He was depressed all the time, Felix said.

In December 1942 Felix's family was ordered to join others being transported from the ghetto to a transit camp known as Kielbasin. A German who was commandant of one of the two Grodno ghettos, Kurt Wiese, came personally to the family's apartment to implement the order.[81] Felix's uncle Sender showed Wiese papers proving he was an engineer, and Wiese (later convicted and given a life sentence as a war criminal, thanks in part to Felix's testimony) allowed him and his immediate family to stay. But the rest were taken to the synagogue so they could be "sent" (which meant marching many hours in bitter snowy weather) to the concentration camp Kielbasin.

The camp was everything Felix had feared—filthy, cold, crowded. "I understood instinctively that Kielbasin was a stop on the way to death," he said.[82]

Within a few days, a Jewish policeman accepted a bribe from Felix (a watch and a loaf of bread) to tell him how he might escape. Felix's family did not want him to chance it, but he thought he had no other option. So his parents bade him a tearful farewell. Then, as wagons that had delivered bread to the camp were leaving, Felix jumped on the last one and rode it out of the camp, as he had been instructed to do by the policeman.

Fifteen minutes outside the camp, German soldiers on motorcycles came up to the line of seven wagons and ordered all to return to camp. Instead of going back with them, Felix jumped off his wagon, rolled into a ditch full of snow, and buried himself in it to stay hidden. From there he made his way back to the Grodno Ghetto and found that his family was still there—Sender and Sarah, Kushka and Lina, Lisa and Mula, and Grandma and Grandpa Frejdowicz. But Felix now had no legitimate identity papers to be in the ghetto, so he had to hide when police came to check papers each night. The rest of Felix's family who had stayed in Kielbasin were ordered back to the ghetto on January 1, 1943. Felix said they were among the several hundred people who had hidden to avoid being transported to the Treblinka death camp.

Despite the temporary reprieve of a return to the ghetto, Felix said it now was clear that the Germans were intent on murdering all the Jews. All illusions were gone. So while Felix's family members dreamed up escape possibilities, they also created hiding places in their ghetto building. Felix and his family at this point lived with fourteen other families in one building, and they created a false partition in an attic, behind which up to sixty people could hide. They also found what they thought was a much more secure crawl space above a kitchen. It had space for eight and was reachable by a ladder. A trapdoor to that crawl space could be closed and locked from the inside. Felix was chosen to be one of the eight to hide in this apparently more secure space.

In the middle of January, the Germans sealed off the ghetto and ordered all but essential workers—such as Sender, Kushka, and their families—to come to the synagogue for deportation. The people in Felix's building quickly moved to their hiding spaces—all but Felix's grandfather, Nahum Frejdowicz, and three small children, who could not be kept quiet in a hiding place. Grandpa Frejdowicz volunteered to stay with those children, two of whom were his grandchildren. In fact, he stayed with them to the end, protecting them as best he could as he and they were sent to their deaths. Felix said his grandfather knew they would be killed and could have gone into hiding, too. But he did not want the children to feel they were abandoned. So he decided to stay with them, even if only for the few hours before they would be murdered. "He's my biggest tragic hero," Felix said with tears in his eyes as he recounted this story.[83]

Two of the eight people hiding with Felix were his aunt Fania and her husband, Berko, who had left their one-year-old boy Haim with Grandpa Frejdowicz. But after a day or two in the crawl space, Fania was desperate to know what was happening outside and whether her child was still there. Eventually, Felix decided that he would leave the hiding place to see what he could learn about what had happened below.

"Fania and Berko were scared to go out, but I couldn't stand Fania's suffering so I decided to go out," Felix said.

Because the ladder was gone, he slid down a pipe after the trapdoor was opened. He searched the downstairs of the house but found it empty. When he tried to get back into the crawl space, however, he was unable to get back up the pipe, despite his best efforts and help from those above. Finally he quit trying and went to the attic to hide in the less secure location.

A day or so later Germans entered the house. The people in the attic could barely breathe for fear of being found. But the searchers never got to the false partition. When, a day or so later, after the deportations stopped, Felix and others ventured out, they were shocked to discover that the people in the crawl space had all been found and taken away as part of what became known as the "Transport of Ten Thousand" from the Grodno Ghetto. Felix, unable to get back into the crawl space, had been spared again. German authorities, Felix later learned, had been led to the crawl space by Isser Schwartz, the same Jewish policeman whom Sender and Kushka had bribed so he would divert any attempt to find the place.

Several of the people hidden in the crawl space managed to get away from the transport later and return to the ghetto, including Felix's uncle Berko and aunt Fania. The two had become separated, and while Fania was alone she went to the home of Jan Puchalski and Anna Puchalska. They had been the caretakers of the rural summer cottages of the Frejdowicz family. But Fania, anxious to be with Berko, stayed with the Puchalskis just one night before returning to the ghetto. As Felix listened to Fania describe Anna's willingness to help, he decided he would go to the Puchalski house if he ever needed a place to hide.

That need came soon. Felix had acquired new identification papers and was assigned with a work crew to do some remodeling work at the home of Heinz Errelis, the head of the Gestapo office for the whole Białystok district who later was convicted as a war criminal in the same trial with Kurt Wiese, overseer of the Grodno Ghetto. While Felix slipped off one morning from the work site to buy a bottle of vodka to take back to the ghetto, word came that the ghetto was being sealed for another deportation. Learning of this from his fellow workers, Felix quickly took off walking to look for a hiding place to avoid being taken back and sent to a death camp. When the woman who sold him the vodka refused to hide him, he returned to the Errelis house, but by then the work crew had been taken away. After another failed effort or two to hide, he made it to the home of the nanny who had watched Sender's children for a week or so before returning them because she was too fearful of being caught.

The nanny allowed Felix to sleep in the barn for the night. "And I was scared of whom in the barn? Of the cow. She had horns," Felix told us. The next morning the nanny gave Felix some porridge and sent him on his way. Without her help, he said, he may not have made it. From there he headed to Losossna, the village where Anna Puchalska lived. It took him until late morning to walk there, but eventually he knocked on her door.

"I had nothing," he told us, "nothing. I didn't have a penny on me. I said, 'I just want one night. That's enough.' She said, 'What do you want to do afterward?' I said, 'I just want to go to the partisans afterward. I don't know where.' I was talking nonsense. It was cold with snow up to the knees maybe. She said, 'You won't go any place. You stay with me. You will be with us.' I said, 'Do you understand what may happen if they find me?' She said, 'I know exactly what happens. God sent you.'"

That's what Anna Puchalska believed. "Extraordinary," Felix told us. "It just shows you a gesture of somebody doing something that could endanger her family, including five children. I didn't know that my grandmother helped her. She never talked about it." But Anna now was willing to take the risk of having her whole family murdered if he were found. Even decades later, Felix Zandman had trouble understanding how she could have risked so much. "Those people who helped me, I just have no words for it. Probably saints from God. How a mother could have the courage, the guts, the inspiration to risk the life of her five children. Herself, maybe. But five children?"

He said he once was asked by a television interviewer whether he would have done what Anna Puchalska did. "I said, alone, a bachelor, maybe I would have considered it. Not sure—but consider. But as a father to five children? What gives me the right to risk my five children? But she did it. She had a big heart, a big heart." And she was wise, too. For instance, she told her children that when they went to confession at their Catholic church, they must never mention anything about the family hiding Jews in case the priest might also be secretly working for the Germans.

Anna's eagerness to help for the long haul when Felix arrived at the Puchalski house was not his only surprise that day. As he was falling asleep that evening in a small room in the house, his uncle Sender burst in, having narrowly escaped an attempt on his life that day by Kurt Wiese, who fired a submachine gun at Sender as he fled from groups being lined up for transport. As he ran from Wiese, Sender found a temporary hiding place in an apartment building occupied by a member of the *Judenrät* who was a Jewish liaison with German authorities, Mottl Bass, and his wife, Goldie. At Sender's request, Mottl went back to the lineup area from which Sender had escaped and obtained a gold piece from Sender's brother Kushka—who, unlike Sender, had been sent to the survivors' line that morning. Sender wanted the money in case he had to bribe someone. He then told Mottl about his plan to run to the Puchalski home, and he offered him and Goldie the opportunity to do the same as a reward for bringing him the gold from Kushka. By then, Sender knew that his wife, Sarah, and their children had been taken away, and he suspected they either were—or soon would be—dead.

Anna moved Sender and Felix to the attic to avoid not just nosy neighbors who might drop in but also the curiosity of her own small children. Within a day Mottl and his wife, Goldie, arrived at the Puchalski house along with two others, Borka Shulkes who, like Mottl, had been a liaison member of the *Judenrät* and Meir Zamoszczanski, a Jewish policeman.

The crowd was too big for Anna's comfort. She sent all of them to stay in the potato cellar behind the house. But that was no long-term answer. It was thirty yards from the house, and anyone searching for hidden Jews would look there first.

They needed a different hiding place, and Sender had an idea. He talked the Puchalskis into letting them dig a small cellar—a hole, really—under a corner of the house where Jan and Anna's bedroom was located. They cut a small part of the floor away under one of the beds to make a trapdoor that Anna could use to lower food in and to take out the bucket used for human waste.

So in mid-February 1943, Felix and five others descended into the hole. There was room for three people to lie down and three to sit up, though they were all tight next to each other. It was, Felix told us, "pitch dark." The only occasional light came from a small petrol lamp they would light to see their food.

The first few days in the pit were horrible. There simply were too many people, and Anna Puchalska was convinced it would not work like this. But Shulkes and Zamoszczanski had possible hiding places elsewhere, so they left. Despite Anna's nervousness, Sender talked her into letting four people stay in the hole—him, Felix, and the Basses. But they had to be silent any time people were in the house and when the smallest Puchalski children (Wladek and Wanda, ages three and one, respectively) were not asleep so they would not know about them and inadvertently give away the hiding place to visitors.

When the four of them settled back in, Sender did something that Felix came to understand helped to save them. He established rules. Indeed, Felix told us he gives Sender credit for their ability to survive together in an astonishingly cramped place, a model of which now is on display at the National Liberty Museum in Philadelphia. "He was such a strong and intelligent man. First of all he set rules, not to fight. This is very interesting. I was trying to analyze how intelligent he was. He told us right away that we don't know how long we'll be here. If we don't have rules which we obey we'll get crazy, and we'll fight with each other. We didn't fight, and we came out from the hiding place as friends."

Sender's first rule was no sex. Sender was thirty-two years old, Mottl and his wife were in their late twenties, and Felix was fifteen. Next, he said, there would be a strict schedule of switching places every two hours. Third, he made a rule about food. He and Goldie would alternately divide what was sent down.

"The one who did not do the dividing," Felix said, "got to choose what portion either Sender and I or Mottl and Goldie would get. You have to have some regulations if people want to live together. There is no way out. And you have to have some civility and some decency to live together. The law is not enough."

After that, it was a matter of getting used to the lice, the worms, the dampness (which stayed despite some straw on the floor), the filth, the smell, the crowd, the long, long hours in the dark. And the uncertainty. Sender told them to plan on being there for a long, long time, but no one knew for sure.

We asked Felix whether they got to leave the hole and take a shower. He laughed. "What was a shower? There was no shower in the house. In those seventeen months, we went out maybe four or five times. Every few months. It was very complicated to get out because of the kids. So at night we would go out to the kitchen, and there Janova would bring a very big tub and put hot water inside it, and we'd sit in it. My uncle, with a bucket of hot water, would wash me and I would wash him and then go down to the hole. Once we had to go down fast, wet," to avoid being caught. While they bathed, Jan and the three oldest children, Sabina, Irena, and Krystyna, were assigned to lookout duties outside.

Once a German officer came to the property with a dog, and this started the

Puchalski's dog, Muszka, barking. Just before the man got to the house, Anna scattered pepper on the floor and around the outside wall by the pit so as to throw off the dog's sense of smell. It worked. The German left without discovering anything unusual.

At regular intervals, Mottl Bass gave Anna some twenty-dollar gold pieces to use to buy food—gold he said one of Goldie's uncles had given to her before he died. Anna also picked up old newspapers, and to avoid suspicion, because she was illiterate, she told people she wanted to wrap food in them. The real purpose was to let the people in the hole know what was happening in the world.

As time went on, day by day, week by week, eventually month by month, a daily rhythm of sorts developed. It gave the people in the hole time to daydream about freedom, about the family members they had lost, about what was happening outside, but it was hard to talk about such intense topics. So mostly they spoke to each other only about mundane matters. But Sender, an engineer, decided to use some of their hiding time to teach young Felix some math. We asked Felix how this process worked.

"He talked to me," he said. "He just talked to me. I remember he taught me trigonometry by heart. That's very difficult to do. Then he would give me some formulas. For me it wasn't difficult at all. For him it was difficult. Imagine how he would have to construct this in his mind, how to pass this information [on] to me without a book. From time to time we had a piece of paper and a pencil. From time to time, maybe once a week, we'd light a little candle and he would examine me. And I'd just write it down. But it was 90 percent by heart."

After the war, when Felix went back to school, he found he could look at long equations on a blackboard in class and quickly come up with the answer without having to use a pencil, slide rule, or anything else. It impressed his teacher, who wanted him to study math in college, but Felix had other ideas.

More than halfway through the seventeen-month stay, in February 1944, the number of people in the hole jumped from four to five. They were joined by Esther Hajdamak-Shapira, the Jewish wife of a non-Jew who had been helpful to Anna in providing for those she was hiding. Esther's husband, in fact, once provided dental equipment that allowed Felix to pull a painful abscessed tooth out of Sender's mouth.

Esther's husband had been arrested when the Germans discovered he was working for the *Armia Krajowa*. Esther had been hiding with her mother-in-law, but she threw her out when her son was arrested. Esther had learned about the Puchalski hiding place from her husband and showed up seeking to be hidden there, too.

"Thank God, thank God, he had told her about that hiding place in case of trouble," Felix said. "And she came. All of a sudden this trapdoor opens up and she drops in. And we are five."

But the group adjusted to her, and Esther quickly adjusted to the group's rules for discipline. It turned out there were no problems adding another person except for having to live in even tighter quarters. For one thing, the people in the hole knew that the Soviets were beginning to drive the Germans back to the west. Eventually, they hoped, they might get as far as Grodno and Losossna and liberate them.

But first things got worse. As the Germans retreated in July 1944, a unit of the German army gathered near the Puchalski house. For a few days, with Germans in and around the house, there was no possibility for Anna even to bring food or remove the excrement bucket. And on July 16, the worst nightmare of the people in the hole materialized. Anna and her family were forced to leave the house, which was taken over by the German soldiers. But she had the foresight to speak loudly enough about what was happening so that the people in the hole had some idea something unusual was happening.

German soldiers came and used the house as a place to sleep. Mottl, who spoke German well, listened to their plans. Then Sender slipped out of the hole briefly to get a better sense of their predicament. They decided to escape the next night and run toward a small flour mill at the end of a nearby river. But they had to concoct a believable story if they were caught once they had managed to get out of the house. Mottl and Goldie had good fake papers, as did Esther. Sender would pretend to be Esther's husband and Felix their child. If caught, they would tell the Germans they were running from the Soviets.

As the evening light was finally dying in the summer sky about 9:30, they waited in the otherwise empty house for dark and their chance to get out. But just then a German soldier came to the house and went to sleep on a couch just outside the bedroom under which they were hiding. Soon, however, Sender heard him snoring, so they quickly and quietly—it took only about a minute— left the house through a window and began to move away from it. Then they realized they were in the middle of a battle, with shells flying around.

When they had walked just a few dozen yards, they heard a voice telling them to stop and give a password. A flashlight shone on the five, and they raised their hands in surrender. After much discussion with German officers, who were frustrated at having to deal with people wandering around in a battle zone, the five were ordered to spend the night behind a nearby hill. The next morning they were interrogated again, but eventually they were told to get out of the area and not come back on pain of being shot. The Germans never figured out that the five were Jews who had been hiding thirty yards from the place they were arrested. Goldie and Sender went to see a Polish woman whom Goldie's family knew, and though the woman refused to hide them, she pointed them to a vacant nearby cottage and said she would try to bring them food. Which she did. Later another man brought them food, too, which they paid for with their wedding rings. Even later German soldiers came to the cottage, being convinced the five were Polish non-Jews. Those soldiers, too, brought food for the five refugees.

They stayed in the cottage for a few more days until, finally, the Soviets drove the Germans from the area. Felix and the others then returned to the Puchalski house, but the family was nowhere around. So they headed back to Grodno, where they were met by a Soviet patrol. The leader, showing disdain for them, demanded to see their papers.

Sender said, "We're Jews. We don't have papers."[84]

They were taken to the Grodno prison, where a Soviet soldier who was Jewish apologized to them for the behavior of the patrol leader. Felix and the others went back to the family home on Brygidzka Street and found it empty. Over the next few days, other hidden Jews arrived back in Grodno, including Anna Schiff, whose story is told in another chapter of this book. Anna gave Felix a quilt.

"After the war we had nothing," Felix told us. "But somehow Anna recovered some clothes, and she gave me and my uncle a bedcover, a quilt. And I used it for ten years probably. When I went to France as a student I still used it."

Felix walked around Grodno that first day back, meeting a few other friends who survived. They told their survival stories to each other. And when he returned to the house on Brygidzka Street that evening, there was Anna Puchalska, who had feared Felix and the others hiding under her house had been caught. She and her family, driven out by the Germans, had retreated to a family member's home some miles away before finally coming back to their own house, which by then was empty. So she went to Grodno to see what she could learn about Felix and his companions.

By then Felix Zandman was seventeen years old. He weighed ninety pounds. So he moved back with Anna and spent a week or so eating and getting his stamina and health back.

The Soviet Union annexed eastern Poland again, and with it Grodno, so the Basses moved to Białystok in Poland. Later Felix joined them for a time. Still later he decided to be smuggled out of Poland so he could move to a kibbutz in what would become Israel. But a friend, whom Sender sent to find Felix, stopped him and eventually convinced him not to go.

After the War

Felix did some gun smuggling for the Haganah, the Jewish paramilitary organization that would become the basis of the Israeli army. He did some currency speculating, and some moving around, even at one point ending up in Gdansk to help run a bakery that Sender had bought. It was while he was in Gdansk, where many of the local residents were Germans, that he was nearly overcome with a desire to kill Germans.

"I could have killed Germans," he told us. "I had no problem with doing that. I was ready to do it. I swore to me that I would do it. However, looking at women, children, some old German people, I just couldn't do it."

Instead of doing that, however, he eventually got what he called his "vengeance in the form of victory over the Nazis" by surviving, by creating a family, by becoming a successful businessman and, in various ways, helping Israel economically by creating four thousand jobs making products for export, and by inventing special systems for Israeli tanks.

While living in Gdansk, Felix started taking college classes, at Sender's insistence. He even became, briefly, the president of the Jewish Students' Union of Gdansk. In that position, he received an invitation—with visas—to be part of a group of sixty Jewish students to go to a conference in France. He and others used the opportunity to escape Poland permanently.

When Felix arrived in Paris, he once wrote, "I felt I was breathing clean air for the first time in my life."[85]

The rest of Felix Zandman's life story is described in his own book, *Never the Last Journey*. In brief, he obtained a Ph.D. in physics from the University of Paris, Sorbonne. He eventually emigrated to the United States, invented a technology used for stress measurements in airplanes, later invented a new technology for electronics components that are used in high-tech electronics, and with a few thousand dollars founded Vishay Intertechnology Inc., which today has plants in several countries. It employs twenty-eight thousand people, including four thousand in Israel, a country in which he holds citizenship today, along with his American citizenship.

But the Holocaust never left him. "It's small things," he told us. "You wouldn't believe it. I go to the toilet, for example, in a hotel, and I think, 'How many Jews could I hide in this toilet stall?' It's always there."

Every day he would remember the hole where he hid from the Germans. "It is always with you?" we asked him.

"Yes," he said. "Always."

A good way in which this experience stayed with him has been his continued connection to Anna and Jan Puchalski's children, of whom four out of five were still alive when we did the interviews for this book. Felix was in regular contact with them and supported them in various ways.

"They have a good economic life," he said. "I am satisfied it is."

It has been the Holocaust, Felix discovered, that has motivated him every day. He told us this story: "I sat one day with a writer, who asked me, 'What is driving you?' I didn't answer because I had never asked myself a question like that. He said immediately, 'The Holocaust is, for sure.' Then I started to think about it, what is driving me, and in fact it is that.

"I should have been dead since 1943, many times dead. And every day I live is a God-given day. I feel I should accomplish something. Accomplish what? And for whom? I want to do it for my people, which is the Jewish people. I had this discussion with a director for TV, and he was continuously looking for me to say that I seek vengeance. But I don't. I seek victory, and maybe that is my vengeance."

When Felix testified at the war crimes trial of Kurt Wiese in Cologne, Germany, in the 1960s, he said, he was surprised to discover that "this guy is a *gornisht*, he's nothing, a nothing. He's a louse." At the trial, Felix said, Wiese started to lie, saying, "I didn't do anything. I didn't kill anyone. I wasn't there."

Here was a man who, to young Felix Zandman, "was a god of death. You understand? An omni-powerful devil. He believes in this. He has the power. He believes he has to kill me and kill everybody. Then I see he can't even stand up for his ideas. It probably wasn't his ideas anyhow. I just looked at him while he was lying and said the hell with that."

So Felix Zandman is the last known survivor of the people who spent time in the pit under the Puchalski house—with the possible exception of Esther Hajdamak-Shapira, with whom Felix lost touch after the war. He has lived with some guilt, but he also has lived with the knowledge that he has achieved amazing things—including becoming a husband to Ruta, the father of three children, Gisele, Ariele, and Marc, and the grandfather of nine. He has received countless honors, been awarded dozens of scientific patents, and employed thousands of people around the world, including in his beloved Israel.

Meeting Two Puchalski Sisters

Using a translator, we spoke with two of Anna Puchalska's daughters, Krystyna Maciejewska and Sabina Kazimierczyk, in Gdansk, where they both live. We asked them why their family members risked their lives to save Jews.

"Felix's grandmother was very, very good to us," Sabina said, "and our families were tied together. When we were children we played with each other."

But did their mother have the right to jeopardize their lives to save other people's lives? Krystyna responded this way: "We children at that time had no rights. The families decided, and that's how it was. But we had no qualms. Our family was very religious, and these were people who needed help." At this, Krystyna began crying. Later she said it has been hard for her to think about this time of war because it almost inevitably has made her cry. Among the memories she disliked dredging up: "The Germans would induce children with chocolate to get them to talk. But we were very tough. And our mother told us never to talk to them."

Sabina added this memory: "Our house was in the forest. And not only did we have to worry about the Germans who were constantly coming and going, but there were a lot of hooligans who looked in our window, and they weren't such nice people. If they'd found Jews hiding there, they probably would have killed them. No question. They would have killed them."

Both daughters clearly expressed pride in their mother's actions. Sabina, in fact, described a situation after the war in which a neighbor in Gdansk learned that her family had saved Jews. He made a small noose and, showing it to her, said, "You don't belong here, you belong in Israel." At that point, Sabina retorted to the man, "I'm very proud that my mother could give everybody a hand."

If these sisters had the chance to do something similar to what their mother did, we asked, would they do it? Krystyna answered, "There hasn't been an occasion to test me. But I think I would do it. We have it in us what our mother taught us. It is in us."

Four Rescuers

When we were in Poland conducting interviews for this book, we met several of the rescuers who helped to save people we previously had interviewed in the United States. But in four instances, we interviewed individuals who either had outlived the Jews they helped or no longer were in touch with family members of those survivors. We spoke with Maria Nowak, Jozef Biesaga, Jozef Mironiuk, and Pawel Roszkowski at the Galicia Jewish Museum in Kraków, in each case using a translator. Here are their stories.

Maria Bozek Nowak

It was the winter of 1942–1943, and Maria Bozek's good friend and classmate Helena Goldstein was in serious trouble. Maria knew just what she had to do for her Jewish friend. Helena, who had been confined to the Kraków Ghetto since it was created in March 1941, already had lost her father, her mother, and a brother, all of whom the Germans had deported and murdered. Now twenty-one-year-old Helena was in the ghetto alone, depressed, not eating, and frightened.

"After the second deportation," Maria told us, "I had a friend who had a Jewish girlfriend in the ghetto. Somehow he managed to get into the ghetto. So I asked him to check to see whether Helena was all right. He came to me later and said Helena was in very bad shape, physically and mentally, because her mother and older brother had been taken on the second transport. She still had one older brother living inside the ghetto with his fiancée, but they were not living with Helena. So Helena was pretty much alone. And she didn't want to eat. I decided that because Helena was alone, I needed to take her out of the ghetto.

"So I contacted my friend with the Jewish girlfriend in the ghetto. We knew Helena was working outside the ghetto and thus could leave it. This was quite good. Second, we knew she needed a Kennkarte (or identification paper). That meant we had to buy a false one for her. But we could afford to buy only an empty one on the black market. She needed more than one document, such as a birth certificate and a baptism certificate. It was not enough to have only one Kennkarte. You needed as many documents as you could get to prove that you are who you are and you are not a Jew. So we bought an empty one and told Helena she needed to take pictures of herself and send them to us by this Polish boy when he came to the ghetto."

175

Maria was taking charge. In a pattern that was to mark her relationship with Helena until the war ended and both women had survived, Maria chose not to wait until she was asked to help. Instead, she assessed the situation and moved quickly to do what she thought was necessary, even at the risk of her own life.

"So we got this false Kennkarte through our friend, who had contacts and knew where to buy it. But Helena needed a new identity," Maria said.

Again, Maria did not wait but moved to find an answer. "I decided to give Helena my own name. And I gave her some of my own documents. And if she were asked for other documents she was to say that all other documents burned or were stolen."

Maria Bozek Nowak

So Helena went through the secretive process of becoming Maria Bozek. "Helena had pictures taken and the Kennkarte was ready. One day before she was to escape, she smuggled out her luggage. But there was a problem of where to keep her after she escaped because she couldn't stay with my family. We were living around many railroad workers who were friends and many of them knew Helena from before the war. There was a risk that someone would tell, and it would be dangerous." Besides, having Helena around would mean there were two Maria Bozeks in the same dwelling.

This was not a problem that Maria asked Helena to solve. Again, she found a solution for her. Maria elected "to take her to the place of a Polish friend, Roman Bartel, who was living alone. When Helena came out of the ghetto the next day to go to work, I was waiting for her, and I grabbed her by the arm. I took her armband [that identified her as a Jew]. It was winter, and Jews were not allowed to wear fur on their coats. So the first thing I did was to put a piece of fur on her neck so people wouldn't think she was Jewish.

"We knew that Helena could not stay in Kraków because Kraków was too small for two people with the same identity. Also, many people knew Helena. So we had two friends, also Jewish, who previously were living in Kraków. They were living in Warsaw under false papers. So we wrote to ask for help for Helena, our mutual friend. One of these Jewish friends came from Warsaw to Kraków and took Helena back to Warsaw with her."

Helena and Maria had been friends for many years. They met as young girls in school when they were assigned to sit next to one another in the classroom. Maria's parents, Antony and Francesca Bozek, had taught her and her younger siblings, Edmund and Alexandra, to treat all people with equal respect, Maria told us.

When Maria and Helena graduated from high school, or gymnasium, in 1938, at age eighteen (Maria was born January 22, 1920, in Kraków), they and a group of friends—about half of whom were Jews—all signed a letter promising, in a burst of youthful enthusiasm and optimism about the future, to meet on the main public square of Kraków at 8 p.m. on July 1, 1943, for a reunion. By that date, however, Helena was struggling to stay alive.

Maria told us that because many Jews in Kraków were not Orthodox and, thus, were generally quite acculturated into Polish culture, it was not unusual for non-Jews to have Jewish friends. "Even before the war, Helena took me to a concert at her synagogue for a Kol Nidre service. I liked it very much and I remember especially the cantors."[86] Maria knew about antisemitism but said she wasn't aware of much of it among her friends.

After graduating from high school, Maria and Helena began studies at different universities (Maria was studying mathematics), but they stayed in close touch. "We were great friends. Helena was invited often to Christmas celebrations with my family, and I was invited to spend time with this Jewish family at Jewish holidays. During the first years of the war in Kraków, we were helping each other. But in March 1941 the Germans established a ghetto here in Kraków. I said to Helena, 'Don't go to the ghetto. We will find a way to hide you here outside.' But Helena didn't want to leave her parents. She knew they needed to go to the ghetto. I understood this."

In June 1942 the first deportation from the Kraków Ghetto to the Belzec death camp occurred. "Helena's father was sent. At that time Germans were saying they were deporting Jews to a work camp in Ukraine. And people believed this. But my father was working on the trains as a conductor or engineer. He had a friend who worked on the deportation trains. And he learned quickly that those trains were not going to Ukraine. Rather, they were going to some forest and coming back empty. So soon everyone knew what was happening.

"And when there was a second deportation from the Kraków Ghetto, everybody knew what was going on. [The second deportation from the Kraków Ghetto to Belzec occurred in October 1942.] Not everybody wanted to believe this, but it was common knowledge. In this deportation, Helena's mother was on the list. But her oldest son, Helena's brother, decided that he would go instead of his mother. So he went. The mother was hiding in a secret place in the ghetto. The mother heard Germans in the ghetto saying this place would be made free of the Jews. So she decided that she wanted to leave, and she went from her hiding place to the transport. At this time Helena was working outside the ghetto most of the time. People doing such work were pretty much safe," at least temporarily.

So in two transports, Helena lost her father, her brother, and her mother.

Once Helena got to Warsaw, friends of Maria helped her get a job doing public address announcements in a railway station. It was a perfect fit for her because she was fluent not just in Polish but also in German. But, Maria said, one day there was a small party in the office where Helena worked. People were drinking and having a good time. Helena joined in the fun by singing, in Polish, an anti-German song. But then she realized she had left the public address microphone on, and the song was broadcast into the whole railway station. Helena had to flee.

After that, Maria told us, Helena got a job as a housekeeper. "She soon found out that the people for whom she was working were members of the Polish underground home army. But just before the Warsaw Uprising in August 1944, they knew they had to run away because Germans were very close to this house and were figuring out the people there were members of the underground. So Helena knew she had to change her identity. One way to do this was to have a false marriage so [as to] get a different name. She did this. Her new name was Maria Szymczak. And then she never again saw her supposed husband. But she had no job, so she had to go to a German unemployment office, and they sent her to another city, Hirschberg, in Germany, to do forced labor."

From then until January 1945, Maria had no contact with Helena and worried constantly about where she was and what she was doing. Then she received a letter from Helena under the name Maria Szymczak that assured Maria she was all right and was working in a laundry. Once again, Maria took the initiative.

"I decided to send her some things. So my mother cooked some food and I had a nice new green beautiful dress, which wasn't easy to buy. We needed special favors to get it. But I decided to send this dress to Helena. So we sent this package. Then the Russian offensive started, and I was afraid that this package was destroyed in the bombing. We had no contact until April, but in April Helena came to Kraków wearing my green dress."

Helena elected to stay in Kraków with her one surviving brother, who also had returned to Kraków with his wife. Helena and her brother managed to get back part of the apartment in which they had lived before the war.

With the Germans defeated, Helena then had to decide who she was going to be. She chose to return to her original first name and to give up the name Maria. But she kept her false last name, Szymczak. And she and Maria again were close friends with frequent contact. Indeed, Maria was head of a pharmacy in Kraków, and in 1981 she hired Helena as an accountant there. But one night in 1986, Maria got a call telling her to come quickly to the hospital to see her friend Helena. "But when I got there she was already dead. So we were together in the beginning and at the end."

We asked Maria why she thought their friend Roman Bartel agreed to risk his life to give Helena a hiding place. To Maria, that decision was no mystery. "We were very close friends and he wanted to help. Second, he had a Jewish girlfriend in the ghetto so since he was helping her it was no different for him to help another Jew."

We also asked Maria why she put her own life in danger on behalf of Helena. She said, "Helena was like family. She was a friend and I wanted to help her, and there was no need for her to say anything to me about it. She was like a sister for me. I knew my life was in danger by helping Helena, but all life was in danger at this time. In the winter, if there was snow lying on the street next to your house, you could be killed for this, for not sweeping it off."

Another question we asked Maria was what people should be taught so that more of them will behave in the way she did on behalf of Helena.

"The most important thing," she said, "is to teach that there is no difference between people. Under our skin we're all the same. If you understand this, you understand that you will do whatever is possible to help other people."

Maria and her late husband, Alfonse Nowak, who died in 1987, had a son and a daughter, and Maria has two grandchildren, a boy and a girl.

Jozef Biesaga

Dawid Nassan, carrying only a Jewish prayer book, was naked, frightened, and exhausted when he showed up at the farm home of Jozef Biesaga and his family in 1942 seeking shelter. Dawid had escaped from a Jewish cemetery in nearby Skala, where he had watched German troops shoot scores of Jews—people whose bodies he then was asked to check for jewelry.

"Dawid and his family, plus some friends, were caught by the Germans, and the Germans locked them in a building near a Jewish cemetery in Skala," Jozef told us. "They kept those Jews in this locked place for a few hours and were planning to shoot them in the evening. They ordered them to undress. Dawid was chosen by the Germans to check the bodies and clean this place, but his wife said to him, 'Run away, run away,' so he ran. The Germans were shooting at him as he ran, but they missed him, and he escaped, naked, and came to our house." He survived the war by hiding with the Biesaga family for thirty-seven months.

The Germans had ordered Polish firefighters from a nearby town to dig the graves in that cemetery for the Jewish bodies. Jozef said these firefighters were aware later that Dawid was going to run away but they chose not to stop him. The firefighters watched as the Germans shot Jews, who tumbled into the graves they had dug. "But," Jozef told us, "the father of Dawid somehow was only wounded. The Polish firefighters tried to help him and take him from this grave. But the Germans ordered them to put him back in the ground, so they buried him alive."

Jozef, born March 9, 1931, outside of Kraków, was eight and a half years old when the war began. Dawid was thirty-six years old when he came to hide with the Biesaga family, which included Jozef, his parents, Jozef and Stefania, an older brother, and two younger sisters. The family farm was in the village of Smardzowice, north of Kraków and just south of Skala.

It was not surprising that Dawid would appear at the Biesaga home seeking refuge. After all, Jozef said, "my family knew Dawid's family before the war." Dawid's wife was a seamstress in Skala, and Dawid bought and sold horses and was in the meat business, too. "We had a lot of contact with this Jewish family. We needed each other to survive."

Indeed, Dawid and his family were regular visitors to the Biesaga home before the war, and "a few times we would give them shelter for the night, even in the first years of the war."

But Dawid's desperate appearance at the Biesaga farm after his cemetery escape and his request to hide there caused an immediate family rift. "When he came," Jozef told us, "my mother did not want to help him by keeping him in our house because she was afraid. She said to my father, 'Are you stupid? You have your own children and you're risking their life to save this one person.' But my father had a strong belief in Christ and was a strong Catholic, and he felt that there was no other choice. He had to help. There was no discussion. So we did it. When Dawid came, I was about eleven years old, but I had to grow up fast."

Jozef said that his father's word was final in the family, but he said that he, too, agreed then and agreed decades later when he recounted the story that "there was no other choice but to help because this is what Christ taught." Jozef explained

Jozef Biesaga

his own willingness to help, this way: "My father raised me as a human being." Indeed, we asked Jozef whether he had heard anti-Jewish propaganda when he was growing up. "Yes, I heard antisemitic things growing up. But in the true church I learned that we must love others no matter who they are."

Once the decision was made to hide Dawid, the family had to figure out the safest place. They created a special room for him. "Next to the barn," Jozef explained, "was a small shed for tools and next to the shed was a doghouse. The entrance to the hiding place was through the doghouse. The dogs knew Dawid so they wouldn't bark every time he went by them to get to his hiding place. The dog was very mean, and everyone was afraid of him. There also was a second hiding place in case of an emergency. In the barn there was a big mound of hay on the second floor. And it was prepared in case of danger he could in one move make this mound of hay collapse and hide him."

Naturally, Jozef's parents created strict rules because of Dawid's presence. "My parents told us we could not tell anyone about Dawid, and if we did tell anyone we're all going to die. My youngest sister was taught to call Dawid not Dawid but Kitek." In addition to the immediate Biesaga family on the farm, Jozef's grandmother lived next door with one of Jozef's uncles and one of his cousins, and all of them knew where Dawid was hiding.

Over the time of Dawid's hiding with the Biesaga family, Jozef was appointed to do various things to care for him and keep him undetected. "Every day I had to bring him food. He was hiding in the stables, which was twenty-five meters from the main building. But I had to take it during the night so it wouldn't be obvious that I was taking baskets to the stables. A second very important duty was that every day I had to spy on the Germans to check where they and the police are. In case the Germans were in our village that day, I had to go tell Dawid to run and hide in the forest."

From peers, Jozef learned various skills to help keep Dawid safe. "I had a friend my age in a nearby village. The Germans came to that village one day, looking for some family who was hiding a Polish underground soldier. This ten-year-old boy directed them the wrong way, so he was like a hero to me."

Another task given to Jozef was to scout out places in the forest where strawberries and other edibles were growing so he would be able to tell Dawid where to find them if he needed them. But, Jozef told us, "often there was nothing to eat. Sometimes my father would take the horse and go out and do work with him and get us something to eat. Often people just ate what they could find in the forest, like mushrooms. But very often there was nothing to eat."

Jozef said that most of the time that Dawid hid with the Biesagas, his life was repetitious and remarkably boring. "Dawid had nothing to do all day. The only thing he had was a prayer book, and he prayed often, but besides that, nothing. For me it seemed funny that the prayer book started from the back. He was a very religious man. In fact, for Yom Kippur he fasted, even though we didn't have much to eat to start with."

Day after day, year after year, Dawid hid and the Biesaga family protected him until, finally, the Germans were defeated. We asked Jozef whether, after the war, his neighbors were critical of what his family had done when they learned about Dawid.

"No," he said. In fact, "our neighbors knew something was going on even during the war. They knew we might be hiding a Jew. But no one mentioned it. We had a strong connection with people in the village and solidarity. So no one betrayed us. After the war, no one asked us accusingly, 'What have you done?'"

Even before the war, Dawid was a poor man, Jozef said. "They had just a small piece of land, and after the war Dawid said to my father, 'I will give you this land.' But my father said, 'Are you stupid? I don't want such a prize because God will give me a prize in heaven.' But after the war, on Christian holidays, Dawid would come and give us small gifts."

Dawid eventually moved to Israel, where he lived until his death. Jozef said Dawid did not send money to the Biesagas from Israel, though he stayed in touch and once sent Jozef a pair of military boots.

Jozef's father died in 1972 and his mother in 1976. We asked him if he thinks of them as heroes. "Yes, I think my parents were heroes because they risked their lives to save another's life. I think of myself partly as a hero because the heritage of my father to help other people still is living in me."

Jozef spent much of his career as a government transportation employee. He fathered a son and a daughter and has three grandchildren and one great-grand-child.

"It is my duty to tell these stories, to tell my story truthfully," Jozef told us.

Jozef Mironiuk

Helping people in need—whether Jewish or not—was "in our family's blood," Jozef Mironiuk told us. For instance, his uncle Mikolaj Iwaniuk had taken several Jews into his home when it became clear that their lives were in danger. But soon so many Jews started coming to Iwaniuk seeking help that he ran out of room and had to find other places for them.

"My uncle knew many Jews," Jozef said. "He hid one and the word got out that it was a safe place to hide." After Jozef's uncle had hidden three Jews (Perla Goldszaft, Mendel Rybkowski, and Noach Rodzynek), eight more came to him after having escaped from a labor camp called Malaszewicze. They were Dawid Finkelsztajn, Perec Radlewicz, Izrael Kaufmann, brothers Szlomo and Motel Goldszeft, Wolf Englender, and brothers Pinkus and Szlomo Ajzenberg.

So the uncle sent the latter five of this group of eight to stay with Jozef's family (Iwaniuk was the brother of Jozef's mother) on their farm near the village of Jakowki, not far from Janow Podlaski.[87] Jozef's father had died in late 1941. "The Germans beat me and my father. Then my father got typhus, and on Christmas Eve he died." But Jozef's mother, Juliana, and his seven siblings (two brothers and five sisters) took in these Jews and hid them until the war was over.

Jozef even knew one of the Jews whom his uncle sent to hide with his family. It was Englender, who ran a candy shop from which Jozef occasionally would purchase sweets before the war. Jozef, born September 12, 1923, was almost six-

Jozef Mironiuk

teen years old when the war began. So when his family decided to resist the Germans by helping to save the lives of Jews, Jozef was old enough to be given quite a few responsibilities.

His family needed as many helping hands as possible, because hiding Jews on the Mironiuk farm was no easy task, Jozef said. There was, after all, "no food like butter or meats. Some days we had a chicken but basically we fed them vegetables. We were farmers so we had potatoes, cucumbers, carrots, and cabbage. But the biggest problem was with medicine, because people very often got sick and it wasn't easy to get medicine. Also, people became suspicious when we bought medicines, asking who was ill. So we learned that we had to be very careful because it was the death penalty for saving Jews."

In the midst of all this seriousness, Jozef said, some odd situations arose that, much later in life, caused him to laugh. "There was one funny situation in which one of the men who was hiding needed soap, and it was strange because no one used soap much or perfume. So it was a risk. But one of my sisters went to the city and bought some soap."

In addition, of course, the Mironiuks had to worry about suspicious neighbors. One day, Jozef said, a neighbor heard voices coming from the barn where some of the Jews were hiding. But Jozef, known to be a member of the Polish underground home army, told the neighbor that the voices had to do with that group. "I told them that there were partisans here. In another shelter that we built and used for the Jews there was danger because of dogs and their keen sense of smell, but we used manure to hide the smell of humans." Jozef said he and his family were able to prevent neighbors from knowing that they were hiding Jews. And it helped that "we had one rule: less talking is better."

In the division of work among family members helping to hide Jews, one of Jozef's sisters, Weronika, was assigned the task of spreading manure around to confuse the dogs. One of Jozef's many tasks was to stay alert for Germans in the area and to send out a warning if need be.

In addition to hiding Jews, the Mironiuks also tried to help in other ways, Jozef said. "There also were Jews we helped who asked about food and clothes but who went elsewhere to hide. I found one Jewish girl in a barn where corn was kept. I helped her get new clothes and food. She stayed a few days and then moved on. She spoke both Polish and Yiddish but I told her she must speak Polish," because a Yiddish-speaker would be recognized immediately as a Jew and thus be in danger.

When he was growing up, Jozef said, he didn't hear much antisemitism. "What I mostly saw was friendly and good relationships between Catholics and Jews. My father had business dealings with Jews, buying and selling corn, sheep, and so on. Jews were buying poultry and sheep and other livestock from my father, who was a farmer."

Still, Jozef was aware of differences. And yet he was the only Polish citizen we interviewed to say to us that both Jews and non-Jews were citizens of Poland. We found it much more typical for people to draw a distinction by referring to "Poles and Jews," as if Jews were not also Polish. But Jozef, without any prompting, made the point that they were all Poles. "Jews were Polish citizens," he said. "They were praying in other places, but that didn't matter."

That attitude, he said, was shaped by his parents and other members of his extended family. "My family and I thought and think that everyone is a human being. And people should help other people without regard to who they are. If they need help, it's right to help." In fact, when Soviet troops first had taken over the area where the Mironiuks lived early in the war, before being driven east by the Germans in 1941, Jozef's family helped various Russians who needed assistance, he said, even though they were considered enemy occupiers of their country.

We asked Jozef whether, after the war, neighbors either praised or denounced his family for having saved Jews. Neither, he said. "After the war there was no issue about us hiding Jews. People didn't ask us children about it at all."

Just before the Soviets liberated that area of Poland from the Germans in 1944, Jozef was arrested by German authorities and imprisoned. What was the charge? "Being Polish, basically," Jozef told us.

He escaped the prison, "and two days later I went to Janow Podlaski and visited my family. Then I was arrested by Polish police." Those officials, Jozef said, were under orders from the Soviets to search for partisans and underground army members. But, as it happened, a Jewish police officer who had escaped to the east when the Germans took over the area and came back with the Soviet liberators "knew me and knew I had helped to save Jews, though I didn't know him. He asked me if I had work at home. I said, 'Yes.' So the policeman said, 'Go home.'" Which is exactly what Jozef did.

After the war Jozef married, joined the Polish air force where he spent forty years in uniform, and became the father of a son and a daughter. He also became grandfather of four. "My children and grandchildren know the story, but the grandchildren really don't understand yet how great the risk was." We asked him to think about his children and grandchildren and tell us whether he might risk their lives in the way his mother had risked his to save the lives of others.

His response was slow in coming. "It's a good question," he finally said. "During the war, the time was different. Life wasn't so precious. First they decided to kill Jews and Gypsies, then they could decide to kill the rest of the Polish people. Today it's different, but I'm sure I would help by giving medicine or food."

Then he remembered the brutality of what was happening all around him in World War II and told us this: "During the war when I risked my life and realized that Germans could come and kill me and my family, I wanted to be killed first because my brothers and sisters were so young and innocent."

We asked him if he felt like a hero. "No," he said. "I don't feel like a hero, but I'm happy that I could help."

After the war Jozef stayed in touch with several of the people he helped to save. Though some of them moved to the United States, he and they continued to share occasional correspondence and holiday greetings.

Pawel Roszkowski

In 1941 Pawel and his mother, Anna Krupa-Roszkowska, were living in a house in Jedlnia owned by her cousin Alexander Blasiak when their lives suddenly changed. Blasiak "one day came with a Polish Jew who was dressed like a German," Pawel told us, "and he said to my mother, 'Anna, don't be afraid. He's a Jew.'" Blasiak asked them to hide the man, "and Mother said, 'Of course we can.' But he needed other clothes. So we burned those clothes. My mother was full of life and very active. I was sure that she would agree" to Blasiak's request to help.

The Jewish man was Jozef Kon, and soon Pawel and his mother were hiding not only him but also his wife, their two daughters, and his wife's sister—and not just for a few days or weeks. They hid them for nearly four years, until the war ended.

Pawel and his mother were not well-off. Anna was a divorced social worker struggling to put food on the table for herself and her son. But she was resourceful enough to figure out how to hide and feed extra people.

Pawel, born May 20, 1927, was twelve years old when the war broke out and thus was old enough to help his mother considerably when she agreed to hide the Kon family. Although he was born in Radom, by the time the war started he and his mother lived thirty kilometers away in Pionki, a small town with a gunpowder factory.

In grade school Pawel shared a bench with a Jewish student whom he came to think of as a good friend. As he told us, "My mother taught me humanity." He adopted his mother's open and welcoming view of people regardless of their religion or ethnic background. Some of this attitude developed through personal experiences with Jews other than schoolmates. For instance, he told us, "I remember other Jewish friends from those days and from our town. One ran a bakery that was in competition with a Polish bakery. But no more than 20 percent of Pionki's population was Jewish."

Another foundational memory came from November 1939. "My mother knew some firemen, one of whom was Jewish. He was very poor. He had five children. But I remember that he gave a liter of milk to my family. He was poor but he shared." And it made a lasting impression on Pawel.

Despite such experiences, however, Pawel was well aware of anti-Jewish sentiments from many sources. Although he had many Jewish friends at school, he said, "It wasn't considered good to share a bench with Jews. Even the priest told me, 'Remember, if you sit with a Jew you can be circumcised.'" As he told

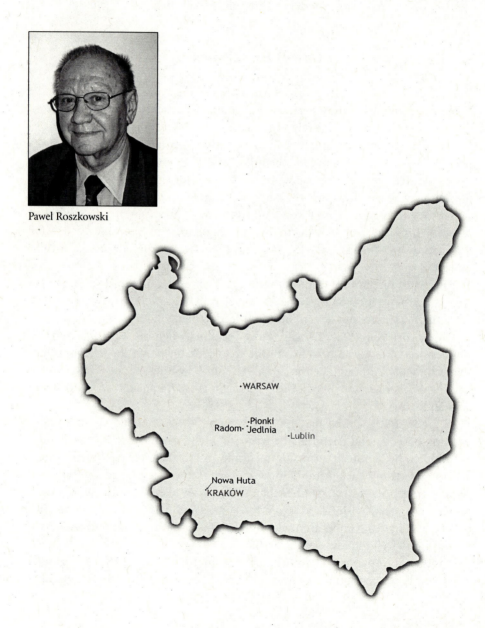

Pawel Roszkowski

us about this more than sixty years after hearing it, he shook his head at such superstitious foolishness.

Pawel said he did not remember hearing that kind of antisemitic nonsense from the pulpit of his Catholic church, but he did recall the Polish government adopting and promoting antisemitic policies even before Germany invaded the country. And he remembered seeing a non-Jew, who was wearing a fur collar on her coat, shopping at a store owned by Jews. As she emerged from the shop, Pawel said, "people threw red paint on her fur" as punishment for patronizing a Jewish-owned business.

In December 1939, because of a house fire and run-ins with German authorities, Anna and Pawel moved to her cousin's house in Jedlnia. After the move Anna was looking for ways to earn money, so she began buying and selling meat on the black market—an activity, Pawel said, that he was told could have brought a death penalty had she been caught.

The house in which Blasiak lived was in the center of Jedlnia. It would have been much harder for him to hide Jews there because of all the activity around it. By contrast, the house to which Anna and Pawel moved was at the edge of town, relatively isolated, and thus a safer place for hiding people.

Pawel said he was not sure exactly how Kon and Blasiak knew each other, but he thought they may have been distant relatives due to intermarriage some generations before. At any rate, Blasiak felt obligated to do what he could to help Kon and his family survive. And once Anna agreed to shelter Jozef Kon, he told her he wanted to try to save the rest of his family, then living in Tomaszów Mazowiecki. "So the question was whether my mother had a place to hide two daughters and his wife, and is it possible to bring them from Tomaszów Mazowiecki. She said, 'Of course. It's not a problem.' Well, it was a problem, but she said yes."

Keeping the Kon family's presence a secret was not easy. When they first moved in, another Blasiak relative was renting one of the ground-floor rooms in the house, but Blasiak did not want that person to know about the Kons. So the Kons' arrival and presence required great stealth. Soon, however, that relative moved out, allowing the Kons to live in the ground-floor space while Anna and Pawel lived on the second floor.

Special arrangements, however, were required for Jozef himself because he was circumcised, and thus the Germans could easily have identified him as a Jew. "Blasiak made a shelter for Jozef under the stairs. There was a door that could be opened only from the inside. And Kon was sitting there almost all the time. He hid there from the end of 1941 until 1945, almost four years."

But that was far from the only difficulty. At one point German soldiers commandeered one of the ground-floor rooms next to where the Kon women were living. That was a temporary problem, however, and everyone survived, though not without some close calls. Pawel described one of those incidents this way: "Kon had a problem with needing to urinate very often. One night the pot in his shelter was full. During the night he generally threw it outside, but the German soldiers took to standing next to the window he used to do this." One night Kon threw out the liquid, which landed near the soldiers, "but they thought some other soldier was dumping things out the window." They did not investigate further to find Kon.

Anna and Pawel also had to deal with Kon's restlessness and adventurous nature. One time Kon simply left his shelter and showed up in Jedlnia at a store that Blasiak operated about two kilometers from the house. Kon told Blasiak that he would watch the store while Blasiak ran some errands. So Kon was in the store, and a woman came in, saw Kon, and quickly left. Kon was very smart and realized she had recognized him as a Jew. So he jumped out the window and escaped. This customer came back with a soldier, to whom she said she recognized Kon. By that time, however, Kon was gone, and Blasiak was back in charge of the store. The soldier, Pawel said, dismissed the woman, calling her "insane."

We asked Pawel whether during the war, or later, he ever got angry at his mother for risking his life. "No, not at all," he said. "My mother talked to me about it at the time, and I wasn't afraid."

In fact, he told us that he was "scared only once in the war," and it had to do with a time that German authorities rounded up people, such as Pawel, who had received special identification papers indicating they were craftsmen. When Germans stopped them and demanded to see their identification papers, they would show them, and normally the Germans would let them go.

One time, however, "we were caught, and although we showed them these i.d.s, we were taken by the Germans to a car. One of my friends said, 'Oh, we're probably being sent to Germany.' But the Germans led us to an armaments manufacturing plant, and there was a gallows there where people were hanged. That day there were sixteen people there to be hanged, and we had to watch it."

Pawel was married twice and had two daughters, three grandsons, a granddaughter, and a great-granddaughter. He spent his career as an engineer at a big factory in Nowa Huta, a planned community built under Soviet auspices on the outskirts of Kraków.

We asked Pawel whether he would consider risking his life or the life of his family to save others, the way his mother did. He was careful to say that he would risk just his own life, but then he said, "I want to say a sentence that I said at the Yad Vashem ceremony [honoring him]: 'Don't let governments create the kinds of laws that dehumanize people.'" He noted that Nazi Germany passed laws legitimizing antisemitic policies and genocidal actions. He also said that every time he finishes a speech on this subject to youth from various countries, "I say 'Let no nationality or religion to divide the nations. When you get old you should be able to say this with a clear conscience: "I was righteous and friend to every man.'"

And he said he continued to worry about the effects of antisemitism and its sources in modern Poland. "Maybe, as a good Pole, I should not say this, but I realize that there are some forces in the nation which cause antisemitism and some forces in the nation use the Catholic faith to express antisemitism. There also are forces in the government that do this. After all, antisemitism may be caused also for cultural reasons. Of course, officially it is said that there is no antisemitism in Poland, but there is. As for me, I believe what Pope John Paul II said, which is that the Jews are our older brothers in faith."

As a Yad Vashem honoree, who is active with a group of other honorees through the Galicia Jewish Museum in Kraków, Pawel said, "I have a lot of meetings with people from different countries and I try to fight antisemitism in a good way."

After the War

A Brief Chronology of Events Related to Rescuing Jews in Poland

1939

September 1	Germany invades Poland, marking the beginning of World War II.
September 3	In fulfillment of their promise to protect Poland's borders, Britain and France declare war on Germany.
September 17	The Soviet Union invades Poland from the east.
September 21	SS General Reinhard Heydrich issues instructions that Jews in Poland are to be gathered into ghettos near railroads for the "final goal." He orders a census and the establishment of Jewish administrative councils in the ghettos to implement German policies and decrees.
September 26	The *Armia Krajowa* (the Polish home army) is formed in Warsaw to resist the Germans.
September 27	A besieged Warsaw surrenders.
September 28	Germany and the Soviet Union agree on how to divide up Poland. Much of Poland's west is incorporated into the Third Reich, while much of central Poland is made part of the General Government, ruled by Germany. Much of Poland's east comes under Soviet control. More than 2 million Jews reside in German-controlled areas, with 1.3 million in the Soviet area. Hitler is given control of Lithuania.
September 29	Poland formally surrenders.
October 8	A ghetto is ordered established in Piotrków-Trybunalski, making that city the first one in Poland to implement Heydrich's September 21 instructions.
October 12	Hans Frank is appointed head of the General Government with the title of governor general.

October 26	Frank issues a forced labor decree for Jews in the General Government who are between fourteen and sixty years of age.
November 23	Jews living in the General Government are ordered to wear special markings on their clothing.
November 28	Frank issues an order requiring establishment of Jewish Councils to carry out German orders for Jews. This order takes effect December 7.

1940

January 24	Hans Frank orders the registration of all Jewish property in the General Government.
March 27	Heinrich Himmler, chief of the SS, signs an order starting the construction of the Auschwitz-Birkenau death camp.
April 30	The Łódź Ghetto is sealed off, with about 164,000 Jews inside.
November 16	The Warsaw Ghetto is sealed off. Originally some 330,000 people were sent there. Later some 120,000 more Jews were ordered to be there.

1941

June 22	Germany invades the Soviet Union.
June 25	Just days after German and other Axis troops attack the Soviet Union, major Russian forces are nearly surrounded near Białystok by Panzer units of Army Group Center. Panzer Group 1 captures Lutsk and Dubno, in what, before September 1939, had been eastern Poland.
December 8	The first group of Jews from the Łódź Ghetto is deported to Chelmno.

1942

July 19	Himmler orders "Operation Reinhard," deportations of Jews from the General Government to the death camps of Belzec, Sobibor, and Treblinka.

1943

April 19–May 16	The Warsaw Ghetto uprising.
June 11	Himmler orders the destruction of all ghettos in Poland.

1944

January 6	Soviet troops advance into Poland.
July 24	Soviet troops liberate Majdanek.
August 1–October 2	The Warsaw Uprising takes place.

1945

January 17	Soviet forces liberate Warsaw.
January 27	Auschwitz is liberated.
May 8	VE Day. The war in Europe ends.

Sources

Two Web sites of the U.S. Holocaust Memorial Museum: http://www.ushmm. org/education/foreducators/resource/chronology.pdf and http://www.ushmm. org/wlc/article.php?lang=en&ModuleId=10005170.

http://fcit.usf.edu/holocaust/resource/document/DocFrank.htm.

http://www.yadvashem.org.

The Holocaust: The Fate of European Jewry, by Leni Yahil (Oxford University Press, 1990).

Yad Vashem

Yad Vashem (the Holocaust Martyrs' and Heroes' Remembrance Authority) in Jerusalem bestows the title "Righteous Among the Nations" on non-Jews
who helped Jews survive the Holocaust. But not on all such non-Jews. Why
not?

There are many reasons that people considered for the title do not meet
the criteria, even though their actions may be quite laudable and even heroic.
Names proposed for the honor of "Righteous" must go through a long and
arduous investigative process.[1] Sometimes even widely admired people do not
receive this designation. The German Lutheran martyr Dietrich Bonhoeffer,
whom Germany executed in April 1945 for participating in a conspiracy to
assassinate Adolf Hitler, is a good example of someone who has not been given
the "Righteous" title because he was not a "rescuer" of Jews as the Yad Vashem
program defines it.

Among the reasons some non-Jews fail to receive the "Righteous" title is that
they did it just for the money and, thus, did not act out of righteous motives,
even though their deeds may have saved Jewish lives. In other cases, those who
were saved did not live long enough after World War II to testify to what the non-
Jews did for them. There are cases in which the survivors are afraid to recognize
their helpers because they promised the non-Jews money that they were unable
to pay when the war ended and now they worry the non-Jews will try to collect.

Yad Vashem describes its overall mission this way:

> One of the principal duties of Yad Vashem is to convey the gratitude of the
> State of Israel and the Jewish people to those non-Jews who risked their lives to
> save Jews during the Holocaust. . . . The Righteous honored by Yad Vashem come
> from 44 countries; they are Christians from all denominations as well as Muslims,
> religious and agnostic, men and women, people from all walks of life, of all ages,
> educated professionals and illiterate peasants, rich and poor. The only common
> denominator is the humanity and the courage they displayed by standing up for
> their moral principles.[2]

And here is Yad Vashem's description of the "Righteous" program:

> In 1963, Yad Vashem embarked upon a worldwide project to grant the title of
> Righteous Among the Nations to non-Jews who risked their lives to save Jews dur-
> ing the Holocaust. To this end, Yad Vashem set up a public committee headed by

a retired Supreme Court justice, which is responsible for granting the title. This project is the only one of its kind in the world that honors, using set criteria, the actions of those individuals who rescued Jews during the war.

The Righteous program and the trees planted on the Avenue of the Righteous Among the Nations have received world coverage, and the concept of Righteous Among the Nations coined in the Yad Vashem Law has become a universal concept and an important symbol. [As of January 2008, 22,211 people have been recognized as Righteous among the Nations.] In addition, Yad Vashem has been developing a comprehensive encyclopedia—The Lexicon of the Righteous Among the Nations— that will eventually include the stories of all the Righteous Among the Nations. The garden of the Righteous Among the Nations, in which marble plaques have been engraved with the names of the rescuers according to country, was inaugurated in 1996. Ceremonies in which the title of Righteous Among the Nations is granted are held in the garden.

Since 1963, a commission, headed by an Israeli Supreme Court justice has been charged with the duty of awarding the title "Righteous Among the Nations." The commission is guided in its work by certain criteria and meticulously studies all pertinent documentation, including evidence by survivors and other eyewitnesses. In order to arrive at a fair evaluation of the rescuer's deeds and motivations, the commission takes into consideration all the circumstances relevant to the rescue story, including the following:

- How the original contact was made between the rescuer and the rescued.
- A description of the aid extended.
- Whether any material compensation was paid in return for the aid, and, if so, in what amount.
- The dangers and risks faced by the rescuer at the time.
- The rescuer's motivations, in so far as this is ascertainable; e.g., friend-ship, altruism, religious belief, humanitarian considerations or others.
- The availability of evidence from the rescued persons [an almost indis-pensable precondition for the purpose of this program].
- Other relevant data and pertinent documentation that might shed light on the authenticity and uniqueness of the story.

In general, when the data on hand clearly demonstrates that a non-Jewish person risked his (or her) life, freedom, and safety in order to rescue one or several Jews from the threat of death or deportation to death camps without exacting in advance monetary compensation, this qualifies the rescuer for serious consideration to be awarded the "Righteous Among the Nations" title. This applies equally to rescuers who have since passed away.

A person recognized as a "Righteous Among the Nations" is awarded a spe-cially minted medal bearing his name, a certificate of honor, and the privilege of his [or her] name being added to those on the Wall of Honor in the Garden of the Righteous at Yad Vashem in Jerusalem. (The last is in lieu of a tree planting, which was discontinued for lack of space.)

The awards are distributed to the rescuers or their next of kin in moving ceremonies in Israel or in their countries of residence through the good offices of Israel's diplomatic representatives. These ceremonies are attended by local government representatives and are given wide media coverage.

The Yad Vashem Law authorizes Yad Vashem "to confer honorary citizenship upon the Righteous Among the Nations, and if they have passed away, the commemorative citizenship of the State of Israel, in recognition of their actions."

Anyone who has been recognized as Righteous Among the Nations is entitled to apply to Yad Vashem for the certificate. If the Righteous Among the Nations is no longer alive, his/her next of kin are entitled to request that commemorative citizenship be conferred on the Righteous Among the Nations who has passed away.

To date, more than 22,000 men and women have been recognized as Righteous Among the Nations. This figure includes family members who shared in the rescue of Jews and represents over 8,000 authenticated rescue stories. Yad Vashem's policy is to pursue the program for as long as petitions for this title are received and are supported by solid evidence that meets the criteria.[3]

In this book, we have included some individuals who have not been recognized by Yad Vashem and whose acts ranged from seemingly minor to quite significant, because that was the reality in the Holocaust. The rescuers who deserve praise are those who did it for unselfish reasons and who showed courage—even if they have not been nominated for or received the Yad Vashem "Righteous" designation. But not all non-Jews mentioned in this book acted with righteous intentions. The first farm family that hid Maria Devinki and her family, for instance, did it for money. By contrast, the man who arranged payment to the farmers helped out of the goodness of his own heart.

The Holocaust produced a wide range of experiences among Jews who survived with some non-Jewish help. In some cases, a non-Jew did one simple act that allowed a Jew the chance to survive by his own wits. In other cases, non-Jews daily risked their own lives—and the lives of their families.

Yad Vashem keeps a running record by country of the number of non-Jews who have been designated "Righteous." Here is the list as of January 2008 (these figures are not necessarily an indication of the actual number of Jews saved in each country but, instead, reflect material on rescue operations made available to Yad Vashem):

Righteous Among the Nations—per Country and Ethnic Origin—January 1, 2008

Albania	63
Armenia	10
Austria	85

Belarus	587
Belgium	1,476
Bosnia	35
Brazil	2
Bulgaria	18
Chile	1
China	2
Croatia	106
Czech Republic	118
Denmark[4]	22
Estonia	3
France	2,833
Georgia	1
Germany	455
Great Britain (including Scotland)	14
Greece	279
Hungary	703
Italy	442
Japan	1
Latvia	111
Lithuania	723
Luxembourg	1
Macedonia	10
Moldova	73
Montenegro	1
Netherlands[5]	4,863
Norway	42
Poland	6,066
Portugal	1
Romania	54
Russia	124
Serbia	127
Slovakia	478
Slovenia	6
Spain	4
Sweden	9
Switzerland	44
Turkey	1
Ukraine	2,213
USA	3
Vietnam	1
Total [2]	22,211

From the stories in this book, here is a list of the people whom Yad Vashem has honored with the title "Righteous Among the Nations":

- Jozef Biesaga for Dawid Nissan.
- Zbigniew Bolt for Irene Bau.
- Maria Bozek Nowak for Helena Goldstein.
- Maciej and Zofia Dudzik for saving Zygie and Sol Allweiss.
- Jusick Gondorowicz and his wife, Antonina-Gabriela Gondorowicz, for Maria Devinki.
- Pawel Harmuszko for Anna Schiff.
- Hanka Janczak and her father, Adam Zak, for Rose Gelbart.
- Sister Klara Jaroszynski (mentioned in the Weksler-Waszkinel chapter) for several children, not including Weksler-Waszkinel.
- Helena Konarzewska, Edward Konarzewski, Marianna Konarzewska, Michal Orlik, and Kazimierz Orlik for Feliks Karpman.
- Jozef Mironiuk for Dawid Finkelsztajn, Perec Radlewicz, Izrael Kaufmann, Szlomo Goldszeft, Motel Goldszeft, Wolf Englender, Pinkus Ajzenberg, and Szlomo Ajzenberg.
- Hanna Morawiecka for Andre Nowacki.
- Jan Puchalski, Anna Puchalska, Krystyna Maciejewska, Sabina Kazimierczyk, and Irena Baginska for Felix Zandman.
- Pawel Roszkowski and his mother, Anna Krupa-Roszkowska, for Jozef Kon and his family.

The Jewish Foundation
for the Righteous

"Righteous Among the Nations," that is, non-Jews who helped Jews survive the Holocaust, if they face financial hardship, can receive regular payments from the Jewish Foundation for the Righteous (JFR). The foundation was created in 1986 by Rabbi Harold M. Schulweis and Dr. Eva Fogelman and seeks to fulfill the Jewish commitment to *hakarat hatov,* or searching out and recognizing goodness.

The organization started by helping to support eight individuals. In 2003 the number of "righteous" receiving JFR support peaked at 1,750. Since then, the number has fallen to about 1,200 in more than twenty-five countries. When these rescuers showed courage by helping Jews, they did not do it for money, and as a rule they are reluctant to ask for financial help in their older years. Most rescuers receiving JFR help live in Eastern Europe. More live in Poland than in any other country. Rescuers use the funds to cover costs of food, heating fuel, medical care, medication, and emergency needs. JFR also awards small grants, on request, to help with funeral expenses. Depending on availability of funds, the foundation also provides onetime grants to cover food for the Christmas and Easter seasons to rescuers living in Poland and other Eastern European countries.

The foundation recognizes that, as time passes, the number of aged and needy non-Jews who risked their lives to help Jews will continue to decline, so it is making a transition to put more emphasis on its educational programming. Already JFR runs programs that educate teachers and students about the history of the Holocaust and rescue. An important part of the foundation's education program is a JFR publication called *Voices & Views: A History of the Holocaust.* This publication uses short selections from leading scholarship to introduce teachers both to the history of the Holocaust and to the scholarly literature in the field.

The foundation is tax-exempt under section 501[c]3 of the Internal Revenue Code. JFR's work is supported primarily through donor contributions. It does not receive or use government funds, although it continues to work closely with the Conference on Jewish Material Claims against Germany (now known as the "Claims Conference"), which provides significant financial support to the foundation. Since 1951 the Claims Conference has worked in partnership with Israel to negotiate for and distribute payments to survivors and rescuers.

The money comes from Germany, Austria, other governments, and certain industries.

Close to 90 percent of JFR expenditures go to program activities, such as rescuer support and education, with the biggest part going directly to the rescuers. In 2007, direct support for such persons amounted to $3.8 million. Rescuers receive a stipend three times a year.

Stanlee Joyce Stahl, who spent twenty years working for the U.S. Department of Health and Human Services, is the foundation's executive vice president. JFR maintains offices at 305 7th Avenue, 19th Floor, New York, New York, 10001. More information is available at the foundation's Web site, www.jfr.org, from which much of the information in this chapter is drawn.

Notes

Introduction

1. Most of the rescuers mentioned in this book also have been honored as "Righteous." Their names can be found in the short chapter on Yad Vashem at the end of this book.

2. Historian Saul Friedlander reports that "of the 3.3 million Jews who had lived in Poland in 1939, some 300,000 survived the war; among these some 40,000 at most survived in hiding on Polish territory." *The Years of Extermination: Nazi Germany and the Jews, 1939–1945* (New York: HarperCollins, 2007), 632.

3. Friedlander goes so far as to say that "no Jew in occupied Europe imagined what the German measures would be." Ibid., 488.

4. Nechama Tec, *When Light Pierced the Darkness: Christian Rescue of Jews in Nazi-Occupied Poland* (New York: Oxford University Press, 1986), 6.

5. Bernard D. Weinryb, *The Jews of Poland: A Social and Economic History of the Jewish Community in Poland from 1100 to 1800* (Philadelphia, Pa.: Jewish Publication Society, 1972), 17, 311.

6. This is the way Leni Yahil reports some of the statistics: "Of the 3.5 million Jews to be found in Poland before the German conquest, 2,350,000 were living in the area that came under German control and 1,150,000 were in the Soviet-controlled sector. When the war began, some 60,000 Jews fled from the western districts of Poland into the area that was to become the *Generalgouvernement* (General Government); about 300,000 managed to cross the border from the *Generalgouvernement* into the Soviet zone. During the first weeks of the fighting, some 30,000 managed to escape the area of German occupation and leave Poland altogether, going primarily to the Baltic states and via Slovakia to Hungary and Rumania." Leni Yahil, *The Holocaust: The Fate of European Jewry, 1932–1945* (New York: Oxford University Press, 1990), 136–37.

7. The prewar borders of Poland were different from the borders today. See the two maps in the front of this book, showing Poland as it existed in 1939 and Poland's borders today. In these six death camps as many as 2.7 million Jews were murdered, along with tens of thousands of others, including non-Jewish Poles, gypsies, Soviet prisoners of war, and others. For more details about the camps, see the Web site of the U.S. Holocaust Memorial Museum, at http://www.ushmm.org/outreach/ncamp.htm, accessed March 7, 2009, and the Web site of Aktion Reinhard Camps (hereafter ARC), at http://www.deathcamps.info, accessed March 7, 2009. See also Friedlander, *Years of Extermination*, esp. 356–65.

8. Michael Phayer reports that only 1 to 3 percent of the Polish population participated in rescue work. *The Catholic Church and the Holocaust, 1930–1965* (Bloomington: Indiana University Press, 2000), 113. He attributes this figure to Wladyslaw T. Bartoszewski, "Polish-Jewish Relations: A Current Debate among Polish Catholics," *Research Report* 7 (October 1987).

9. For readers who want to delve into more scholarly works about rescue and, more broadly, the nature of altruism, we suggest at a minimum the following works (as well as other books listed in the bibliography): Eva Fogelman, *Conscience and Courage: Rescuers of Jews during the Holocaust* (New York: Anchor Books, 1995); Samuel P. Oliner and Pearl M. Oliner, *The Altruistic Personality: Rescuers of Jews in Nazi Europe* (New York: Free Press, 1988); Mordecai Paldiel, *The Path of the Righteous: Gentile Rescuers of Jews during the Holocaust* (Hoboken, N.J.: KTAV Publishing House, 1993); works by Nechama Tec, including *When Light Pierced the Darkness;* and works by Yehuda Bauer, particularly *A History of the Holocaust* (London: Franklin Watts, 1982) and *Rethinking the Holocaust* (New Haven, Conn.: Yale University Press, 2002).

10. Bauer, *Rethinking the Holocaust,* xv.

11. Ellen Land-Weber, *To Save a Life: Stories of Holocaust Rescue* (Urbana: University of Illinois Press, 2000), 187.

12. Christopher Browning, speech given at Kansas State University, Manhattan, Kansas, on February 18, 2008, audiotape in the possession of Tammeus. Browning is best-known as the author of *Ordinary Men: Reserve Police Battalion 101 and the Final Solution in Poland* (New York: HarperCollins, 1992).

13. Bauer, *Rethinking the Holocaust,* xi.

The Stories

1. The local honor was announced in 1999 at the Holocaust Memorial Center's annual dinner. Yad Vashem honored Maciej and Zofia Dudzik as "Righteous" in 2007, at a ceremony in Poland attended by several Dudziks as well as by Zygie and his daughter Esther Ingber.

2. ORT was founded in the eighteenth century. The name is derived from the Russian words for "Society for Trade and Agricultural Labor among the Jews in Russia." It later became known as World ORT. See www.ORT.org.

3. Irene said she and her mother were among about forty-one thousand Kraków Jews who were moved in that way, by the time the Kraków Ghetto was created in early March 1941.

4. The term *Volksdeutsch* refers to ethnic Germans living outside of Germany.

5. The *Armia Krajowa,* often referred to just by its initials A.K., was the Polish underground army.

6. Yahil reports that the Polish underground in general, and the A.K. in particular, "displayed little interest in the Jews and certainly took no action to defend them." Indeed, the A.K. "was led by prewar professional officers and imbued with antisemitism." Beyond that, "many individual Jews and whole groups were liquidated in [the] forests by the right-wing and extremist sections of the Polish underground." Yahil, *The Holocaust,* 457. So Bolt's experience with the A.K. was highly unusual.

7. We interviewed Sheila in late March 2007. She died of leukemia on October 6 of that year.

8. For a description of life in Chełm then, see the Jewish genealogy Web site affiliated with the Museum of Jewish Heritage, http://www.jewishgen.org/yizkor/chelm/che179.html, accessed March 4, 2009.

9. It's likely that this occurred in what became known as the December 1939 *Aktion,* a German word referring to the roundup of Jews for deportation to labor camps or death camps. These *Aktionnen* (the plural) were carried out in Poland as well as in eastern occupied territories.

10. One online source indicates a Jewish population of more than 70 percent. See the Jewish genealogy Web site affiliated with the Museum of Jewish Heritage, www.jewishgen. org/KRsig/Townlist.htm, accessed March 4, 2009.

11. Another version of this story was told to Maria's son, Sam Devinki, in 2007 when he went to Poland and spoke to two of Jusick's sons. They told him that this gun incident occurred later, after the farmer had begun to run out of food, which forced Jusick to bring the farmer flour in order for him to continue feeding Maria and the others under the barn. In either case, the farmer knew Jusick was protecting Maria and the others.

12. Sam Devinki said that Jusick's sons came to believe that it was Wladyslaw Chelowski, the first farmer who hid Maria and others, who killed Maria's brother David. But Maria said she doubts that account.

13. For more information on the population of Sokołów at that time, see www. edwardvictor.com/Ghettos/Sokołów_Podlaski.htm, a Web site maintained by a collector of Holocaust educational material, accessed March 4, 2009, and the Jewish genealogy Web site affiliated with the Museum of Jewish Heritage, www.jewishgen.org/Yizkor/Pinkas_poland/ pol7_00339.html, accessed March 4, 2009.

14. Aaron Elster and Joy Erlichman Miller, *I Still See Her Haunting Eyes: The Holocaust and a Hidden Child Named Aaron* (Peoria, Ill., BF Press, 2007), 25. See also Aaron Elster's Web page, www.aaronelster.com.

15. Ibid., 30, 44.

16. Ibid., 57, 58.

17. Ibid., 67, 68.

18. Ibid., 90.

19. Ibid., 91.

20. The *Shema,* found in the book of Deuteronomy, is a Jewish prayer recited each morning and evening. Traditionally these are the last words a Jew says prior to death.

21. Elster and Miller, *Haunting Eyes,* 100.

22. Ibid., 106. For more information see the Web site of the U.S. Holocaust Memorial Museum, at http://www.ushmm.org/education/foreducators/resource/pdf/idcards.pdf, accessed March 7, 2009 (see page 9 of this document).

23. Elster and Miller, *Haunting Eyes,* 108.

24. Ibid.

25. This claim from a non-eyewitness contradicted what both Aaron and Irene described.

26. For more information about the population of Sosnowiec at that time, see the Web site for Yad Vashem, http://yad-vashem.org.il/about_holocaust/month_in_holocaust/december/ decenber_lexicon/SOSNOWIEC.html (accessed March 7, 2009).

27. The Bund was a Jewish political party that espoused a form of Jewish socialism and secular Yiddish culture, both of which stood in tension with Jewish Orthodoxy. The Bund was active in a number of European countries from the late nineteenth century into

the 1930s. Friedlander (*Years of Extermination,* 219) reports that the Bund was created in Vilna [or Vilnius], Lithuania. For a good online explanation of the Bund, see the Web site of the Institute for Jewish Research, http://www.yivo.org/digital_exhibitions/index.php?mcid=76&oid=10, accessed March 4, 2009.

28. For details about Srodula, see the Web site of the Shoah Education Project, www.shoaheducation.com/GHETTOMAP.html#kielce, accessed March 4, 2009.

29. For Yad Vashem's account of what happened to the Jews of Srodula, see the Yad Vashem Web site, http://www1.yadvashem.org/about_holocaust/month_in_holocaust/december/decenber_lexicon/SOSNOWIEC.html, accessed March 4, 2009.

30. Roman told us that there is a drawing of the room in which he was hidden in Srodula, in Art Spiegelman, *Maus: A Survivor's Tale* (New York: Random House, 1986), the Pulitzer Prize–winning illustrated narrative of Holocaust survival.

31. Immediately after the war, Roman did attend a Catholic school, but not for long. He said "not only the kids but the nuns" made life miserable for him there because he was Jewish. "They punished me a lot."

32. For more information on the population of Kalisz at this time, see the Web site of the U.S. Holocaust Memorial Museum, http://www.ushmm.org/wlc/article.php?lang=en&ModuleId=10005789, accessed March 7, 2009.

33. For more information on the population of Rzeszów at this time, see the ARC Web site, www.deathcamps.org/occupation/rzeszow%20ghetto.html, accessed March 7, 2009.

34. Felicia Graber, "And She Lived Happily Ever After," an essay in *And Life Is Changed Forever: Holocaust Childhoods Remembered,* ed. Martin Ira Glassner and Robert Krell (Detroit: Wayne State University Press, 2006), 95.

35. Ibid., 88. For more information on the population of Tarnów at this time, see the ARC Web site, www.deathcamps.org/occupation/tarnow%20ghetto.html, accessed March 7, 2009.

36. See the ARC Web site, http://www.deathcamps.org/belzec/belzecoverview.html, accessed March 7, 2009.

37. Graber, "Happily Ever After," 89.

38. Ibid.

39. Ibid., 85, 88.

40. Today the official address puts it in Jaktorow woj Mazowieski, into which it was incorporated.

41. Graber, "Happily Ever After," 87.

42. From the start of the twentieth century and even earlier, in fact, Góra Kalwaria was an important center of the Hasidic movement, first under the leadership of the Gerer rebbe (*rebbe* is the title given to Hasidic spiritual guides) Yehuda Aryeh Leib Alter, who died in 1905, and then under the leadership of his son, Rabbi Avraham Mordechai Alter (sometimes the name is given as Mordecai Abraham Alter). The Gerer, or Kotsk-Ger, sect of Hasidic Judaism was founded in 1859 in Góra Kalwaria, according to www.everything2.com/index.pl?node_id=1262822, accessed March 7, 2009. Hasidic pilgrims came to Góra Kalwaria from all over the world. Indeed, a special railroad was constructed from Warsaw to help bring the pilgrims. When Feliks was a boy, he said, Góra Kalwaria had two synagogues. One was open every day, and one was open just for Sabbath services and for holidays.

43. The 1900 Jewish population of Góra Kalwaria was 2,019, according to the Jewish genealogy Web site affiliated with the Museum of Jewish Heritage, http://data.jewishgen. org/wconnect/wc.dll?jg~jgsys~shtetm~-502357. And in 2006 the total population of Góra Kalwaria was 11,438, according to this source: http://wikimapia.org/4098339/G%C3%B3ra_ Kalwaria. Both sites accessed April 18, 2009.

44. Feliks's memory of the time he was at the labor camp is in tension with reports concerning the camp in books by historian Martin Gilbert. Gilbert states that "the Germans began to 'liquidate' various labor camps" in December 1942, and near the end of that month, some four hundred slave laborers at Karczew were murdered. Martin Gilbert, *The Second World War: A Complete History* (New York: Holt Paperbacks, 2004), 386. In another book, Gilbert reports a slightly earlier date, December 1, for the four hundred deaths at the Karczew camp. Martin Gilbert, *The Holocaust: A History of the Jews of Europe during the Second World War* (New York: Holt Paperbacks, 1987), 503. So there's a difference of fifty people between the Gilbert and Karpman estimates of the number of people in the camp, and there's the clear inference in Gilbert's work that the Karczew camp had ceased to exist by January 1943. When we interviewed Feliks, he insisted that he was at the camp until mid-1943.

45. The U.S. Mint started producing twenty-dollar gold coins, called double eagles, in 1907. Although they carried the twenty-dollar denomination, the coins contained one ounce of gold and the value thus fluctuated. Feliks did not tell us how he obtained the coin.

46. For an account of the conflict between the pope and Radio Maryja's founder, Reverend Tadeusz Rydzyk, see www.spiegel.de/international/0,1518,413976,00.html, accessed March 7, 2009.

47. Jewish population figures for other-than-large Polish cities at the start of the war can be difficult to verify. Jerry remembered that Pruszków's Jewish population was several thousand and made up as much as 10 percent of the city's total population. The Jewish genealogy Web site affiliated with the Museum of Jewish Heritage (http://data. jewishgen.org/wconnect/wc.dll?jg~jgsys~shtetlmaster2, accessed March 5, 2009) lists the 1921 Pruszków Jewish population at 971. But the Holocaust Chronicle Web site (http:// www.holocaustchronicle.org/StaticPages/216.html, accessed March 5, 2009) reports that on January 31, 1941, some 3,000 Jewish deportees, mostly from Pruszków, arrived at the Warsaw Ghetto. Pruszków's total population in recent census counts is reliably reported as more than 50,000 by several sources, including a Web site maintained by Jan J. Lahmeyer, who has collected population statistics for decades (http://www.populstat.info/Europe/ polandt.htm, accessed March 5, 2009).

48. We visited Otwock in the late summer of 2007 to see what remained of this health resort (the city was granted this status in 1923). The year before World War II began, the Otwock area was host to some forty thousand patients annually, mostly from Warsaw. Otwock is much less a getaway location for Warsaw residents today, but there still are remnants of the famous old Abram Gorewicz Spa, which at one time was described as the biggest wooden construction in Europe. Andre and his mother stayed briefly either there or somewhere similar when they were hiding in this community. About the only remaining sign of Jewish life in the Otwock area now is an abandoned Jewish cemetery in a wooded

area in Otwock itself and a relatively new fence around the smashed and ruined Jewish cemetery in nearby Karczew. In the latter cemetery we saw human bones lying about on the sandy soil amid broken tombstones.

49. Yad Vashem, *The Encyclopedia of the Righteous among the Nations: Rescuers of Jews during the Holocaust—Poland,* ed. Israel Gutman, Sara Bender, and Shmuel Krakówski (Jerusalem: Yad Vashem, 2004), 1:436.

50. For more information about this agency, which assists people honored by Yad Vashem as "Righteous Among the Nations," see the Jewish Foundation for the Righteous Web site, at www.jfr.org, accessed March 7, 2009. See also our chapter about it in this book.

51. In 1918 Grodno (or Hrodna, in Belarusian) was part of the Russian Empire, but it became part of a reconstituted Poland after the Treaty of Versailles ended World War I. Grodno still was part of Poland at the start of World War II. Today Grodno is just over the border from Poland, in Belarus.

52. While one source (the "Virtual Guide to Belarus" Web site started by Belarusian natives now living around the world, www.belarusguide.com/cities/hrodna, accessed March 5, 2009) suggests that about thirty thousand of Grodno's approximately fifty thousand residents at the time were Jewish, another source (the ARC Web site, www.deathcamps. org/occupation/rzeszow%20ghetto.html, accessed March 6, 2009) indicates the proportion of Jews in the general population was shrinking and by 1939 was down to just under 42 percent.

53. Anna Schiff has given videotaped testimony to the USC Shoah Foundation for Visual History and Education. More information is available at the USC Web site, http://college. usc.edu/vhi, accessed March 5, 2009.

54. For more information on the ghettos in Grodno, go to the Yad Vashem Web site, http://www1.yadvashem.org./about_holocaust/lost_worlds/grodno/grodno_the_german_ occupation.html, accessed March 7, 2009.

55. Władysław Bartoszewski and Zofia Lewinówna, eds. *Righteous among Nations: How Poles Helped the Jews, 1939–1945* (London: Earlscourt Publications, 1969), 29–30.

56. Halinka had gone into hiding without her husband and child because of marital difficulties, Anna said. Halinka later learned that both her husband and child perished.

57. In Polish, a wife's last name will end in –ska when her husband's last name ends in –ski.

58. For more on the Cologne trial, go to the Yad Vashem Web site, http://www. yadvashem.org./about_holocaust/lost_worlds/grodno/grodno_the_german_occupation. html, accessed March 7, 2009.

59. *Hitlerites* was a common Polish term for Germany's troops and Nazi authorities.

60. For a brief history of the relationship of Vilna to Poland and Lithuania during the twentieth century, see Friedlander, who notes that right after World War I the Baltic countries "became independent, but Lithuania lost Vilna to Poland." *Years of Extermination,* 219, 220.

61. The Shoah Visual History Foundation is an organization that has gone by several names. At present it is known as the USC Shoah Foundation Institute.

62. For a historical account of Ponary, see the ARC Web site, www.deathcamps.org/ occupation/ponary.html, accessed March 5, 2009.

63. Stare Swieciany then was in Poland; today it is part of Lithuania and is known as Svencionys.

64. Essay called "Where Is My Homeland?" by Romuald Weksler-Waszkinel, at the Web site of the Institute of Central and Eastern Europe, www.intesw.ebox.lublin.pl/ed/2/weksler.html.en, accessed March 5, 2009.

65. Yad Vashem's account of this reports that Batia left the baby Romuald on the balcony of the house where Piotr and Emilia lived. The account says Emilia stepped out onto the balcony a bit later and screamed, "A baby! A baby!" and then undid the blanket in which Romuald was wrapped so that neighbors who had gathered around could see that the child was not circumcised. But Romuald told us Yad Vashem got this part of the story wrong, and that he was in fact circumcised, though he did not know that until much later. Gutman et al., *Encyclopedia of the Righteous,* 2:853.

66. Ibid.

67. Even today that quest goes on among some people in Poland who were hidden as children in the war and who today are beginning to rediscover and reclaim their Jewish identity. Michael Schudrich, chief rabbi of Poland, says such people come to him almost every day now seeking to reconnect to their Jewish pasts.

68. Weksler-Waszkinel, "Where Is My Homeland?"

69. Weksler-Waszkinel, "Memory and Conscience," a lecture delivered on September 16, 2003, to the DePaul University College of Law.

70. Weksler-Waszkinel, "Where Is My Homeland?"

71. Ibid.

72. Weksler-Waszkinel, "Memory and Conscience," the DePaul lecture.

73. Ibid.

74. An essay describing the history of anti-Judaism in Christian history and how it contributed to modern antisemitism is available at http://billtammeus.typepad.com, the author's "Faith Matters" blog. Click on "Anti-Judaism in Christian History" under the headline "Check this out" on the right side of the opening page.

75. Weksler-Waszkinel, "Where Is My Homeland?"

76. For more information concerning the population of Grodno at that time, go to the "Virtual Guide to Belarus" Web site started by Belarusian natives now living around the world, www.belarusguide.com/cities/hrodna, accessed March 6, 2009.

77. In the rural Polish custom, Anna Puchalska was known as Janova, which means wife of Jan.

78. Felix Zandman, with David Chanoff, *Never the Last Journey* (New York: Schocken Books, 1995), 8, 89.

79. Ibid., 37.

80. For details on the fate of the people living in Ghettos One and Two, see the ARC Web site, www.deathcamps.org/occupation/grodno%20ghetto.html, accessed March 6, 2009.

81. For more information about Kurt Wiese, see the Yad Vashem Web site, http://www1.yadvashem.org./about_holocaust/lost_worlds/grodno/grodno_the_german_occupation.html, accessed March 7, 2009.

82. Zandman with Chanoff, *Never the Last Journey,* 69.

83. Decades later, Felix arranged for a monument to be erected at Yad Vashem in Israel

in honor of his grandfather, and he made it possible for members of the Puchalski family to be honored, too.

84. Zandman with Chanoff, *Never the Last Journey,* 136.

85. Ibid., 168.

86. "Kol Nidre" means "all the vows" and is a worship service on the eve of Yom Kippur. In the central prayer in the service, people seek release from vows and promises they have made as individuals in the previous year but that they have been unable to fulfill.

87. Today Janow Podlaski is just west of the Poland-Belarus border, almost straight east of Warsaw.

After the War

1. Irena Steinfeldt, director of Yad Vashem's Righteous Among the Nations Department, says "it is indeed 'a long and arduous investigative process,' but what is more important is that the decision to award the title is taken by an independent commission that is headed by a retired justice of the Supreme Court (of Israel) who reviews every decision." Steinfeldt email to Bill Tammeus, August 7, 2008.

2. See the Yad Vashem Web site, http://www1.yadvashem.org/righteous_new/index_righteous.html, accessed March 7, 2009.

3. See the Yad Vashem Web site, http://www1.yadvashem.org/righteous/index_righteous.html, accessed March 7, 2009.

4. The Danish Underground requested that all its members who participated in the rescue of the Jewish community not be listed individually, but as one group.

5. The numbers for the Netherlands includes two people who were originally from Indonesia but who were residing in the Netherlands at the time.

Bibliography

Ackerman, Diane. *The Zookeeper's Wife: A War Story.* New York: W. W. Norton, 2007.

Bartoszewski, Władysław, and Zofia Lewinówna, eds. *Righteous among Nations: How Poles Helped the Jews, 1939–1945.* London: Earlscourt Publications, 1969.

Bauer, Yehuda. *A History of the Holocaust.* London: Franklin Watts, 1982.

———. *Rethinking the Holocaust.* New Haven, Conn.: Yale University Press, 2002.

Bauman, Janina. *Winter in the Morning: A Young Girl's Life in the Warsaw Ghetto and Beyond, 1939–1945.* New York: Free Press, 1986.

Browning, Christopher. *Ordinary Men: Reserve Police Battalion 101 and the Final Solution in Poland.* New York: HarperCollins, 1992.

Dodd, Monroe, ed. *From the Heart: Life before and after the Holocaust—A Mosaic of Memories,* by Trudi Galblum. Kansas City: Midwest Center for Holocaust Education and the *Kansas City Star,* 2001.

Dwork, Deborah, ed. *Voices and Views: A History of the Holocaust.* New York: Jewish Foundation for the Righteous, 2002.

Elster, Aaron, and Joy Erlichman Miller. *I Still See Her Haunting Eyes: The Holocaust and a Hidden Child Named Aaron.* Peoria, Ill.: BF Press, 2007.

Fogelman, Eva. *Conscience and Courage: Rescuers of Jews during the Holocaust.* New York: Anchor Books, 1995.

Friedlander, Saul. *Nazi Germany and the Jews: Volume 1, The Years of Persecution, 1933–1939.* New York: Harper Perennial, 1998.

———. *The Years of Extermination: Nazi Germany and the Jews, 1939–1945.* New York: HarperCollins, 2007.

Gilbert, Martin. *The Holocaust: A History of the Jews of Europe during the Second World War.* New York: Holt Paperbacks, 1987.

———. *The Righteous: The Unsung Heroes of the Holocaust.* New York: Owl Books, 2004.

———. *The Second World War: A Complete History.* New York: Holt Paperbacks, 2004.

Goldberger, Leo, ed. *The Rescue of the Danish Jews: Moral Courage under Stress.* New York: New York University Press, 1988.

Graber, Felicia. "And She Lived Happily Ever After." In *And Life Is Changed Forever: Holocaust Childhoods Remembered,* ed. Martin Ira Glassner and Robert Krell, 85–96. Detroit: Wayne State University Press, 2006.

Gross, Jan T. *Neighbors: The Destruction of the Jewish Community in Jedwabne, Poland.* New York: Penguin Books, 2001.

Gutman, Israel, Sara Bender, and Shmuel Krakówski. *The Encyclopedia of the Righteous among the Nations: Rescuers of Jews during the Holocaust—Poland.* Volumes 1 and 2. Jerusalem: Yad Vashem, 2004.

Hallie, Philip Paul. *Lest Innocent Blood Be Shed: The Story of the Village of Le Chambon and How Goodness Happened There.* New York: Harper and Row, 1979.

Hirschfield, Brad. *Remember for Life: Holocaust Survivors' Stories of Faith and Hope.* Philadelphia, Pa.: Jewish Publication Society, 2007.

Huneke, Douglas K. *The Moses of Rovno: The Stirring Story of Fritz Graebe, a German Christian Who Risked His Life to Lead Hundreds of Jews to Safety during the Holocaust.* New York: Dodd Mead, 1985.

Land-Weber, Ellen. *To Save a Life: Stories of Holocaust Rescue.* Urbana: University of Illinois Press, 2000.

Marks, Jane. *The Hidden Children: The Secret Survivors of the Holocaust.* New York: Fawcett Columbine, 1993.

Matas, Carol. *Greater than Angels.* New York: Simon and Schuster Children's, 1998.

Mendelsohn, Daniel. *The Lost: A Search for Six of Six Million.* New York: Harper Perennial, 2006.

Mendelsohn, Ezra. *The Jews of Central Europe between the World Wars.* Bloomington: Indiana University Press, 1987.

Oliner, Samuel P., and Pearl M. Oliner. *The Altruistic Personality: Rescuers of Jews in Nazi Europe.* New York: Free Press, 1988.

Paldiel, Mordecai. *The Path of the Righteous: Gentile Rescuers of Jews during the Holocaust.* Hoboken, N.J.: KTAV Publishing House, 1993.

Paulsson, Gunnar. *Secret City: The Hidden Jews of Warsaw, 1940–1945.* New Haven, Conn.: Yale University Press, 2002.

Phayer, Michael. *The Catholic Church and the Holocaust, 1930–1965.* Bloomington: Indiana University Press, 2000. (See especially chapter 7, "Catholic Rescue Efforts during the Holocaust.")

Rittner, Carol, and Sondra Myers, eds. *The Courage to Care: Rescuers of Jews during the Holocaust.* New York: New York University Press, 1986.

Spiegelman, Art. *Maus: A Survivor's Tale.* New York: Random House, 1986.

Tammeus, Bill. "Anti-Judaism in Christian History." In "Faith Matters" blog, http://billtammeus.typepad.com.

Tec, Nechama. *Defiance: The Bielski Partisans: The Story of the Largest Armed Rescue of Jews by Jews during World War II.* New York: Oxford University Press, 1994.

————. *Dry Tears: The Story of a Lost Childhood.* New York: Oxford University Press, 1984.

————. *When Light Pierced the Darkness: Christian Rescue of Jews in Nazi-Occupied Poland.* New York: Oxford University Press, 1986.

Tomaszewski, Irene, and Tecia Werbowski. *Zegota: The Council of Aid to Jews in Occupied Poland, 1942–1945.* Montreal, Canada: Price-Patterson, 1994.

Weinryb, Bernard D. *The Jews of Poland: A Social and Economic History of the Jewish Community in Poland from 1100–1800.* Philadelphia, Pa.: Jewish Publication Society, 1972.

Weksler-Waszkinel, Romuald. "Memory and Conscience." Lecture delivered September 16, 2003, to the DePaul University College of Law. Found at http://www.law.depaul.edu/institutes_centers/ihrli/pdf/reverend_memory_conscience.pdf.

————. "Where Is My Homeland?" Essay at www.intesw.ebox.lublin.pl/ed/2/weksler.html.en, accessed March 5, 2009.

Yahil, Leni. *The Holocaust: The Fate of European Jewry, 1932–1945.* Translated by Ina Friedman and Haya Galai. New York: Oxford University Press, 1990.

Zandman, Felix, with David Chanoff. *Never the Last Journey.* New York: Schocken Books, 1995.

Readers' Guide

This book raises profound questions about how people make excruciatingly difficult decisions, choices that can result in life or death. We think that the stories we tell in this book can be useful tools for asking such questions of ourselves, our families, our students, our congregants, and our friends. There is no way to know specifically how we might act in traumatic times, of course, but perhaps we might not be caught completely off-guard by trouble and by our reaction to it if we have thought through various options before disaster strikes. This kind of preparation might even lead us to do the right thing when all around us people are doing the wrong thing. In the end, we may be better able to respond more humanely to crises.

So we offer the questions in this readers' guide as a way of helping you think through the implications of the stories we have gathered for this book. If *They Were Just People* and your discussion of it raise questions that we have not asked, please share them with us. Our contact information can be found on the Web site, www.theywerejustpeople.com, along with lots of other information we think you might find helpful. Tell us, too, how you have used this guide. Are you, for instance, a teacher who found it helpful in leading the discussion with your students? A member of the clergy who used it with members of your congregation? Or perhaps a grandparent who shared it with your grandchildren?

Before we get to the more specific questions pertinent to each chapter, we offer here some broader questions that arise from the whole history of non-Jews who risked their lives to save Jews during the Holocaust.

General Questions

- Under what circumstances, if any, is it a morally defensible choice to risk not just your life but also the lives of your family members to save the life of someone else?

- How long should one whose life was saved feel an obligation toward the person or persons who saved it? Does the debt ever end? Asked from the other perspective, if you risked your life to save another person's life, what does the person you saved owe you? And for how long?

- If you survived when all the odds suggested you would die, how do you then live in a way that acknowledges the gift of life you've been given? And is this somehow a different way of living than the way you might otherwise live?

- Scholars tell us, correctly, that memories of eyewitnesses to traumatic events can be untrustworthy. And yet sometimes memories are all we have to understand our past. How do you decide whether you can accept the version of the past that memory has created?

- In most of the cases reported in our book, the Jews who were saved knew the people who saved them before the war. One lesson to draw from this is that it can be helpful to have friends outside your own faith and ethnicity. Do you know such people who would be willing to come to your aid or whom you would be willing to help?

- Here is a question we have asked ourselves, because one of us is a Jew and one is not. Is it possible for non-Jews to understand the Holocaust in the way that it's possible for Jews to understand it, viscerally? If not, is it possible to describe what non-Jews don't get about the Holocaust?

- Many Holocaust survivors were amazingly resilient and achieved remarkable success after the war, becoming major contributors to their nations and the world (see, for instance, the Felix Zandman story). Does it matter why? In other words, does it make a difference whether they were motivated by wisdom achieved through trauma, by a feeling of guilt for having survived at all, or by something like anger or revenge, or whether they succeeded simply because of their innate wisdom and skills?

- Many survivors say the Holocaust was the central event in their lives—just as some people say this or that war, the Great Depression, or the 9/11 terrorist attacks defined their existence. Is it possible to live a healthy and balanced life if just one event overwhelmingly shapes that life?

- We met members of rescuing families and survivors with various scars and flaws. For instance, some rescuers adopted antisemitic attitudes while some were so consumed by the actions they performed in the Holocaust that they appeared to us to be arrogant. And some survivors were so internally focused that they struck us as almost insufferable (as, perhaps, we seemed to them). If someone has performed a great and saving deed, do his or her later actions, however destructive, diminish that act? And how tolerant of self-centeredness must we be toward people who have suffered much? Does their suffering excuse such behavior?

- Just to survive, some people learned how to cheat the system, how to deceive others, how to engage in what they acknowledged would have been immoral behavior in other circumstances. If they sometimes engage in such behavior now, long after the traumatic period in which they learned it, should others excuse it because of that history?

- One survivor we met experienced almost nothing but trouble, trauma, and evil from childhood until after the war ended. But despite this absence of goodness in his life, he is today a thoughtful, caring, and nearly always positive man. Is this just because of good genes? Or is it possible to identify factors that can lead to such a good result?

And now we have study questions specific to each story in our book:

Zygie Allweiss

- For a good part of the time they were in hiding, Zygie and his brother Sol were armed. Would it have been morally defensible for them to shoot German soldiers any time they could? Is there ever a time when self-defense is *not* a justification for committing violence against someone who is truly threatening you with violence?

- Zygie cut his way out of the back of a truck that was taking him and others to die in a cemetery. When it's necessary to take individual action to save yourself from violence or death, what responsibility, if any, do you have for helping to save others in your same situation?

- The Dudziks, who hid Zygie and his brother, were friends with the Allweiss family before the war. When, if ever, does friendship obligate you to risk your life to save a friend? Speaking of that friendship, the Allweiss boys and the Dudzik family lost contact after World War II and got reconnected only in 1999 when the daughter of one of the Dudzik girls found Sol Allweiss through an Internet search. Before the Internet made such connections so much easier, how much of a search effort would you have made if you were the Allweisses and how much if you were part of the Dudzik family?

- Zygie's sister, certain on one particular day that she would perish, asked Zygie this: "Why do I have to die today?" He could find no words to explain it, so he said nothing. In the midst of trauma, when is silence the best answer?

Irene Bau

- Zbigniew Bolt was in love with Irene, and that was one reason he risked his life to save her. When someone does something for you because of love, do you have a moral obligation to respond or to reciprocate in a way that matches that act? Or is simply receiving the gift of that act enough?

- Irene's mother had hidden some jewelry in case she needed to retrieve it and sell it to get money to survive. Many Jews debated how real the threat from the Nazi regime was. When is preparation for disaster just good planning? When is it evidence of paranoia? How have you prepared for whatever catastrophes you may encounter?

- Like many other Jews trying to survive the Holocaust, Irene pretended to be a Catholic. Under what circumstances, if any, is it right to deny your religion? And given the long history of martyrdom among Christians and the even longer history of mass oppression and murder of Jews, is it likely that followers of those two traditions might answer this question differently?

- Zbigniew Bolt considered asking Irene to marry him. He was Catholic, she was Jewish, and they did not marry. What are the possible difficulties of interfaith marriage? What are the possible benefits of interfaith marriage? Would it be understandable—or even expected—if the eventual spouses of people who had shared a traumatic time in history might feel some jealousy?

Sheila Bernard

- The man who hid and saved Sheila and her mother had done a lot of bad things in his life and wanted to do something good before he died. Does one right action cancel out a lot of wrongs in life?

- Sheila said the Germans destroyed a seven-hundred-year-old synagogue in her hometown of Chełm, Poland. What are the various ways that destroying historical artifacts can affect people whose history those artifacts represent? What obligations do people have to preserve the history of groups other than their own?

- When Sheila was a little girl, she witnessed German authorities murder her aunt right in front of her. Under what circumstances, if any, might it be possible to forgive such an atrocity? Why might forgiveness be helpful for the survivor? Are there times when it is simply wrong to forgive someone?

- Sheila died after we had interviewed her, and after she had the chance to approve our writing about her. Thus, it fell to her daughter to give us final permission to use her story in this book. What obligations do children have to preserve their parents' history? Where would you draw the line in deciding how much of that history to make public?

Maria Devinki

- Maria and her family paid a huge amount of money each month to hide under the floor of a barn to survive. How much would you pay? Is any price that allows you to keep living too high?

- The man most helpful in helping Maria survive said he had help from family and friends to resist the pressure to turn Jews into the authorities. Can you resist evil alone? Does it sometimes (or even always) require help?

- Maria lived in holes under barns for more than two years, and often there was little or nothing to do. How would you pass the time if you were required to hide for that long? What internal resources would you need in order to survive? Do you have them? If not, where will you get them? After the war Maria built several successful businesses. Does simply surviving a traumatic situation give people the insight and skills necessary for later success in life? If not, what else does it take?

- At one point Maria and those with whom she was hiding had to move from one barn to another. On the way, they avoided being caught by people who called out to them to ask who they were and what they were doing. Maria said their escape was a miracle. A widely used Jewish prayer book says that "we walk sightless among miracles." What constitutes a miracle? Have you ever experienced one?

Aaron Elster and Irene Budkowski

- When Aaron was ten years old, his mother sent him away from her to try to survive on his own. If you were a mother, under what circumstances could you do that? If you were the child sent away, what would you feel toward your mother?

- Near the end of the war, with bombs exploding around them, the Gorskis told Irene and Aaron they could not join them in the safety of a potato cellar because they did not want to die with Jews. Why do you think the experience of having saved two Jewish children was not enough to undo their antisemitic attitude? More broadly, can the roots of hatred run so deep that it's impossible to destroy them?

- At the start of the German occupation of their town, the parents of Irene and Aaron bribed German authorities to let them continue operating their butcher shop. When, if ever, is it morally acceptable to do things you normally consider illegal or immoral?

- Irene told about a dream Mrs. Gorski had in which she learned where to find a bottle containing some kind of red liquid painkiller she used to stop Irene's terrible toothache. If you believe in God, do you think God speaks to us through our dreams? If not, how do you explain such stories?

Roman Frayman

- Because of what happened to him, Roman said he's a "firm believer in miracles." Do you, too, believe in miracles? If so, do you think they always, sometimes, or never require human participation to accomplish them?

- Roman remembers that when he was three years old, he saw a German soldier shoot a woman in the head. Have you ever witnessed anything close to such violence? If so, have you recovered from it? What does it take to heal such a brutal memory?

- Even long after the war, Roman's father tried to protect his son from some of his starkest memories of the Holocaust. When, if ever, is it helpful to get people to forget what they've experienced? When is it more helpful to help them remember, no matter how painful? Are there times when, if it were possible, it might help someone simply to erase a memory?

- Although in all likelihood Roman's younger brother died as an infant, Roman still retains at least a little hope that he's still alive somewhere. Faced with such a situation, when should we abandon hope? What does it cost to hope? What does it cost to give up hope? Beyond that, is there a difference between giving up hope and letting go of something you can't control?

Rose Gelbart

- Rose's first memory of the war as a child was of many people running away from her home city and bombs and guns being fired around her. If that was one of your earliest memories, would you feel vulnerable and unprotected even as an adult?

- Like many Jews in Europe in World War II, Rose and her family lived for a time in a closed ghetto. How would it affect your view of yourself, your family, and others around you if authorities separated you physically from the rest of your city or town? Would you wonder what was wrong with you? Or would you wonder what was wrong with the people who ordered this?

- Hanka Janczak, the woman who helped save Rose, told us that her father, Adam Zak, and Rose's mother were in love but not lovers. When might romantic tensions fatally compromise efforts to achieve a mutually desired goal, such as survival in the midst of turmoil? Are there circumstances under which they might contribute to a solution?

- To protect her Jewish identity, Rose's mother destroyed any photographs she had of Rose's father and grandparents. Under what circumstances, if any, would you be willing to obliterate your family's history by destroying photos and documentation?

Felicia Graber

- It wasn't until well after the war that Felicia found out she was Jewish and that the man she thought was an uncle was her father. To protect your children from death, what lies would you be willing to tell them? Would there be anything you would not lie about to protect them?

- Felicia said that her disrupted childhood left her with "feelings of insecurity, of being inadequate," and with a "constant need for approval." In what ways can going through traumatic times damage people? In what ways can it strengthen them?

- Felicia and her brother described their father both before and after the Holocaust as an ordinary man with ordinary skills and problems. But during the Holocaust, they said, he rose to the occasion and found creative solutions to the crisis. Do we need crises to bring out the best in us?

- At one point Felicia's father feigned an injury to avoid being taken to a slave labor camp. Are there any limits on behavior if its purpose is to defeat what clearly seems to you to be an evil system? Is there, in other words, a point at which you add to the evil in the world to try to defeat evil?

Feliks Karpman

- Feliks's wife, Marianna, was a member of the non-Jewish family who helped him survive the Holocaust. Although Feliks grew up Jewish and Marianna grew up Catholic, neither has been active in their religions during their marriage. In such so-called mixed marriages, is it somehow an advantage if neither spouse is religiously observant? Or might different religious commitments add strength to the union?

- When we were in Góra Kalwaria, Feliks showed us the old Jewish cemetery, which was in bad shape, with many of the headstones destroyed, despite his efforts to maintain it. Across the street the Catholic cemetery was in excellent shape. Do non-Jews in Góra Kalwaria have an obligation to help maintain the Jewish cemetery just because it's part of their community's history? Or should it just be allowed to disintegrate once Feliks is gone? When we visited that Jewish cemetery, Feliks showed us the grave of a woman who first had been buried in the Catholic cemetery, but because she had been born a Jew, Feliks and others moved her casket across the street. Did Feliks and his cohorts do the right thing? On what basis do you judge that?

- Feliks told us that "Marianna's family was not antisemitic. I knew which family I could trust." How do you decide whom to trust in a crisis? How sure can you be that people you think you know well will behave as you hope they will in a catastrophic situation?

- Marianna told us that she preferred to tell people the story of how her family helped save Feliks, "even before we got married so there would be no problems later when they learned about us." Clearly she knew some antisemitic people would object to the marriage. Can you think of any legitimate reasons to be opposed to interfaith marriages?

Jerry Koenig

- Jerry's father made a business deal with a man named Jan Góral to hide his family in exchange for becoming the owner of the Koenig family's farm after the war. Góral risked his family's life by doing this, but did he act honorably or morally if he did it for profit?

- The adults hiding in the bunker with Jerry and his family decided they had to poison a newborn baby to silence her so her crying wouldn't give away their hiding place. This was not an uncommon occurrence in the Holocaust, but was this justifiable as self-defense? Was it simply murder?

- A farm on which Jerry and his family were staying for a time before they went into hiding was quite near the Treblinka death camp and sometimes they could smell the bodies being burned there. Can you imagine any action you might have taken in such a situation that might have effectively opposed the Treblinka operation? Or would you have been completely out of options?

- The Góral family ended up having to feed eleven people hiding in their barn. Imagine trying to feed that many extra people without anyone realizing what you were doing. What kind of evasive action would you have to take?

Andre Nowacki

- When he was a small boy in the Holocaust, hiding from Germans, Andre said he was made to feel that "I did not exist." If such an idea is imprinted in a child's young mind, will he or she be more likely or less likely to value life later?
- To avoid having Andre appear to be Jewish, his parents did not teach him Yiddish. Can you list all that gets lost when people are forced to deny and forget—or never learn—their own heritage?
- We met and interviewed Andre at the offices of the Jewish Foundation for the Righteous in New York. The foundation helps provide financial and other support to non-Jews who risked their lives to save Jews in the Holocaust. Do Jews generally have a moral obligation to do that? Should non-Jews who helped expect such support? Or should any such support be based on altruism rather than obligation?
- Some boys almost forced Andre's mother to acknowledge he was Jewish by showing them his circumcision. If such a religiously mandated physical marking could mean punishment, harassment, or even death, would you violate the rules of your religion?

Anna Schiff

- Not long after the ghetto was created in Grodno, Anna's husband and infant son died at the hands of German authorities. Even late in her life, she told us, she felt as if "something is always missing." What does "getting on with your life" mean after sustaining such a major loss?
- Anna said her father was not very religious, but he had great reverence for Jewish traditions. If all religion disappeared tomorrow, what traditions rooted in religion would you want to preserve?
- Even though conditions in the barn where Anna and others hid were miserable, she said they all remained friends. Do hard times help to create good human qualities? Or do they simply reveal such qualities that already exist?
- Pawel Harmuszko, the man who saved Anna, put his own life in jeopardy to save several other Jews, too. If you had been one of them, how would you have shown gratitude to him? And do the children, grandchildren, great-grandchildren, and even succeeding generations have some kind of obligation to people who saved their ancestor?

Barbara Turkeltaub

- A Catholic priest and Catholic nuns, who did not know Barbara or her little sister, saved them, making this story different from most others in our book in which the non-Jews who saved Jews knew them before the war. Is there something more honorable about risking one's life for a stranger than for a friend or acquaintance? Or are degrees of honorability in these kinds of matters meaningless? Did the priest and nuns bear a special obligation to save lives because of their religious commitments?

- Barbara said the treatment of Jews by the German occupiers of Lithuania was "a campaign to humiliate, belittle, and demean." Where does the desire to conduct such a campaign come from? Is it an inevitable result of human nature? If so, can it be controlled?

- At one point in her girlhood, Barbara witnessed German troops murdering Jewish women at the edge of a forest. Can such a memory ever be healed? Is it inevitable that people who experience such things live with unrelenting fear or at least an increased sense of their own vulnerability?

- When Barbara's mother finally found her two years after the end of World War II, Barbara had so accommodated herself to life in a Catholic convent that she insisted she would not return to her mother unless her mother converted from Judaism to Christianity. Are there any circumstances under which you would agree to convert to a different religion to achieve a goal? Are there any circumstances under which you would ask someone else to do that?

Father Romuald Jakub Weksler-Waszkinel

- Romuald did not know for sure that he was born a Jew until his adoptive Catholic mother finally acknowledged that truth more than a decade after he was ordained a Catholic priest. What might be some legitimate reasons for concealing the truth of someone's origin from him or her?

- As a child Romuald knew he did not look like either his (Catholic) mother or father and he wondered why. What are the measuring sticks children use to determine how and where they fit into their family's story? When things don't add up in a child's mind, what can relieve the anxiety this creates? After discovering his Jewish background, Romuald lived with that secret until a nun helped him find his family origins and helped him meet his Jewish relatives. Can holding secrets over a long term have negative ramifications on how we live?

- Even after discovering he had been born a Jew, years passed before Romuald knew his original family's name. How much of your identity and sense of self is tied up in your last name and your family history? Romuald told us that Jesus is his rabbi, and he had to find a way to relate to his Jewish relatives in Israel once he found them. Have you ever had to reconcile major differences in life experiences so that you wind up crossing unusual bridges? What's the most constructive way to accomplish that?

- When Emilia and Piotr Waszkinel agreed to take baby Romuald as their own and try to save him from death at the hands of the Germans, they were motivated by religious reasons. Does religion provide the only understandable rationale for altruism? Are there nonreligious reasons that make as much sense?

Felix Zandman

- The woman most responsible for saving Felix Zandman from death in the Holocaust felt she was returning a favor to Felix's grandmother. Can you think of an instance in which what you considered a minor obligation resulted in you being repaid more generously than you ever could have imagined?

- An act of destruction by a thief inadvertently allowed Felix and others in his family to escape German authorities in hot pursuit of them. How is it possible that seemingly evil deeds sometimes yield good results?

- Felix's father insisted that the family not join the Jewish police, formed under German rule, so they would not be collaborators with the occupiers. When does cooperation with oppressive forces cross the line between survival tactic and appeasement—or even encouragement—of evil?

- By hiding Felix and others, Anna Puchalska put not only her own life in jeopardy but also the lives of her husband and five children. When putting yourselves and others at risk really is a choice, does anyone have the right to endanger the lives of family members when those members are not old enough to make that choice for themselves? If you are the one for whom others are risking their lives, could you live with the knowledge that your existence is jeopardizing the lives of others?

Four Rescuers

- Maria Bozek Nowak helped her Jewish friend Helena Goldstein survive by giving Helena her own identity so there were two Maria Bozeks. If you did such a thing, would you feel your identity was somehow diminished or in jeopardy?

- Jozef Biesaga's family hid a Jewish man for more than three years. If you had no idea when a crisis would end, what would keep you going so you wouldn't give up?

- Jozef Mironiuk was sixteen years old when the war began and was given quite a few responsibilities in his family's efforts to save Jews. Are people who have lived through difficult times inevitably more mature and wise than people who have never been profoundly challenged by trouble?

- Pawel Roszkowski told us that "my mother taught me humanity," and he adopted a welcoming attitude toward all people because of it. In what ways is our attitude about life shaped by our parents? How can we overcome destructive ideas they might teach us?

Authors Bill Tammeus and Rabbi Jacques Cukierkorn are available for speaking engagements about this book. For contact and additional information, visit www. theywerejustpeople.com.

Index

About the Authors

Bill Tammeus, a former nationally syndicated columnist for the *Kansas City Star*, is the author of *A Gift of Meaning* (University of Missouri Press) and lives in Kansas City, Missouri.

Rabbi Jacques Cukierkorn, descended from Polish rabbis, is the spiritual leader of the New Reform Temple in Kansas City, Missouri, and author of *Accessible Judaism: A Concise Guide.*